THE BIBLE AND CHRISTIAN LIFE

THE BIBLE AND CHRISTIAN LIFE

A Collection of Essays

C. E. B. CRANFIELD

Emeritus Professor of Theology
University of Durham

T. & T. CLARK LTD,
59 GEORGE STREET, EDINBURGH

Copyright (©) T. & T. Clark Ltd, 1985

Typeset by C. R. Barber & Partners (Highlands) Ltd.,
Fort William, Scotland,
printed and bound by Page Bros (Norwich) Ltd., England,

for

T. & T. CLARK LTD
EDINBURGH

First printed 1985

British Library Cataloguing in Publication Data

Cranfield, C.E.B.
   The Bible and Christian life: a collection of essays.
   1. Bible. N.T.—Criticism, interpretation, etc.
   2. Christian life—Biblical teaching
   I. Title
   248.4   BS2545.C48

ISBN 0-567-29125-1

PREFACE

Of these eighteen essays fifteen are, I think, intelligible without a knowledge of Greek (the meaning of those Greek words which occur in some of them is indicated either in brackets or by the context). The exceptions are XII, XIV and XV. Articles, which were preparatory to the writing of commentaries on Mark and Romans, have almost all been excluded from this collection both because of the amount of Greek they contain and also because readers desiring a fuller discussion than is to be found in those commentaries are likely to have access to the journals and composite works in which the articles were published.

Grateful acknowledgement for permission to republish material is due to the editors and publishers of *Epworth Review*, *The Expository Times*, *Interpretation*, *Irish Biblical Studies*, *New Testament Studies*, and *Scottish Journal of Theology*; to the Rev. Dr. J.I.McCord, the Rev. Dr. T.H.L.Parker and the Epworth Press; to Dr. Robert Banks and the Paternoster Press; to Prof. Morna Hooker, Prof. S.G.Wilson and the S.P.C.K.; to the Rev. D.W.Torrance and the Handsel Press; and to the Akademie-Verlag, Berlin.

My gratitude to my wife for all her help and unfailing patience through the years, during the course of which all but the earliest one of these papers were written, is too deep for words.

April, 1985   C.E.B.C.

CONTENTS

I
THE PREACHER AND HIS AUTHORITY[1]

I wonder whether you have ever thought what a strange object a traditional Christian pulpit is, elevating its occupant above his hearers as it does in a way that no lecturer's or public speaker's platform claims to do. How can an ordinary mortal dare to climb up into such a construction, in order to address his fellows from a position of such evident superiority? To do so is surely intolerable presumption, unless one really has a quite special and transcendent authority. Has the Christian preacher such an authority? For those of us who have declined to succumb to that fashion which would replace the sermon by something more modest, an address or a talk or maybe a dialogue, and who still from time to time make bold to ascend the pulpit stairs in the hope of delivering a sermon, this question of the preacher's authority is surely extremely urgent. So I make no apology for directing your attention to it this afternoon.

It has been the conviction of the Reformed Church that the crucial thing here is Holy Scripture – that the preacher's authority has to do with the Bible. This conviction was given notable expression in the speech which William Shakespeare put into the mouth of Prince John of Lancaster in *King Henry the Fourth*, Part Two, Act 4, at the beginning of Scene 2. There the assumption is, I think, plain to see that it is by his 'exposition on the

[1] The Shergold Memorial Lecture delivered at the Autumn Synod of the Northern Province of the United Reformed Church in Newcastle upon Tyne, 26 October, 1974, and first published in *Epworth Review* 2 (1975), pp. 95–106.

1

holy text', which he is able to give because he is 'deep . . . within the books of God', that the preacher is

> 'The very opener and intelligencer
> Between the grace, the sanctities of heaven,
> And our dull workings.'

The justification for setting the preacher up aloft in his towering pulpit and even claiming that his mouth is God's or Christ's mouth, as both Luther and Calvin did,[1] was the expectation that he was going to try humbly to expound Holy Scripture. What are we to make of this in the eighth decade of the twentieth century?

The question of the preacher's authority may be resolved into two main questions: first, the question of the authority of the Bible, and, secondly, the question of the relation of the preacher to the Bible's authority. To consider either of these questions at all fully would require a great deal more time than I can have. All I can do is to try to set before you as clearly as I can an outline of what seem to me to be the main things which ought to be said on these two questions.

1   The Authority of the Bible

I must begin by admitting frankly that I cannot *prove* to myself or to you or to anyone else that the Bible is the Word of God. To prove that it has, or at any rate some parts of it have, the authority of really great literature,

[1] Cf., e.g., Luther as quoted by K. Barth, *Church Dogmatics* I/1, Edinburgh, 1936, p. 107; Calvin in Sermon 42 on 1 Samuel (CR 57 (*Calvini Opera* 29), col. 705, and Commentary on Isaiah (CR 64 (*Calvini Opera* 36), col. 240).

that it has as a whole the authority of moral grandeur, is, of course, possible enough; but the authority of great literature and the authority of moral grandeur are not the same thing as divine authority. That it has divine authority, that it is God's own Word, this I cannot prove. I simply confess it. I confess it, because I am forced to do so, forced by the Bible itself. It has imposed its authority upon my mind and conscience by virtue of its contents, and I know that now I cannot refuse to acknowledge its authority as the authority of God's own Word without trampling on what personal moral and intellectual integrity I possess. So I join with my fellow-Christians in confessing what neither I nor they can prove, but both they and I know with the deepest conviction of mind and heart to be assuredly true.

What I have just been saying is of course no new insight. It is essentially what, as I understand it, the first chapter of the Westminster Confession of Faith implies, when it says that 'The authority of the holy scripture . . . dependeth not upon the testimony of any man or church, but wholly upon God (who is truth itself), the author thereof' and when it refers to 'the heavenliness of the matter, the efficacy of the doctrine, the majesty of the style, the consent of all the parts, the scope of the whole . . . , the many other incomparable excellencies' but goes on to state that 'our full persuasion and assurance of the . . . divine authority thereof is from the inward work of the Holy Spirit, bearing witness by and with the word in our hearts'. And in this the Confession of Faith is true to the insight of Calvin, who had spoken in this connexion of the inward testimony of the Holy Spirit (*testimonium Spiritus Sancti internum*),[1] and had used the Greek word *autopistos* to express the fact that the Bible is self-

---

[1] See *Institutes* 1.7.4f; 3.1.1, 3f; 3.2.15, 33–36.

authenticating.[1] And, if you think about it, you will see that it is not at all surprising that we cannot *prove* that the Bible is the Word of God; for, if we men really could do this, that would mean that we were somehow above the Bible, in a position to sit in judgment upon it, provided with a measure independent of it by which to measure it, and in that case the Bible would certainly not be the Word of *God*.

I begin then from the confession that the Bible is the Word of God, and proceed now to try to indicate how I understand this statement, 'The Bible is the Word of God'.

(1) The Bible does not make claims for *itself*. On the contrary, it points away from itself, beyond itself, to an authority other than itself. So, for example, in the first chapter of St John's Gospel it refers to the Word of God in a way that makes it quite clear that it is not claiming to be itself that Word. The Bible attests a Word that is other than itself as the Word of God, as its authority. It witnesses to the Word which is Jesus Christ Himself. And this is the first thing which must be said about the Bible as the Word of God. It is as the primary witness to Jesus Christ that it is the Word of God. Only He is the Word of God in the fullest, the absolute, sense. The Bible is not the Word of God independently of Him, but only in relation to Him, as testimony to Him. It is the Word of God, that is, 'the Word of God written', by virtue of its content, by virtue of the fact that it is the primary witness to Him, attesting Him as God's self-revelation, 'the Word of God revealed'.

But the Bible is related to Jesus Christ in a further way, inasmuch as He actually uses this primary witness to Himself as the medium, the vehicle, of His personal

[1] *Institutes* 1.7.5.

presence with His Church. The Bible attests itself to us as the Word of God by the fact that the living and exalted Christ, the Lord of the Church, Himself speaks to us through it and we hear His voice and recognize it by the working of His Spirit. It is here that we have the vital key to the right understanding of the statement that the Holy Scriptures are the Word of God – in the recognition that in them we have to do with Christ's keeping His promise to be with His Church 'alway, even unto the end of the world' (Mt 28.20). This promise of Jesus has to be understood in the light of another saying of His, which on the surface seems flatly to contradict it, the saying, 'ye have the poor always with you; but me ye have not always' (Mt 26.11 = Mk 14.7). There is a real sense in which, in the time between His ascension and His coming again, Christ is absent from His disciples. He is no longer with them in the way in which He was with them during the days of His earthly ministry, and not yet with them as He will be in God's coming day. We do not see Him, but have to 'walk by faith, not by sight' (2 Cor 5.7). And yet during this time of His real absence, in which His Church's situation is that pictured in the parable of the absent master in Mk 13.34ff, He is also with us no less really, though indirectly, through the Holy Spirit, coming to us again and again in the trysting-places of His own appointment, of which the first is Holy Scripture. The Bible attests itself to us as God's Word in that, as we hear and read and study the written testimony to Christ ,consisting of the ancient words of prophets, apostles and others, He Himself comes to us, using their testimony as the vehicle of His personal presence and of the conversation He desires to hold with us. Thus the authority of Scripture is not just the authority of a sacred book, but the authority of the living Lord of the Church and of the universe, who in His freedom uses its ancient

5

testimony for His own purposes as and when and where it seems good to Him. It is this real presence of the Lord Jesus Christ in and through Scripture which is the innermost secret of its authority, of its being God's own Word.

(2) We have been considering the authority which pertains to the Bible as the primary witness to Jesus Christ which both points to Him as God's self-revelation and also is used by Him as the means of His own presence with us and of His speaking to us. The second thing which must be said is that the words of the Bible through which the Lord Jesus Christ speaks to us are the words of *men*. To confess rightly that the Bible is the Word of God does not mean denying this; for the Bible is at the same time both the Word of God and the words of men. What then is the status of these human words of the Bible, these human writings, in and through which Christ speaks to us?

In this connexion the NT speaks of inspiration. Thus 2 Tim 3.16 contains the words 'Every scripture inspired of God', and in 2 Pet 1.21 we read that 'men spake from God, being moved by the Holy Ghost'. And Jesus Himself is reported as having introduced a quotation from one of the Psalms with the words, 'David himself said in the Holy Spirit' (Mk 12.36). This language has been variously understood by Christians. One view is that it means that the human words of Scripture must be infallible, inerrant. People have spoken of the Holy Spirit's 'dictating' to the human witnesses. It is often assumed that this is the view of the sixteenth-century Reformers and, in particular, of John Calvin. But, while this view certainly did become prevalent in the period of what is called Lutheran and Calvinist Orthodoxy, it seems clear that it was not held by the Reformers themselves. Luther, in a famous sentence of his preface to the OT, likened the Scriptures to the swaddling-clothes in which the infant Jesus was laid:

'Poor and mean are the swaddling-clothes, but precious is the Treasure, Christ, that lies therein.' And Calvin too, though it is true that he frequently speaks of the Holy Spirit's 'dictating', makes it clear that he regards the Scriptures as fully human documents as well as recognizing in them the Word of God, and he freely admits the presence of inaccuracies. So, for example, commenting on Mt 27.9, he says: 'I confess I do not know how the "Jeremiah" came in here, and I do not worry much. Certainly it is an obvious mistake to put Jeremiah for Zechariah, for we do not find this saying or anything like it in Jeremiah.' It is clear that Calvin understood the Bible to be the Word of God in a way which does not exclude its also being at the same time the words of men.

The true meaning of the inspiration of the Bible is surely that the men whose testimony we have in its pages were truly chosen and used by God and enabled by Him to bear effective witness, but not that they were lifted above all human weakness and fallibility. It is a matter of the gracious and merciful God's condescension to use men in their humanity, that is, in their fallen, sinful humanity, for His own gracious and merciful purpose. Their fallen humanity was not obliterated. Their words are not infallible. They could make mistakes, and did make them (as, for example, the 'Jeremiah' for 'Zechariah', which Calvin noted). But the mistakes, so far from being a reason for doubting the Bible's divine authority, are evidences of the graciousness of God who has condescended to speak to us in and through the weak words of men like ourselves. Inspiration is not the secular marvel of a mechanically infallible book, but the divine miracle of God's free grace which condescends to use frail and sinful men and their stumbling witness as the vehicle of His own Word. Its true nature as divine miracle and mystery is well indicated by St Augustine of Hippo, when

7

in his first homily on St John's Gospel he says: 'I dare to say, my brothers, that maybe not even John himself has spoken the truth as it actually is, but even he has spoken it as he was able, because he was a man speaking about God. He was indeed inspired by God, nevertheless he remained a man. Because he was inspired, he was able to say something; if he had not been inspired, he would have been able to say nothing. But because he was an inspired man, he did not speak the whole truth, but spoke what a man could speak.'[1]

The doctrine of verbal infallibility maintained by some Christians seems to me to be an all too human doctrine, for it flatters our human egotism by leading us to suppose that we may gain control of God's Word and use it for our own purposes. If it were really true that the words of the human witnesses were raised above human weakness and liability to error, that there is no serious tension between the human words and the divine Word, that the divine Word and the words of the witnesses are simply identical, then we might indeed hope to possess God's Word, to have it more or less under our control, an instrument in our hands which we could make use of for our own purposes. But God does not give Himself into our hands in that way. In giving Himself He always remains the Lord who is free. The presence of the divine Word in and through the written words is a mystery and a miracle of divine grace: it is not like the presence of a fossil imprisoned in a rock.

But let no one conclude from what I have been saying in the last few minutes that, since the biblical writers were not miraculously preserved from the possibility of error, it must therefore be sensible to assume that they were generally incompetent, naïve, credulous, even addicted to

[1] Quoted by Barth, *CD* I/1, p. 128.

deliberate deception! There are some people who imagine that, when they approach the study of the biblical text with such assumptions, they are being scientific. I do not wish to give any encouragement to an attitude which I regard as thoroughly perverse. To adopt a patronizing stance with regard to the biblical writers is certainly not a proof of one's superior intelligence: it merely proves one's ignorance.

(3) In the third place, it must be stated with emphasis that the authority of the Bible is the authority of the Bible *as a whole*. The Bible is a unity, and the secret of its unity is the person of Jesus Christ, to whom the whole Bible bears witness and who uses the whole Bible as the vehicle of His personal presence with His people.

On the surface it is, of course, highly paradoxical to talk about the unity of the Bible; for the Bible is not one book but 66 books (39 in the OT and 27 in the NT), and Shakespeare was perfectly right to refer to 'the books of God', using the plural. Holy Scripture is, in fact, a whole literature written over a period of more than a thousand years – a period considerably longer than that between Geoffrey Chaucer and the present day. Indeed, it is hardly just one literature, since three languages (Hebrew, Aramaic and Greek) are involved. It embraces a very wide variety of types of literary production, cultural backgrounds and points of view. It includes elements which in some respects are strongly opposed to one another. But in very different ways and from very different viewpoints the various elements of the Bible all attest Jesus Christ. The OT is like a great multitude of forefingers spread far and wide but all pointing in the same direction, some from a very great distance, some from close at hand, towards something which God was to bring to pass, God's coming salvation; and the NT is like another group of forefingers, this time a group of fingers pointing backward to what was in relation to them the quite near past. And at the centre, at the place towards which all the fingers point, stands Jesus Christ, the fulfilment of all God's promises to Israel, the true fulfilment of all Israel's hopes. The testimony is bafflingly manifold, until we begin to see it in relation to Christ; but, when once we do see it all in relation to Him, we begin to find that even the apparently most unlikely, even the really offensive, elements have a part to play in the total testimony by which we are enabled to see Jesus as the Christ of Israel, the Saviour of the world, the Lord of the universe, in His full splendour, majesty and graciousness.

In view of what has just been said, it is clearly of vital importance that we should recognize that, while every particular part of Holy Scripture is truly part of the whole testimony and Christ deigns to make use of every part of the whole, no part is to be regarded as the Word of God in isolation from the rest. It is only in its relation to all the rest of Scripture that each particular part is the true and authentic Word of God. Even those passages which are most obviously sublime are not to be isolated from the rest. So, for example, the narratives of the Crucifixion in the four Gospels are not the true Word of God unless they are understood in the light of the testimonies to the Resurrection which follow them, and the narratives of the Easter days are not the Word of God apart from the preceding narratives of the Passion, and St John's Gospel needs the Synoptic Gospels and the Synoptic Gospels need the Gospel of St John. And the OT is not rightly understood except in the light of the NT, and the NT cannot be fully understood apart from the OT. If we hold fast to the principle that every part must be understood in its context and in relation to the whole, then we shall be able to take even such offensive things as the bloodthirsty nationalistic vindictiveness expressed in the 137th Psalm

('Happy shall he be, that taketh and dasheth thy little ones against the rock') in our stride.

But this interpreting every particular part in relation to the whole is not just a matter of allowing one over-emphasis to correct another, of collecting contradictory statements and then letting them cancel each other out. We have to understand each part not just in relation to the whole, but in relation to the whole understood as testifying to Christ. It is He Himself who is the unity of the Bible. So every part is to be understood in relation to Him – though not, of course, in any naïve way like that which insists on explaining every mention of wood as a reference to the Cross.

Let me conclude the first part of this lecture (the discussion of the authority of the Bible) by quoting a memorable sentence from Wilhelm Niesel's very valuable book, *Reformed Symbolics: a comparison of Catholicism, Orthodoxy, and Protestantism.*[1] 'In the Church of the Gospel,' he says, 'it is not a question of an infallible book, a "paper pope", but of Christ clothed in the words of His witnesses, the apostles and prophets, of the Christ who by His Spirit proves Himself a living Lord who still uses the words of His messengers to announce His presence today, where and when He wills.'

2   The Relation of the Preacher to the Bible's Authority

I turn now to the second of the two questions I mentioned at the beginning – the question of the relation of the preacher to the Bible's authority.

I shall not labour the point that the preacher does stand

[1] Eng. tr. by A. D. Lewis, Edinburgh, 1962, p. 231.

in a relationship to the Bible. I am aware, of course, that there are some preachers who think to by-pass Scripture and are quite persuaded that to take a text from it is just old-fashioned and out of date. But I hope that I need not argue this point, but may assume that, as members of the United Reformed Church, we should all agree that to try to by-pass the Bible in preaching is as perverse as attempting to celebrate the Holy Supper without bread or wine, that it is, in fact, to show oneself ignorant of what real preaching is all about.

If then the preacher does stand in a close relationship to the Bible, what exactly is this relationship?

One view of the matter which contains a very important element of truth and yet is misleading and dangerous is that which sees the preacher's relation to the Bible as that of the expert to the subject of his expertise. The element of truth in this is obvious. The preacher certainly ought to try very hard to be as expert in the Bible as he possibly can. This cannot be said too strongly. And it is true that, though, physically, he stands behind the pulpit Bible, there is a sense in which his situation is between the Bible and the congregation, a sense in which he is a sort of middleman, working on the Bible in order to obtain from it a message which he then passes on to his people. The dangers here are less obvious, and they are all the more dangerous for not being obvious. Such a view of the matter is liable to lead very quickly to a sort of obscurantism which presents the preacher as someone who by virtue of his superior knowledge is in a position to patronize the congregation, doling out to them according to his discretion convenient portions of Bible message neatly prepacked and guaranteed suitable for the non-expert's consumption. But the preacher is in a perilous condition, when he has begun to think of himself in this way, and the more a preacher does know about the Bible, the less inclined will he be to think of himself as such an expert. Moreover, such a view of the relation of the preacher to the Bible encourages the rest of the Church to imagine that they are free to leave the serious study of the Bible to those who preach, forgetting the truth, which the Reformers saw so clearly, that the Bible is for all God's people. Most serious of all, such a view suggests that the Bible is just a subject like other subjects, which, like them, can be mastered by undergoing a sufficiently long course of study and instruction; but, while it is of course true that there is a vast amount of information and discussion concerned with the Bible, comparable with the matter of any subject of academic study, the essential thing about the Bible is the fact that the living Christ Himself speaks to us in and through it; and He who spoke yesterday wills to speak also today and tomorrow, and must therefore be heard afresh again and again.

So, while the preacher should most certainly try to be as expert as he can be in the Bible and in those studies which relate to it, his relation to it is not to be thought of as that of the expert to the subject of his expertise, but as something more humble, the relation of a hearer and a servant. His task is to lead the congregation in the work, which is common to him and to them, of hearing the Word of God. He stands in the pulpit as the servant of the Word, to render service in connexion with the expected event of Christ's presence and conversation with His people, to lead and encourage the congregation in their waiting upon that event. In so far as he does serve Holy Scripture thus humbly and honestly, and only in so far as he does so, we may make bold to refer to his very human talking as itself the Word of God ('the Word of God preached') and to his mouth as 'the mouth of God'.

The preacher's place, then, is, metaphorically speaking, under the Bible; he stands under its authority. He should remember, if he is conducting worship in one of those churches where the Bible is solemnly carried in before the preacher and if it is also the custom for the congregation at that point to rise, that they rise – at least if they know what they are doing! – not in honour of him, but in honour of 'the Word of God written', of which he is only the humble and unworthy servant. His relation to the Bible is certainly not that of someone who has taken its authority to himself and is now in a position to wield that authority as his own. He is the servant of Jesus Christ, 'the Word of God revealed', by being, not the master, but the lowly servant, of the Bible, 'the Word of God written'.

The traditional pulpit, which we mentioned at the beginning of this lecture, is not raised aloft above the congregation in order to indicate the elevation of the preacher's person: it is raised aloft to indicate the majesty of that event upon which preacher and congregation together wait, namely, Christ's presence and speaking through the written testimony of prophets and apostles. It is because it is the place where the attempt is again and again made to expound the Bible in the confident expectation of that event that the pulpit is raised so high. Alas for the hapless preacher who imagines that it is raised high in order to be a platform for the exhibition of his learning, eloquence, humour and impressive personality, forgetting that it is the throne of Jesus Christ from which He alone is to rule His people!

That the preacher's task in any sermon is to expound a passage of Scripture honestly and clearly, explaining its meaning in its context (not quite independently of its context, as is sometimes done!) and in relation to the Bible as a whole and to Christ to whom the whole Bible bears witness, and apply it as simply and directly as possible to the concrete situation of his hearers, should go without saying. That the passage has to be applied needs to be stressed; for the temptation to take refuge in generalities and vagueness is very strong, and far too many sermons leave matters in the air. The preacher's work has not been done, until the scripture-passage has been allowed to bring home to the hearers quite explicitly and concretely its bearing on their particular lives. Where the preacher faces the same congregation Sunday by Sunday, there is a lot to be said for his attempting from time to time to preach through a biblical book, expounding it section by section consecutively, as John Chrysostom, for example, did, and John Calvin, both of them magnificently, and as has been done recently with notable success by some continental preachers (for example, Eduard Thurneysen and Walter Lüthi in Switzerland). It is good for us to remind ourselves that the biblical writers, like most intelligent writers, wrote their books with the intention that they should be read through in order from the beginning to the end, a fact which some recent compilers of lectionaries seem to have been determined to ignore, preferring that Scripture should be read in church in about as jumbled an order as they could well devise.

It is clear that, if the preacher is going to fulfil his task faithfully, he must apply himself seriously and diligently to the study of the Bible. May I, therefore, in conclusion, make five points very briefly by way of general advice on the study of the Bible?

(i) There is a memorable quotation from the great eighteenth-century German NT scholar, J. A. Bengel, printed at the head of the introduction of the widely-used Nestle Greek Testament.[1] The first part of it (*Te totum applica ad textum*) means: 'Apply thy whole self to the text'. That is the first point. Since the Lord Jesus Christ Himself wills to use Holy Scripture as the means of His

---

[1] It has been omitted from the 26th edition (1979) – in our view, an unhappy omission, whether accidental or deliberate.

conversation with us, we must commit everything that we are to the study of the text. To bring anything less than our whole selves, when we wait upon Christ's speaking to us, would be to insult our Lord and King. Whatever intellectual ability we possess, the fullest diligence and conscientiousness of which we are capable, all our sense of humour, all our seriousness of purpose and concern, all our experience of life and affairs, must be applied. If we can read the Bible in the original languages, then that too we must bring. If we are professional theologians, then, of course, we must make the fullest possible use of all the help which scholarship can afford. And here I would say to you that there is no need to be afraid of critical studies, provided always you remember to be as rigorously critical of your own ideas and of the views and claims of modern biblical scholars as you are of the scriptural text. The trouble comes of not being critical enough. Some NT scholars are unbelievably uncritical when it is a matter of their own ideas. We need not be afraid for the Bible's safety: it is an anvil which will wear out very many hammers. But, as far as scholarly study is concerned, how much the particular person is required to do will vary greatly from person to person. Remember that we are required to bring what we are and have, not what we are not and do not have. What is inexcusable is the carelessness which neglects to use the gifts God has given. 'God has promised,' Calvin once said,[1] 'that His blessing shall be upon the hands of those who work . . . . If I should enter the pulpit without deigning to glance at a book, and frivolously imagine to myself, "Oh well, when I preach, God will give me enough to say", and come here without troubling to read, or thinking what I ought to declare, and

[1] Sermon on Deut 6.15–19 (CR 54 (*Calvini Opera* 26), cols. 473–474), as quoted by T. H. L. Parker, *The Oracles of God: an introduction to the preaching of John Calvin*, London, 1947, p. 69.

not carefully consider how I must apply Holy Scripture to the edification of the people – then I should be an arrogant upstart!'

(ii) Secondly – and I shall make the remaining points much more briefly – remember that Christ is not a prisoner in Scripture, not there at our disposal, but the Lord who is free. He comes to us in His freedom as and where and when He wills. He is free not to speak to us in a particular passage at a particular time, as well as to speak; and we must be patient when He does not speak, and not conclude that, because He does not will to speak to us in a particular passage now, He will never speak to us or to others in it. So we should approach the text with a humble prayer, 'Speak, Lord; for thy servant heareth'. We may say that prayer with humble confidence, with confident expectancy, but not with the arrogant presumption of those who imagine they have God under their control.

(iii) Thirdly, remember that we need to be enabled to hear. It is possible for Christ to speak to us, and for us because of our sinfulness, our deep self-centredness, to fail to hear. Therefore we need to pray God to give us His Holy Spirit, to open our ears and minds and hearts, to enable us to recognize the voice of Christ and to understand what He is saying to us. To approach the text without the twofold prayer (for Christ to speak and for the Holy Spirit to enable us to hear) is likely to prove a barren exercise, even though we do bring our own utmost efforts to the task.

(iv) Fourthly, seek the right thing in Scripture. Of course, there are many different things that we may properly look for, such as the enjoyment of splendid poetry and the discovery of interesting historical information about many periods; but there is one thing which we must look for first and foremost and above all, and on which we must try always to keep our eyes fixed, and that is Jesus Christ Himself. We must seek Christ in the Scriptures, must read them expecting to find Him. He is the key to the right understanding of them, and no passage of the Scriptures is properly understood, unless He is seen as its inmost meaning and substance. To remember this always is the sufficient safeguard against any possible misunderstanding of the next point.

(v) Fifthly, and lastly, 'apply the whole matter to thyself'. That is the second half of the quotation from Bengel in the Nestle edition of the Greek Testament – *rem totam applica ad te*. Another German NT scholar, Julius Schniewind, who died a few years ago, once put it like this: 'We cannot properly understand the word of Scripture without applying it right away to our own life.'[1] You remember the words of the prophet Nathan to David (2 Sam 12.7), 'Thou art the man'. We must take the Word of God to ourselves, its judgment of human sin, its measureless mercy, its summons to obedience. On the preacher's obligation to lead the way in obedient response to the Scripture he expounds, Calvin says with memorable vigour: 'It were better for him to break his neck going up into the pulpit, if he does not take pains to be the first to follow God.'[2]

[1] 'The biblical doctrine of conversion', in *SJT* 5 (1952), p. 268.
[2] CR 54 (*Calvini Opera* 26), col. 304, as quoted in Parker, op. cit., p. 60.

II
A STUDY OF 1 THESSALONIANS 2[1]

The contents of 1 Thessalonians 2 bear a close resemblance to those of the preceding chapter; but in chapter 2 there is a considerable increase of detail, and a greater intensity of feeling comes to expression. Both chapters are concerned with the ministry fulfilled in Thessalonica by Paul and his colleagues, Silvanus and Timothy, and with the existence there of a young church as its result. Both chapters strike the note of thanksgiving to God; but, while in chapter 1 Paul's 'We give thanks to God' comes at the beginning, following immediately upon the epistolary prescript, in chapter 2 the words 'we also thank God' occur near the middle (v. 13). We shall take the liberty of making Paul's thanksgiving in v. 13 our starting-point and then dealing with its sequel in vv. 14–16, which includes two very puzzling and difficult verses (v. 15f), before considering the long paragraph consisting of vv. 1–12. We shall then conclude by taking a quick look at vv. 17–20, which, though they are closely connected with chapter 3, throw a valuable further light on vv. 1–12.

I

Verse 13 declares that Paul and his colleagues – it seems more natural here to understand the first person plural in this way (cf. 1.1) than to take it as a writer's plural or any other kind of plural used of a singular subject – 'thank God without ceasing'.[2] The reason for this constant

---

[1] First published in *Irish Biblical Studies* 1 (1979), pp. 215–226.

[2] The first 'also' of the verse (representing the second καί) is by some connected with 'we', by others with 'thank'. In either case, the force of

thanksgiving is indicated in the latter part of the verse:[1] 'that, when ye received from us the word of the message, *even the word* of God, ye accepted *it* not *as* the word of men, but, as it is in truth, the word of God, which also worketh in you that believe'.

There are several details of exegesis to be considered before we attempt to draw out the significance of this as a whole. (i) The Greek word represented by 'message' can denote the ability to hear, the act of hearing, that with which one hears (i.e., the ear), that which is heard, so a report, message (cf. its use in the Isaiah quotation in Rom 10.16). The RV supplement, '*even the word*', is not necessary. For 'from us the word of the message, *even the word* of God' we might well substitute something like 'the word of God spoken by us'. (ii) That Paul used παραλαμβάνειν ('receive') here to denote external reception as opposed to something inward denoted by δέχεσθαι ('accept') does not seem to us very likely, since παραλαμβάνειν, which is a technical term in the NT for receiving teaching or tradition (cf., e.g., Mk 7.4; 1 Cor 11.23; 15.1, 3; Gal 1.9, 12; Phil 4.9), does not naturally exclude the thought of inward acceptance but rather includes it (see, in particular, 1 Cor 15.1 and 3). But the way in which the two verbs are used in this verse does suggest that, while παραλαμβάνειν may be taken to bear its ordinary meaning embracing both the external and the internal aspects, δέχεσθαι does specially bring out, and focus attention on, the element of inward personal decision. (iii) The Greek contains no explicit equivalents

the Greek word is just to give emphasis to the word it is associated with. It is probably better (*pace* B. Rigaux, *Saint Paul: les Épîtres aux Thessaloniciens*, Paris and Gembloux, 1956, p. 437f) to connect it with the verb.

[1] The διὰ τοῦτο ('for this cause') is here used with reference to what follows, anticipating 'that ...'.

of the '*it*' and '*as*' of the RV. It is therefore possible to translate: 'when ye received . . . , ye accepted not the word of men, but . . . the word of God'. Paul's point would then be that, when the Thessalonians had received the gospel message, they had received no mere human word but had received nothing less than the word of God Himself. Rigaux insists that the Greek should be taken this way.[1] But against this it must be said that 'when ye received the word . . . of God, ye accepted . . . the word of God' seems decidedly tautological; that, on this interpretation, the clause 'as it is in truth' seems redundant; that the use of δέχεσθαι with two accusatives[2] in the sense 'accept some one (or "something") as something' can be paralleled (cf., e.g., Thucydides 1.43, where it is used of accepting some one as an ally); and that the presence of 'as it is in truth' tells positively in favour of this 'accept . . . as' interpretation. We conclude that the Latin Vulgate's insertion of *illud* and *ut*, which the AV and RV have followed, gives Paul's meaning correctly. (iv) It is not certain whether the antecedent of 'which' is 'the word' or 'God' (in the Greek the relative pronoun here is masculine, as are both λόγος ('word') and θεός ('God'). The Vulgate and some of the Fathers understood the relative as referring to God;[3] but we are inclined to think that it is rather more natural to take it to refer to the word.[4] But, substantially, there is not a great difference of meaning involved.

[1] op. cit., p. 440.

[2] To understand the first accusative from the participial clause (in Greek: in the RV the clause beginning with 'when') is of course natural enough.

[3] So too J. A. Bengel (in his *Gnomon Novi Testamenti*, first published in 1742), who saw in the introduction here of a relative clause about God an underlining of the fact that the word really is God's word.

[4] Cf. the use of ἐνεργής (RV: 'active') with reference to the word of God in Heb 4.12. If we were to accept Rigaux's contention (op. cit.,

Verse 13 indicates two things about the people who make up the young church in Thessalonica. These two things are, if we understand the verse correctly, that they have recognized the message of the gospel for what it truly is, and have received it as such, namely, as the authoritative word of God; and that this word of God is now working in them, having definite consequences in their lives. The questions which this verse puts to us, as we seek to hear in it God's word for us, are obvious enough: Are those marks of true churches and of true Christians, to which it points, characteristic of the congregations to which we belong and of ourselves? Have we really received the gospel message as the authoritative word of the eternal God – as what it truly is, and not as mere human teaching, as a philosophy or as an ideology or as something for which, as part of our cultural inheritance, we feel a certain sentimental attachment, perhaps rather condescending, perhaps always diminishing? And is the word of God really working in us effectually? Does it make a significant difference to the way we live our lives? Could we honestly say that it is – in some measure at least – moulding our daily lives, disciplining us, curbing our egotism? Does it, for example, affect what we do with our money or the way we vote in parliamentary elections?

II

Verse 14 supports the latter part of v. 13 (note the 'For') by referring to the fact that the Christians of Thessalonica have followed the pattern of those of Judaea, in that, as

pp. 440, 668–670) that ἐνεργεῖται is passive ('is rendered active': RV 'worketh' assumes that it is middle), then the question of the antecedent would be settled in favour of 'the word'; but we are not convinced by his arguments.

the Christians of Judaea have suffered persecution at the hands of their fellow-Jews, so they have been persecuted by their own fellow-countrymen. To share Christ's reproach, to be hated for His sake, this is another mark of the true church and the true Christian. We may compare the words of Jn 15.19f: 'because ye are not of the world, but I chose you out of the world, therefore the world hateth you .... If they persecuted me, they will also persecute you'. The words of William Temple, 'Not all that the world hates is good Christianity; but it does hate good Christianity and always will',[1] are wise words and true. If our lives are even just beginning to be under the discipline of the gospel, they are bound to be in collision with the values and ways of the society around us.

III

Verses 15 and 16 are incidental. Having mentioned the Jews, that is, the unbelieving Jews, in the course of referring to what the Thessalonian Christians have suffered from their fellow-countrymen, Paul adds by the way some statements concerning them. With 'who ... killed the Lord Jesus' we may compare Acts 2.23; 3.15; 4.10; 7.52; also Mk 12.7f and its parallels. Paul is not forgetting the part played by the Romans, but he is underlining the special guilt of God's own chosen people. With 'and the prophets' compare, among other passages, Mt 23.29–37; Mk 12.5; Acts 7.52; Rom 11.3. Of the next four charges levelled against the unbelieving Jews, the first is distinguished by the use of a further aorist participle in the Greek (they have fiercely persecuted[2] Paul

---

[1] *Readings in St John's Gospel*, London, 1950, p. 271f.

[2] The RV takes ἐκδιώκειν here to mean 'drive out'. It is rather more probable that the ἐκ- has here a strengthening force and that the

and other preachers of the gospel), the other three[1] by the use of present participles expressing continuity. The clause which the RV renders 'to fill up their sins alway' is understood by some as final,[2] by others as consecutive. It is difficult to decide between these alternatives. If we take the clause to be consecutive, we may understand the thought to be that their always completing the full measure of their sins results from the rebelliousness against God which has just been described. If, however, we take the clause as final, we may understand the thought to be that God's purpose behind all this rebelliousness of His own people was that they should always complete the full measure of their sins. The expression 'fill up their sins' is biblical (cf. the Septuagint version of Gen 15.16; Dan 8.23; 2 Macc 6.14f).[3] Though the precise sense it has here is not easy to determine, the general sense which we take it to have will become plain from our discussion of the last sentence of this paragraph (v. 16b).

It is this sentence which is the most difficult part of vv. 15 and 16. It is often taken to be a declaration that there is now no hope for the Jews. So the NEB renders the Greek: 'and now retribution has overtaken them for good and all'. If this 'for good and all' really gives the true meaning of the Greek, then Paul's view of the situation of the Jewish people certainly did undergo a most drastic change between the writing of 1 Thessalonians and Romans 11. But the Greek phrase εἰς τέλος is patient of more than one interpretation. It can mean, for example,

---

compound verb is used in the sense 'persecute vehemently'. Cf. A. Oepke, in *TWNT* 2, p. 232f.

[1] In one case the participle is not expressed but has to be supplied – that is, ὄντων with ἐναντίων.

[2] The purpose is understood to be God's.

[3] Cf. also Mt 23.32.

'at last', 'finally', 'to the uttermost'. The most likely meaning of the sentence as a whole in view of what Paul says elsewhere is, in our opinion, that God's wrath has already come upon the Jews to the uttermost in the event of the Cross. In that event the disobedience of God's people reached its climax, and God showed it up in its true character with final and absolute clarity. Moreover, in the act of taking upon Himself the full burden of His wrath against sinners He allowed men to see its awful reality.[1] Paul knew full well that the judgment of the Cross was God's judgment not of the Jews only but of all men, Jews and Gentiles alike. But here he refers specially to the Jews, underlining their special guilt as the people of God. The lesson which Christians ought to draw form v. 16b is most certainly not an encouragement of any antisemitism to which they may be inclined but a reminder of the fact that the Christian Church shares with the Jewish people a specially exposed and dangerous position in relation to God's judgment – 'to whomsoever much is given, of him shall much be required'. And how like the unbelieving Jews of Paul's time we Christians often are! Could it not often be fairly said of us that we 'please not God', and sometimes that, far from being serious about our missionary task, we prevent, in one way or another, those who would hear the gospel from hearing it so as to be saved?

IV

We turn now to vv. 1–12. They tell us a very great deal about the ministry of Paul and his colleagues in

---

[1] For an attempt to expound what Paul meant by 'the wrath of God' and its revelation the reader is referred to the writer's I.C.C. commentary on Romans, volume 1, pp. 106–111, 213–217.

Thessalonica which lay behind the existence of the young church to which this letter is addressed. They deserve a much more detailed and careful study than we shall have space for here; for they do, in fact, provide an outline for what could be a truly notable and worthwhile course of lectures in pastoral theology, and it is on this aspect of them that we shall specially focus attention.

It is perhaps not quite as certain as Rigaux takes it to be[1] that εἴσοδος (RV: 'entering in') is used in v. 1 (and also in 1.9) in its literal sense of 'entrance' or 'visit'; but, even if we take Rigaux's judgment for granted and ignore the possibility that εἴσοδος is here used metaphorically,[2] it is still hardly to be disputed that this chapter as a whole indicates clearly that Paul and Silvanus and Timothy had found an entrance to the Thessalonians' hearts – had shown themselves credible as messengers of God, possessed of that credibility which only God Himself can give but without which no true pastoral work can even be begun, let alone sustained and brought to fruition. (And to say of some one that he or she is a credible minister of the gospel of Christ, in the sense that he or she is some one who can be – and, by God's gracious working, at any rate to a considerable extent, deserves to be – taken seriously as a minister of Christ's gospel, is surely as high praise as one can confer on a fellow-human being.)

In v. 2 Paul refers to the fact that, in spite of the sufferings and humiliating treatment which he and his colleagues had had to bear in Philippi (see Acts 16.19ff), they had 'waxed bold in our God to speak' to the Thessalonians 'the gospel of God', even though in Thessalonica too they met with opposition ('in much

[1] op. cit., pp. 400 and 388f.

[2] See W. Bauer, *Griechisch-deutsches Wörterbuch zu den Schriften des Neuen Testaments* ..., Berlin, 1971 (corrected and expanded reprint of 5th ed. of 1958), s.v. 1.

conflict' – see Acts 17.5ff). The word for us to mark specially here is παρρησιάζεσθαι (RV: 'wax bold'). The substantive παρρησία (its derivation is from the combination of the words for 'all' and 'speaking') was used to denote that freedom of speech which the Athenians claimed as their right and of which they were greatly proud.[1] It was characteristic of a democracy. In the NT the word's range of meanings includes openness in speech, frankness, publicness (publicly, in public), boldness, fearlessness, confidence, joyful confidence.[2] So here in v. 2 ἐπαρρησιασάμεθα is an affirmation that they had proclaimed the gospel of God fearlessly and confidently. Contrast the timidity, the lack of confidence, the hesitancy, by which so often the preaching in Britain at the present time is characterized. It is a rare experience to hear the gospel of Jesus Christ proclaimed with confidence and joy and without apology, that is, with the παρρησία of which it is altogether worthy.

Verse 3 contains three interesting negative phrases. The first of them is 'not of error'. The noun πλάνη denotes a going astray from the truth, a state of being misled. It corresponds not to the active verb πλανᾶν ('lead astray') but to the passive πλανᾶσθαι. For Paul it is clearly a matter of great importance whether the source of his exhortation is the truth of the gospel or error, that is the condition of being astray from that truth. This phrase puts a number of questions to us. To mention just some of them – Do we want to have, or would we rather escape the embarrassments involved in having, that moral and intellectual integrity which compels a person to care seriously about the distinction between truth and

[1] Cf., e.g., Euripides, *Hippolytus* 421–423; *Ion* 670–672; Demosthenes 9.3; Aristotle, *Athenaion Politeia* 16.6; Polybius 2.38.

[2] See, for example, Jn 7.26; 11.54; Acts 4.29; Eph 3.12; Heb 10.19; 1 Jn 3.21.

falsehood? Are our churches and their ministers and teachers at present perhaps so bewildered and confused as to be scarcely conscious of the need to distinguish the truth of the gospel from the fashionable falsehoods of the day? How far is an anti-intellectual prejudice characteristic of our churches? And, if it is, how far is it a reaction against a barren pseudo-intellectualism which has obscured the fact that theology has to do with obedience, that the truth of God is only known when we begin to 'do' it (cf. Jn 3.21; 1 Jn 1.6)? The second negative phrase is 'nor of uncleanness'. While the word ἀκαθαρσία is often used of sexual immorality in particular, it can also denote quite generally the moral condition of the pagan world. We need to ask ourselves how far we could truly claim that the source of our exhortation is uncontaminated by the manifold corruptions of the pagan society in which we live. The last of the three negative phrases of v. 3 is 'nor in guile'. That Paul should be anxious to dissociate himself as strongly as possible from the many charlatans who wandered about in his day claiming to be purveyors of philosophical or religious wisdom is understandable enough, and it is quite likely that he added 'nor in guile' with this purpose in mind. But guile is certainly not a special peculiarity of the ancient world; and we should be wise to consider whether Paul's phrase is not relevant to the position of those who, having ceased to believe those things which in their ordination they have solemnly affirmed that they believed, lack the honesty to resign their ministries (we do not, of course, mean to suggest that every passing doubt or depression or even the experience of a prolonged period of doubt constitutes a proper ground for resigning one's ministry), and so deceive their fellow-men and abuse their trust.

We may take together vv. 4b and 6a (in what follows we shall have to pass over much that is interesting and important). While there is a right pleasing of men which is a Christian duty (see, for example, Rom 15.2f), there is a pleasing of men which is opposed to pleasing God, and this is something which a Christian minister should eschew. So Paul writes: 'not as pleasing men, but God'. And similar is the general purport of v. 6a ('nor seeking glory of men, neither from you, nor from others'). The bearing of these two half-verses on our present-day church life is surely too clear to need exposition.

Verse 5 contains two denials. In support of the former ('neither at any time were we found using words of flattery') Paul appeals to the Thessalonian Christians' own knowledge ('as ye know'); in support of the latter ('nor a cloke of covetousness') he calls God to witness ('God is witness'). The reason for this difference is probably that, while flattery is something which is usually pretty obvious (to the onlookers at least – to the person flattered it is, of course, often not at all obvious), the sort of thing to which the latter denial refers is something which it is much more difficult for human perception to discern. The essence of λόγος κολακείας is the saying of things designed to gratify the vanity of some one with the intention of gaining some advantage for oneself. It is a very common clerical failing, which in situations of extreme boredom may provide some comic relief for any onlooker who is sufficiently hard-hearted to be able to put out of his head the thought of the serious inward damage which the flatterer is doing to himself – and quite often also to the person flattered. The gain which the clerical flatterer seeks, is, of course, often simply general popularity (undiscerning congregations like to be flattered and like those who flatter them!); but it may also be favour in high places and the preferments and promotions which may result therefrom. With regard to the latter denial, the Greek represented by 'a cloke of covetousness' is difficult. The word πρόφασις ('cloke') can have a variety of meanings; πλεονεξία is also an elusive word; and the sense of the genitive is patient of a number of different explanations. Perhaps the most likely explanation of Paul's meaning is that he is denying that he has been guilty of any sort of hidden exploitation of the Thessalonians. There are many ways in which one can exploit another person, that is, use him or her for one's own selfish ends, for self-gratification of one kind or another. Often, of course, a man's exploitation of his fellow-man is open, shameless, blatant. But exploitation of others is sometimes exceedingly subtle; and, among Christians, it can be veiled in various beautifully pious disguises. And not only can it be hidden from its victim and from all human witnesses: it can also be unrecognized by the exploiter himself – unconscious exploitation of others.

We notice next Paul's reference to his gentleness[1] in v. 7: 'But we were gentle in the midst of you, as when a nurse[2] cherisheth her own children'. It is an interesting and instructive feature of this paragraph; for gentleness is an apostolic quality which is by no means common among parish ministers and priests. How many of the clergy would be more accurately described as inclined to be arrogant, self-willed, stubborn, domineering, than as gentle! How many are too conscious of their authority, and apt to see it as a personal thing rather than as belonging to the message, of which they are always the altogether unworthy, and are meant to be the humble,

---

[1] On the textual variation between ἤπιοι ('gentle') and νήπιοι ('babes') the reader may be referred to B. M. Metzger, *The text of the New Testament: its transmission, corruption, and restoration*, Oxford, [2]1968, pp. 230–233. ἤπιοι should surely be read.

[2] The Jerusalem Bible is surely right in rendering τροφός here by 'a mother': cf., e.g., Sophocles, *Ajax* 849.

servants! The gentleness to which Paul refers is surely contrary to all pomposity and also to that excessive loquaciousness, which is a besetting sin of many clergy, making them far too often oblivious of the fact that their parishioners need not only to be talked to by, but also to be able to confide in, their pastors (and some parishioners are likely to be too shy and hesitant to be readily able to seize the odd moments when their pastors stop for breath).

From the rest of vv. 1–12 we pick out just three things for notice. The first is the reference in v. 8 to Paul's and his colleagues' readiness to impart to the Thessalonians 'not the gospel of God only, but also our own souls, because ye were become very dear to us', which both gives a precious further glimpse of the tender affection of Paul's relations with his churches and is also a reminder that to be a proper Christian pastor one must give one's very self (cf. RSV; NEB) to those in one's charge, so that, while belonging absolutely to Christ alone, one belongs more to them than to oneself. The second is v. 10: 'Ye are witnesses, and God *also*, how holily and righteously and unblameably we have behaved ourselves toward you that believe'. It should be remembered that Paul is not speaking here of what he has been, or is, toward God (in view of Rom 7.14ff, it may, we think, be safely assumed that the man who wrote these words was well aware that his life had fallen, and still continued to fall, far short of God's absolute standard). He is not claiming that his conduct toward the Thessalonians has been blameless in God's sight; but only that it has been such that before his fellow-Christians he can hold his head erect. A Christian minister, who knows himself altogether unworthy before God, may still be conscious of being a man of relative integrity and of having a right to look his fellow-Christians in the eyes. And,if he is not a man of integrity

31

in this sense, he is scarcely likely to be a credible minister of the gospel. The third is the presence of the words 'each one of you' in v. 11. Paul's giving himself to his churches involved a fatherly concern for each individual in them – one by one. Such a caring for the individual is a mark of every faithful under-shepherd of Him, who – we are told – 'calleth his own sheep by name' (Jn 10.3).

V

We turn lastly to vv. 17–20, in which Paul speaks of his strong desire to see the Thessalonian Christians again and the fact that he (note the emphatic 'I Paul' in v. 18) has more than once wanted to visit them again (though he has not been able to do so), and then goes on to say: 'For what is our hope, or joy, or crown of glorying? Are not even ye, before our Lord Jesus at his coming? For ye are our glory and our joy'. This is surely something decidedly surprising for the apostle to say. John Calvin saw the difficulty: Paul's words seem to be inconsonant with the truth that there is only One, in whom we may properly boast either now or hereafter, God Himself. His comment is sensible: 'we should not take this to mean that he glories in any other than God, but that we are allowed to glory in all of God's favours in their proper place in such a way that He Himself is always our point of aim'.[1] These last two verses of the chapter shed a flood of light on the important question of the scale of values to be recognized by a minister of the gospel, be he a parish minister or a theological teacher. That to glory in our social, academic or ecclesiastical honours or dignities is out of the question

---

[1] *The Epistles of Paul the Apostle to the Romans and to the Thessalonians*, Eng. tr. by R. Mackenzie, Edinburgh, 1961, p. 351.

should be clear to us. Karl Barth wisely recognized that in heaven his eleven honorary doctorates would all have to be handed in at the cloakroom,[1] and even the *Church Dogmatics* would be but waste paper there,[2] where we shall know even as also we have been known. But, if at the parousia of Jesus Christ – notice the words 'before our Lord Jesus Christ at his coming' (the present tense ἐστε in v. 20 is to be understood in the light of v. 19): to glory in our converts now or in the large numbers who maybe crowd the churches where we minister would be premature, since we do not yet know who will endure to the end – there are some who have owed something of their true faith in Jesus Christ to words or deeds of ours, then that is something of eternal worth, in which, as God's favour to us, we may properly glory and rejoice, humbly and thankfully, for ever.

[1] E. Busch, *Karl Barth: his life from letters and autobiographical texts*, Eng. tr. by J. Bowden, London, 1976, p. 489.
[2] ibid.

III
LIGHT FROM ST PAUL ON CHRISTIAN-JEWISH RELATIONS[1]

In this short essay I shall try to draw out what seem to me to be the main implications for Christian-Jewish relations today of Paul's teaching as I understand it. For the sake of clarity I shall number my sections.

1. We may start from Paul's strikingly emphatic and solemn declaration of his grief in Rom 9.1–5 ('I speak the truth in Christ, I do not lie – my conscience bears me witness in the Holy Spirit – *when I declare* that I have great grief and continual anguish in my heart. For I would pray that I might be accursed *and cut off* from Christ on behalf of my brethren, my kinsfolk according to the flesh . . .').[2] It attests his clear recognition that the central point at issue between Christians (whether Jewish or Gentile) and non-Christian Jews is of transcendent importance. The fact that the great majority of his fellow-Jews reject Him who is, Paul is convinced, the true Messiah of Israel, is proper cause for deep anguish. The first point with regard to Christian-Jewish relations to be learned from Paul is, we submit, that we should recognize with full frankness the reality of the chasm which separates us and not indulge in any attempt to paper it over.

2. But the same passage shows something else, Paul's equally clear recognition that the unbelieving Jews are

[1] First published in D. W. Torrance (ed.), *The Witness of the Jews to God*, Edinburgh, 1982, pp. 22–31.

[2] I hope I may be forgiven both for using in the quotations from Romans my own translation from *A Critical and Exegetical Commentary on the Epistle to the Romans*, Edinburgh, vol. 1, [3]1980, and vol. 2, [2]1981 – for giving me permission to do this I have to thank Messrs. T. & T. Clark, Ltd. – and also for referring the reader to that commentary for the detailed exegesis, which is the basis of much of what I shall say here.

still his 'brethren', still 'Israelites' (note the present tense, *eisin*, in v. 4), still fellow-members of the people of God's choice. If we would be true to Paul's teaching, we must surely repudiate altogether the notion, which is very widespread among Christians and has often been expressed by theologians (including – God forgive him! – the present writer), that the Jewish people, having rejected Jesus Christ, has been dispossessed of its election and simply replaced by God by a new Israel, namely, the Christian Church. The whole of Romans 11 bears this out, set as it is under the sign of v. 2a, 'God has not cast off his people whom he foreknew'.[1] Addressing the Gentiles among the Roman Christians Paul says concerning the at present unbelieving Jews in vv. 28f: 'As regards *the progress of* the gospel they are enemies for your sake, but as regards the election they are beloved for the sake of the fathers; for the gifts and the call of God are irrevocable'. We may compare Rom. 3.3f ('What then? If some have failed to respond with faith, shall their lack of faith render God's faithfulness ineffective? God forbid! We confess rather than God is true, and all men liars . . .').

Paul does indeed recognize that 'not all who are of Israel are Israel' in the sense of standing in a positive relationship to the accomplishment of God's purpose, but that does not mean that only part of Israel is the elect people of God. All Jews, 'all who are of Israel' (Rom 9.6), are members of God's elect people, members of that community which is Jesus Christ's environment, all without exception witnesses to God's grace and faithfulness; but not all of them are Israel in the narrower

[1] The relative clause should not be taken as limiting the reference of 'his people' to those members who are objects of God's secret election (*pace* Calvin); for in v. 1, in the light of 10.21, 'his people' must surely denote the people of Israel as a whole, and it is unnatural to give it a different sense in v. 2.

35

sense of being the company of relatively understanding, willing, grateful witnesses to that grace and faithfulness. Barth was surely right to see in Romans 9–11 the recognition that the people of God exists in two forms in history, on the one hand, as the believing element of the people in OT times, the Israel within Israel, and (continuous with it) the Church consisting of both believing Jews and believing Gentiles, and, on the other hand, that bulk of Israel which is not the inner Israel and (continuous with it) the still unbelieving Jews.[1] While it is only in its existence in one of these forms that the people of God bears a testimony to Jesus Christ which is positive, conscious, voluntary and joyful, even in its existence in the other it cannot help bearing witness to Him, and its witness, though negative, unconscious, involuntary and joyless, is in its own peculiar way impressively eloquent.

3. In Rom 10.1 Paul declares that the desire of his heart and his prayer to God for his unbelieving fellow-Jews are 'that they may be saved', and his declaration indicates a continuing duty of the Christian Church, a duty which includes seriously and wholeheartedly willing, earnestly and faithfully praying for, and therefore also persistently but at the same time humbly, graciously and in a truly brotherly fashion working for,[2] the salvation of the Jews. It would seem to be an indication of the feebleness of faith and absence of serious engagement with Holy Scripture which appear to be characteristic of present-day British church life that one so seldom hears in public worship any specific prayer for the salvation of non-Christian Jews.

4. In the following verse, the last four words of which give expression to very grave criticism, Paul pays to his

[1] Reference may be made to the section on God's election of grace in *Church Dogmatics* II/2, pp. 1–506, as a whole.
[2] Cf., e.g., Rom 11.13f; also Acts 13.14ff; 14.1; 17.1–3, 10, 17; 18.4f; 19.8; 21.39f; 22.1ff; 28.17ff.

still unbelieving kinsmen a most notable tribute: 'I bear them witness that they have zeal for God'. Both 'zeal' and 'for God' are significant. He acknowledges that their zeal has the right object: it is zeal for the one true God. And he acknowledges that it is indeed zeal. It is a double acknowledgement which the Church ought always to remember. It should both encourage a brotherly and open attitude towards the Jews on the Church's part and also contribute to a salutary disturbance of Christian self-complacency (for of how much of the churches' own membership could it be stated with equal confidence that the object of its worship is really the living God and not one or other of the various idols of an acquisitive, spendthrift, corrupt society, and, even where the churches' members are concerned with the true God, how much of their concern could be described with any accuracy by so strong a term as 'zeal'?).

5. We take a look next at the last words of Rom 10.2. The meaning of the words 'yet not according to knowledge' is that, in spite of the earnestness of the still unbelieving Jews' zeal and the fact that their zeal is really zeal for the true God, it contains a grievous flaw – it is 'not according to knowledge'. That does not mean that the persons concerned do not know God: they certainly do know Him (cf. v. 19). But they will not know Him as He really wants to be known, as He really is. There is an incomprehension at the heart of their knowledge and in the centre of their dedicated and meticulous obedience a stubborn disobedience (cf. Mk 4.12). Paul goes on in v. 3 to explain that their ignorance consists in their failure to acknowledge God's righteousness, that is, the status of righteousness before Him which He Himself offers as a gift, and – what is the other side of this failure – their obstinate determination to establish their own righteousness, that is, their claim to be counted righteous

before God by virtue of their own deserts. This is indeed a failure to know God as He really is – in His mercy and faithfulness and in the seriousness of His claims. The disobedience which results from this ignorance is their refusal to 'submit to the righteousness of God', that is, to humble themselves to accept it as an undeserved gift of God's mercy.

6. The meaning of the last four words of Rom 10.2 and the following verse can be properly seen only in the light of their context. From 9.30–32a we learn that Israel, that is, the great majority of the people of Israel, failed to attain to the law of righteousness 'because *they pursued* it not on the basis of faith but as on the basis of works'. They misunderstood that law which God had given them in His graciousness. Instead of recognizing the seriousness of its claims upon them and so allowing themselves to be led to put their trust in God's forgiving mercy and to respond to it by giving themselves to Him in thankfulness and humility (that is, of pursuing it 'on the basis of faith'), they had cherished the illusion that they could so adequately fulfil its commandments as to put God in their debt (that is, they had pursued it 'as on the basis of works'). From vv. 32b and 33 we learn the christological dimension of Israel's ignorance and disobedience: 'They stumbled against the stone of stumbling, even as it is written: "Behold, I lay in Zion a stone of stumbling and a rock of offence, and he who believes on him shall not be put to shame" '. Verses 30–33 as a whole indicate the intimate and essentially positive relation between the law and Christ, which is clinched by the words 'For Christ is the end of the law' in 10.4, in which (in spite of many recent confident assertions to the contrary) 'end' (Greek: *telos*) must surely have the sense of 'goal', 'substance', 'innermost meaning'. Israel has failed to recognize its Messiah because it has failed truly

to come to grips with its own law, and it can never understand its law aright until it recognizes and accepts Him who is the very substance and inmost meaning of the law. So the Messiah, who has been given for Israel's and the world's salvation, can only be, so long as Israel's stubborn perverseness persists, the occasion of Israel's undoing.

7. The guilt of Israel is rendered abundantly clear by Rom 9.30–10.13: it is guilty because it has failed to heed properly its own law for which in its uncomprehending way it has been so zealous. But the fact that it has been given the law, the goal and inmost substance of which is Jesus Christ, does not by itself constitute such a full opportunity to invoke the name of the Lord in the sense of Rom 10.12 and 13 as would render Israel altogether and unquestionably without excuse. For that fullness of opportunity to have been given it was necessary that the message that the divine promises have now been fulfilled should have been proclaimed by messengers duly commissioned by God Himself. So, before going on in Romans 11 to give the assurance that, all human ignorance and disobedience notwithstanding, God has not cast off His chosen people, Paul is concerned to drive home in 10.14ff with final, incontrovertible decisiveness the fact that still unbelieving Israel is altogether without excuse by showing that such a proclamation has indeed taken place. Paul will have it clear beyond any shadow of doubt that the salvation of Jews no less than that of Gentiles is a matter of sheer mercy, without the least handhold for human merit.

8. Jesus Christ, who is the occasion of the deep and grievous division between Jews and Christians which may not be concealed, is also the One who unites them. He, who is the acknowledged Saviour and Lord of all who believe in Him, is Himself a Jew, the Jew *par excellence.*

39

The supreme privilege and dignity of the Jews is the fact that He is, so far as His human nature is concerned, a member of their race (cf. Rom 9.5); and this, their surpassing dignity, can never be taken away from them. To despise them is to despise and dishonour Him, in whom alone there is salvation for men. The Jewishness of Jesus of Nazareth is the final and irrevocable condemnation of every form of antisemitism, whether it be blatant and brutal or subtle and even more or less unconscious, and the unbroken bond between believing Christian and unbelieving Jew.

9. Closely related to this bond between Christian and Jew which Jesus Christ Himself is in His own person is the bond consisting of the OT which bears witness to Him. If the Church heeds St Paul, it will recognize that truly to believe in Jesus is to believe in Him according to the fullness of the OT attestation of Him, which certainly includes believing in Him as the Messiah of Israel. It will recognize too, surely, that statements representing Christ and the OT law as opposed to each other (common though they have been in recent decades among NT scholars) are mistaken and should be repudiated, and that the law should be seen as an essential part of the OT's testimony to Christ, by which Church and Synagogue are bound together. It will recognize that, though at present a veil does indeed lie on the Jews' hearts, when they hear or read the law, it is nevertheless true that in all their engagement with the law, they are, objectively though unconsciously, having to do with Jesus Christ Himself, who is its substance and meaning and who is speaking to them through it, and it will look forward with eagerness to the time when their hearts will turn to Him and the veil be taken away (cf. 2 Cor 3.14–16).[1]

[1] With regard to the substance of this paragraph reference may be made to Cranfield, op. cit., especially pp. 845–870.

10. If Christians and Jews are united by their special relatedness to Christ and by their common commitment to, and engagement with, the OT, they are also further united by the special clarity with which by reason of these things their sinfulness is made manifest and by the specially serious character, which their sinfulness possesses. According to Rom 5.12ff, sin was already present and active in the world before the giving of the law, but it was as yet nowhere absolutely clearly visible and sharply defined. If sin was ever to be decisively defeated and sinners forgiven in a way that is worthy of the altogether good, merciful and faithful God, sin must first be made to increase somewhere in the sense of being rendered clearly manifest. So the law was given, 'in order that in one people (for their own sake and also for the sake of all others) sin might be known as sin. But ... when the advent of the law makes sin increase in the sense of becoming manifest as sin, it also makes it increase in the sense of being made more sinful, since the law by showing men that what they are doing is contrary to God's will gives to their continuing to do it the character of conscious and wilful disobedience'.[1]

It is in Israel and in the Church, where God's grace and God's commandments are most fully known, that human sin is most exceedingly sinful. Nowhere else can it be so hateful. The same evil which, when perpetrated outside Israel and the Church, is monstrous, is, when perpetrated within Israel or the Church, immeasurably more monstrous. 'You only have I known of all the families of the earth: therefore I will visit upon you all your iniquities' – such is the warning of Amos 3.2; and similar is the significance of Lk 12.48 '... And to whomsoever much is given, of him shall much be required ...'.

It is in this context that we should, I think, look at 1 Th

[1] Cranfield, op. cit., p. 293.

2.15f, where Paul says about the unbelieving Jews (according to the RV): 'who both killed the Lord Jesus and the prophets, and drave out us, and please not God, and are contrary to all men; forbidding us to speak to the Gentiles that they may be saved; to fill up their sins alway: but the wrath is come upon them to the uttermost'. The last sentence is the most difficult part of this. It is frequently understood as a declaration that there is now no hope for the unbelieving Jews. So in the NEB the original is rendered: 'and now retribution has overtaken them for good and all'. But, if this 'for good and all' really were an accurate representation of the sense of the Greek, it would be necessary to assume a very drastic change in Paul's thought with regard to the situation of the Jewish people between the writing of 1 Thessalonians 2 and Romans 11; and, while such a change may be conceivable, it seems to us more likely, in view of what Paul says elsewhere, that the meaning of this sentence is that God's wrath has already come upon the Jews to the uttermost – in the event of the Cross. In the first words of v. 15 Paul is not forgetting the part played by the Romans, but is underlining the special guilt of God's chosen people. In the event of the Cross the disobedience of God's people reached its hideous climax, and God revealed it in its true character with final and absolute clarity. And in that special guilt of the Jews the Christian Church should see itself as having a share. For is it not itself, in spite of all its overwhelming privileges, continually putting Christ to shame by its unfaithfulness and wilful disobedience? While the judgment of the Cross is, of course, God's judgment on all men without exception, it is the sinfulness of Christians and Jews which is most starkly revealed by it.[1]

[1] I am grateful to the Editor of *Irish Biblical Studies* for allowing me to use in this paragraph some phraseology from my 'A Study of 1 Thessalonians 2' (reprinted in this volume, pp. 19ff).

11. Paradoxically, in view of what has been said above, and yet perhaps after all not altogether surprisingly, Church and Synagogue are united also in proneness to self-righteousness and complacency. In Romans 2 Paul apostrophizes the typical Jew who is sure of his own moral superiority over the Gentiles. Much of what he says could be applied to very many Christians. But this proneness to self-complacency common to Jews and Christians – though in a good many it has been, and is, to a considerable degree, counteracted by serious engagement with Holy Scripture – is so obvious a matter, particularly to observers from outside, that it need not be laboured here.

12. But the fact that Jesus Christ and the OT, though it is over them that they are so deeply and grievously divided, nevertheless bind Christians and Jews together means that they are also bound together in hope. The importance of the place which hope has in the life of believers, according to Paul, is clear enough from such passages as Rom 5.4f; 8.17–39; 12.12; 15.4, 13. Romans 11 shows that he saw the existence of the still unbelieving Jews also as set by the mercy of God under the sign of hope. To his own question, 'has God cast off his people?', he gives the firm reply, 'God has not cast off his people whom he foreknew' (Rom 11.1–2); and he assures the Roman Gentile Christian that God can graft in again the branches of the cultivated olive-tree which have been broken off (vv. 23 and 24). But his hope for his non-Christian fellow-countrymen does not ignore the need for faith in Christ (v. 23 includes the words, 'if they do not remain in their unbelief'). The salvation of 'all Israel' mentioned in the course of vv. 25–27 would seem to be envisaged as an eschatological event, the coming of the Deliverer out of Zion probably being understood by Paul with reference to the parousia of Christ. The relentless

concentration of the composite OT quotation in vv. 26f on God's forgiveness and on Israel's need of it dashes all Israel's illusory hopes of establishing a claim on God on the basis of its merit. There is hope for Jews as for Christians because for both alike the last word is with God's mercy on sinners.

13. Finally, we must say something with regard to the services which Jews and Christians do, as a matter of fact, whether consciously or unconsciously, render each other, and also with regard to those further services which they may or may not, but which we hope they will, render each other.

It may at once be said that to each of the two communities the very existence of the other continuing through the centuries is a valuable challenge to examine again and again itself, its own foundations and present life. That we ought to show each other, not (as we have too often done) hatred, contempt and cruelty, but brotherly affection, respect and kindness, should surely be absolutely clear without its having to be said. It surely also should be generally agreed that the possibility of blurring differences for the sake of easier and more comfortable relationships ought to be regarded as a temptation to be firmly resisted and that we ought to express to each other what we believe as clearly as possible with the utmost frankness and sincerity.

We shall suggest first a service additional to the services already mentioned (that rendered by our very existence and that indicated in 3 above), which the Church and individual Christians can and surely ought to render the Jews. We owe it to them always faithfully to try to recall them to the Law, the Prophets and the Writings, whensoever they seem to us to have forgotten them or to be in serious danger of forgetting them. We certainly have to do this very humbly indeed in view of all that we

Gentile Christians have on our consciences in relation to them. We dare not forget the monstrous barbarities perpetrated by the Nazis and by many collaborators belonging to other nations, the shameful silence of those who did not wish to know what was being done in their midst, the disgraceful failure of those in power in the various western democracies to act promptly to do what could have been done to save many more Jews from the Holocaust, the long, long record of Christian persecution of Jews which preceded the hideous horror of the Hitler days, and the continuing shame of the existence of antisemitism today whether in cruder or in more subtle forms. But we should only be increasing that burden, if we were to allow it to inhibit us now and in the future from speaking frankly. And we need to be very specially on our guard against the insidious temptation (it may well usually be below the level of conscious decision) to try to settle for making amends for our own sins at others' expense by a sentimental and uncritical commitment to the Israeli state's aspirations, which takes little or no account of the rights of the Palestinians. To succumb to this temptation would assuredly be to add yet more to the great pile of wrongs already inflicted on the Jews by Christians.

We certainly do owe them the clear challenge to examine their national, and particularly their political national aspirations, critically in the light of the Law and the Prophets and the Writings. Are the scriptural foundations of those aspirations as firm and sure as is often assumed? Even the question whether they are wholly illusory ought to be honestly faced. Are there perhaps serious spiritual dangers in Zionism? Is it possible that a good many Jews in their present preoccupation with political national goals and in their determination to attain them – sometimes it seems at any cost – are in danger of losing their own souls? If Jews commit injustice against people whose families God has allowed, in some cases for very many centuries, to dwell in the land once given to Israel and if – O that the suspicions might be proved ungrounded! – they quite often descend to gross inhumanity, are they not trampling upon the Law and the Prophets?

With regard to the service which the Jews do as a matter of fact constantly render to Christians, we may add to what has already been said at the beginning of this section and in section 4, the point that their very survival until now in spite of all that they have suffered is a particularly cogent evidence of the reality and faithfulness of God, a precious testimony presented to us for which we should be thankful.

But there is a further service which they can do to us, and which we should desire to receive from them, and indeed urgently implore them to render us. It is that they should recall us to a proper engagement with the OT – in fact, that they should do us the same service which we suggested that we owe to them. Thereby they would be conferring upon us immeasurable benefits; for the Church today suffers grievous damage from the various forms of Marcionism which afflict it, and where the Church fails to draw nourishment and instruction from the OT it is, not surprisingly, stunted and enfeebled. Serious engagement with the OT is necessary, if the Church is to sustain anything approaching an adequate Christology, a proper Trinitarian doctrine, an adequate soteriology, a satisfactory doctrine of creation, to mention just four examples. But our imploring the Jews to try to recall us to the OT should surely include the earnest entreaty that they should never cease from pointing out to us with the utmost forthrightness and rigour our daily-repeated failures to judge ourselves by the standards of goodness which we and they together possess in the Law, the Prophets and the Writings, our persistent hypocrisy, our double standards, our despicable self-righteousness and complacency, our deliberate flouting of God's commandments, our inhumanity, our godlessness. They are in a specially good position to be perceptive, penetrating critics of the Church and of individual Christians. If they do criticize us in the light of those Scriptures which we hold in common and bring their criticism home to us relentlessly and fearlessly, they will put us for ever in their debt.

IV
THE CHRISTIAN'S POLITICAL
RESPONSIBILITY ACCORDING TO
THE NEW TESTAMENT[1]

The New Testament contains a very considerable amount of material bearing on the political responsibility of the Christian – much more, I think, than someone who has not yet questioned it seriously on the subject would be likely to expect. It will, therefore, be wise for us, before attempting to draw out the NT teaching, to try to get a general idea of the various ranges of material which ought to be taken into account.

These may be very roughly indicated as follows:

(i) *Passages containing direct exhortation on the subject.* These are the passages which first come to mind when the subject is mentioned: Mk 12.13–17 (= Mt 22.15–22 = Lk 20.20–26); Rom 13.1–7; 1 Tim 2.1–7; Tit 3.1–2; 1 Pet 2.13–17.

(ii) *Passages which, while not containing exhortation on the subject, have some sort of reference to the state.* This range of material may be subdivided into (*a*) passages which throw light on the attitude of Jesus to the state: e.g. Mk 10.42 (= Mt 20.25 = Lk 22.25 – the saying about the Gentile rulers' lording it over their subjects); Lk 13.32 (our Lord's reference to Herod as 'that fox'); Mk 13.9 (= Mt 10.18 = Lk 21.12–13 – the reference to standing before governors and kings for Christ's sake); (*b*) the Passion narratives; (*c*) the Birth narratives; (*d*) passages which throw light on Paul's attitude to the state: e.g. 1 Cor 2.6–8 (the reference to the rulers of this world being ignorant of the divine wisdom which he teaches); 1 Cor

[1] A paper read to the Sheffield Theological Society on 16 January, 1961, first published in *SJT* 15 (1962), pp. 176–192, and reprinted in C. E. B. Cranfield, *The Service of God*, London, 1965, pp. 49–66.

6.1–6 (the warning against taking a dispute with a fellow-Christian before a heathen court); Acts 16.19–39 (the account of Paul's imprisonment at Philippi and his insistence that the magistrates should come in person to release him); and the last chapters of Acts from 21.31 onwards; (*e*) Revelation 13 (the passage about the beast from the abyss).

(iii) *Passages which, while not referring to, yet have an important bearing upon, the state and the Christian's political responsibility.* These may be subdivided into (*a*) passages dealing with the rule of the exalted Christ; (*b*) passages concerned with eschatology; (*c*) passages which make clear the reality and universality of sin; (*d*) passages which reveal to us in our fellow-man 'the brother for whose sake Christ died'; (*e*) passages containing ethical teaching, especially those which are concerned with love to one's neighbour; and perhaps we should add (*f*) passages concerning the law.

The above survey is by no means exhaustive, but it is enough to show that there is no lack of NT material relevant to our subject. It should also have made it clear that, while the passages mentioned under (i) are of very great importance for our present purpose, it would be extremely foolish to try to build up a NT doctrine of the Christian's political responsibility upon them exclusively. This has sometimes been attempted in the past – with calamitous results. The passages under (i) will certainly be misinterpreted, if they are interpreted in isolation from the material indicated under (ii) and (iii).

I

The first thing to be noticed about the NT material is that all the passages which were mentioned under (i) in our

49

preliminary survey agree *that the Christian has a political responsibility* which is inescapable, has an obligation toward the state. Thus in Mk 12.13–17, whereas the Pharisees and Herodians in their question use the simple verb 'give' ('Is it lawful to give tribute unto Caesar, or not?'), Jesus in His reply uses the compound verb ἀποδιδόναι (RV: 'render'), which means 'to give or pay back something which one owes as a debt', thereby indicating that they are under an obligation to Caesar. In Rom 13.1–7 the subject of the imperative ὑποτασσέσθω is πᾶσα ψυχή ('every soul', i.e., in this context 'every Christian'). Paul is indicating emphatically that there is no one in the Church who is exempted from the duty to 'be in subjection to the higher powers'. In 1 Tim 2.1–7 prayers 'for all men; for kings and all that are in high place' are that to which the writer exhorts (παρακαλῶ – the regular word for Christian exhortation that is based on the gospel) 'first of all'. The same assumption is to be seen in Tit 3.1–2 and 1 Pet 2.13–17. Common to all these passages is the conviction that every Christian has an inescapable obligation toward the state.

II

In the second place, we have to ask, *What reasons for the Christian's political responsibility are indicated in the NT either explicitly or implicitly?* Why, according to the NT, has the Christian a duty toward the state? A number of reasons may be distinguished:

(i) Once more we begin with Mk 12.13–17. It is important here to remember the occasional nature of the teaching it contains. While the saying of Jesus which forms the climax of the section has far-reaching significance, its shape is to a considerable extent

determined by the question which has been put to Him –
by its limited reference (it is not a general question about
the citizen's duty to the state, but one specifically
concerned with the matter of the tribute) and also by the
fact that it is not motivated by a sincere desire for
guidance but is a deliberate attempt on the part of our
Lord's enemies to trap Him. They knew that, if He
answered 'Yes' to their question, His popularity with the
mass of the people would be at an end, while, if He said
'No,' they could at once denounce Him to the Romans.
But Jesus's response is not just a skilful evasive action; it is
also, as the early Church clearly realized, a piece of
teaching of abiding and general significance. Jesus asks
His questioners to show Him a *denarius*, not because He
does not know what is on it, but because He wishes to
show up their hypocrisy and also because the fact that
they are actually using Caesar's coins is an essential
element of the situation. Those who are taking advantage
of the amenities provided by Caesar's rule are under a
moral obligation to make some payment in return. One
reason, then, why the Christian has a duty to the state is
that he is a beneficiary of it.

(ii) Another, and a more theological, reason is
indicated in Rom 13.1b and c. Verse 1b ('for there is no
power but of God' – οὐ γὰρ ἔστιν ἐξουσία εἰ μὴ ὑπὸ
Θεοῦ) expresses a truth already familiar to the Jews (cf.
Jer 27.5f; Dan 2.21, 37f; 4.17 (cf. 4.25, 32; 5.21); Wisd 6.3;
1 Enoch 46.5), namely, that it is God who sets up (and
overthrows) rulers, and that no one actually exercises
ruling authority unless God has set him up. Verse 1c ('and
the *powers* that be are ordained of God' – αἱ δὲ οὖσαι ὑπὸ
Θεοῦ τεταγμέναι εἰσίν), whether it is a general statement
or, as is perhaps more likely, a particular statement about
the actual authorities with which both Paul and the
Church in Rome had to do, namely, the Roman Emperor

51

and his representatives, is a corollary of v.1b. Verse 2 draws out the implications of v.1b: to fail-to-be-subject (ἀντιτάσσεσθαι) to the authority is rebellion against God's ordinance, and, as such, will not go unpunished by God.

(iii) A third reason is indicated in Rom 13.3f ('For rulers are not a terror to the good work, but to the evil. And wouldest thou have no fear of the power? do that which is good, and thou shalt have praise from the same: for he is a minister of God to thee for good. But if thou do that which is evil, be afraid; for he beareth not the sword in vain: for he is a minister of God, an avenger for wrath to him that doeth evil'). I have argued elsewhere[1] that Paul in these verses is neither just thinking of his own good experiences at the hands of the imperial government nor just speaking ideally, but means that, consciously or unconsciously, willingly or unwillingly, the authority will surely praise the good work and punish the evil, because it is, whether it knows it or not, whether willingly or unwillingly, God's servant appointed by God for the very purpose of helping Christians toward salvation and punishing those who do evil.

(iv) 1 Tim 2.1–7 indicates a reason which to some extent overlaps, but is not identical with, that given in Rom 13.3–4 which we have just considered. The Christian is to pray for those in authority, in order 'that we may lead a tranquil and quiet life in all godliness and gravity. This', that passage continues, 'is good and acceptable in the sight of God our Saviour; who willeth that all men should be saved, and come to the knowledge of the truth. For there is one God, one mediator also between God and men, *himself* man, Christ Jesus, who gave himself a

---

[1] 'Some observations on Rom 13.1–7', in *NTS* 6 (1959–60), pp. 176–192.

ransom for all . . .' It is implied that God wills the state as a means to promoting peace and quiet among men, and that God desires such peace and quiet because they are in some way conducive to men's salvation. It is God's purpose that the state should, by restraining the chaotic tendencies of men's self-assertion, maintain those outward conditions under which the gospel may be preached to all and sundry without hindrance. Thus the state is a provision of God's patience, which desires to give to all men the opportunity to repent and be saved; and we have to serve the state for the sake of men's eternal salvation. Our fulfilment of our political responsibility is therefore a necessary part of our fulfilment of our evangelistic responsibility.

(v) A fifth reason may be inferred from the fact that Rom 13.1–7 is part of the exhortation which begins at 12.1. The Roman Christians' subjection to the powers that be is part of the 'reasonable service' or 'understanding worship' (λογικὴ λατρεία) which they are to offer to God in gratitude for all that He has done, is doing, and will do, for them in Jesus Christ.

(vi) The context of Rom 13.1–7 suggests a further reason. This passage is both preceded and followed by exhortations to love (12.9ff and 13.8–10), and it is no erratic boulder in its context. Since the state serves both the ordinary temporal good of our fellow-men and also their eternal salvation, the right service of the state is an integral part of our debt of love to our neighbours.

(vii) Finally, the fact that not only authority over the Church but 'all authority . . . in heaven and on earth' has been given to the exalted Christ (Mt 28.18) and that He is 'the ruler of the kings of the earth' (Rev 1.5), the 'Lord of lords, and King of kings' (Rev 17.14; cf. 19.16), is a compelling reason why the Christian should view the state and his responsibility to, and for, it with the greatest seriousness. He knows that it is an instrument of Christ's kingly rule.

III

In the third place, we have to ask about *the content of the Christian's political responsibility*. What, according to the NT, does the Christian owe the state? What is the content of the subjection enjoined in Rom 13.1; Tit 3.1; 1 Pet 2.13f?

It is often assumed that ὑποτάσσεσθαι in these passages simply means 'obey'. Thus Sanday and Headlam entitled the section Rom 13.1–7 'On Obedience to Rulers', and stated in their introductory summary to it: 'The civil power ... must be obeyed. Obedience to it is a Christian duty ...'; and, more recently, Professor Barrett in his commentary has used the phrase 'obedience to magistrates'. But, as I tried to show in the article to which I have already referred, ὑποτάσσεσθαι does not always mean 'obey'. This meaning is excluded in Eph 5.21; for here the word is used of a reciprocal obligation ('subjecting yourselves one to another in the fear of Christ'), and obedience cannot be reciprocal. Here it would seem to denote the recognition that one's fellow-Christian has, as Christ's representative to one, an infinitely greater claim on one than one has on oneself, and the behaviour that flows from such a recognition. We may compare the expressions 'in honour preferring one another' in Rom 12.10 and 'each counting other better than (or "superior to") himself' in Phil 2.3. It is therefore not unreasonable to maintain that in Rom 13.1; Tit 3.1; 1 Pet 2.13f, the word ὑποτάσσεσθαι denotes not an uncritical obedience to the authority's every command but the recognition that one has been placed below the authority by God and that, as God's servant and the instrument of Christ's kingly rule, it has a greater claim on one that one has on oneself, and such responsible conduct in relation to the authority as results from such a recognition.

The rightness of this interpretation reached by way of a philological inquiry is borne out by the fact that the NT contains a considerable amount of material which clearly implies that a Christian does not owe the civil government an unquestioning obedience. We may think of Mk 12.17, where Jesus's words 'and unto God the things that are God's' indicate plainly that there are limits to what is owed to Caesar. We may think also of much of the material mentioned in categories (ii) and (iii) in our preliminary survey. For example, our Lord's reference to Herod Antipas as 'that fox' (Lk 13.32) hardly suggests that His attitude to His lawful ruler was one of unquestioning, uncritical obedience; and, according to Acts 16.35ff, Paul himself did not depart meekly at the behest of the magistrates of Philippi but rather sought to recall them to a proper sense of their own true dignity by insisting on their coming in person to release him and Silas. It is hardly necessary to mention Revelation 13 and 14, where it is certainly not implied that Christians should docilely worship the beast or receive the mark of his name. That, whenever the civil ruler's commands conflict with the commandments of God, the Christian 'must obey God rather than men' (Acts 5.29) is in the NT everywhere presupposed. In view of the NT material generally we may say that the subjection to the authority which is enjoined, while it will often include obedience, is never simply obedience and nothing more, is never an uncritical, unquestioning obedience, and in some circumstances will not include obedience at all.

Having dealt with the common fallacy that St Paul enjoined obedience to magistrates *simpliciter* (a misunderstanding which has had many exponents and often calamitous results but which would never have arisen, if Christians had resisted the temptation to expound a particular passage of the NT independently of the rest of it), we must now attempt to discover what elements are (according to the NT) comprised in the subjection or ὑποτάσσεσθαι which the Christian owes the powers that be.

We list, first, six things which the Christian owes the powers that be in the circumstances actually envisaged by the NT writers, namely, in an authoritarian state. All of these are equally obligatory for the Christian citizen of a modern democracy.

(i) *Respect* (τιμή). Thus Rom 13.7 enjoins, 'Render to all their dues: ... honour to whom honour'; and 1 Pet 2.17, 'Honour the king'. To respect the government and its various agents means taking them seriously. It means taking them thoroughly seriously – usually much more seriously than they take themselves – as the ministers (διάκονοι, λειτουργοί – Rom 13.4, 6) of God, as men who have been ordained by God (Rom 13.1) and are accountable to Him for the solemn trust which He has committed to them and therefore have a high and reverend dignity. It will often mean treating with full seriousness for the sake of their office men who themselves have little or no understanding of the true dignity of their office and who in themselves are contemptible. But it certainly does not mean flattery or 'respect of persons'; indeed these are incompatible with a proper respect. Nor does it forbid one to claim whatever legal rights one has over against the government. Paul was not showing disrespect for the magistrates at Philippi, but was rather paying them true respect, when he insisted on his legal rights and thereby summoned them to a proper sense of their own dignity (Acts 16.35ff). And, when rulers or their agents behave unworthily and commit injustice, respect will involve, for those whose position makes it possible, administering rebuke. We may cite John the Baptist's rebuking of Herod (Mk 6.18; Lk 3.19), concerning which Calvin comments: 'Hence we learn with what unshaken fortitude the servants of God ought to be armed when they have to do with princes; for in almost every court hypocrisy and servile flattery are prevalent; and the ears of princes, having been accustomed to this smooth language, do not tolerate any voice which reproves their vices with any severity' and 'John has thus, by his example, furnished an undoubted rule for pious teachers, not to wink at the faults of princes, so as to purchase their favour at this price, how advantageous soever that favour might appear to be to the public interests.'

(ii) *Obedience so far as it does not involve disobeying God*. While it is of the greatest importance to realize that ὑποτάσσεσθαι does not simply mean 'obey' and in some circumstances will not involve obedience at all, it is certainly true that ὑποτάσσεσθαι will usually involve obedience. In Tit 3.1 the words 'to be in subjection to rulers, to authorities' are followed by 'to be obedient' (πειθαρχεῖν). The Christian is under obligation to obey the government of the state of which he is a citizen, its various agents, and the duly enacted laws of the state, in so far as such obedience does not conflict with obedience to God.

(iii) *A serious and responsible disobedience, whenever obedience would involve disobeying God*. We may refer to Acts 4.19f ('But Peter and John answered and said unto them [that is, to the Sanhedrin], Whether it be right in the sight of God to hearken unto you rather than unto God, judge ye: for we cannot but speak the things which we saw and heard') and 5.29 ('But Peter and the apostles

57

answered and said, We must obey God rather than men').

(iv) *Payment of taxes.* The basic text here is, of course, Mk 12.13–17 (=Mt 22.15–22 =Lk 20.20–26) (The Question about Tribute to Caesar). Compare Rom 13.6f ('For for this cause ye pay tribute also; for they are ministers of God's service, attending continually upon this very thing. Render to all their dues: tribute to whom tribute is due; custom to whom custom; ...'). The Christian is under obligation to pay his dues to the state, because, as a beneficiary of it, he owes it some payment in return for the protection and amenities which it provides, and because no state can function without resources, and therefore a fundamental refusal to pay taxes would be a fundamental 'No' to the state as such. We do not exclude the possibility that it might in certain circumstances be right to refuse to pay a particular tax.

(v) *Prayer for those in authority.* Thus 1 Tim 2.1ff: 'I exhort therefore, first of all, that supplications, prayers, intercessions, thanksgivings, be made for all men; for kings and all that are in high place; that we may lead a tranquil and quiet life in all godliness and gravity. This is good and acceptable in the sight of God our Saviour; who willeth that all men should be saved, and come to the knowledge of the truth.' This prayer, earnest, persevering and believing, for the civil authority is an essential part of the debt which the Christian owes it, whether it is Christian or pagan, religiously indifferent or anti-religious, just or unjust.

(vi) *Witness to Christ.* An essential part of the Christian's debt to the powers that be is that he should not fail to bear witness to Christ in word and deed and to play his part in the corporate witness of the Church within the state of which he is a citizen, a witness which has to be borne by preaching and sacrament, by the Church's order and common life, and by its service of the community.

Very often this witness will entail suffering, and sometimes death. 'Take ye heed to yourselves,' says Jesus, 'for they shall deliver you up to councils; and in synagogues shall ye be beaten; and before governors and kings shall ye stand for my sake, for a testimony unto them' (Mk 13.9). This is indeed the most essential service which the Christian owes the government and its agents; for by it he attests their real dignity as ministers of God, servants of Christ's kingly rule, the limits of their authority, and also the promise under which they stand.

We have now, I think, listed all the elements of the Christian's subjection to the powers that be, which are actually indicated in the NT. But the NT writers envisaged an authoritarian state, in which there was no question of the ordinary citizen's sharing responsibly in government. We have therefore to translate what they say into terms of our different political order, if we are to apply it to ourselves without serious distortion. It is clear from what has been set out above that according to the NT the Christian living under an authoritarian system is under obligation to do *what he can* for the maintenance of the state as a just state. The Christian living in a democracy *can* do much more for the maintenance of the state as a just state. It is therefore surely a true drawing-out of the NT teaching to assert that the extra which the Christian living in a democracy can do for the maintenance of the state as a just state is obligatory for him, is an essential part of his proper subjection to the powers that be, and that for him to fail to render this extra would be to resist the power and so be guilty of rebellion against the ordinance of God (Rom 13.2) just as much as to fail to fulfil obligations (i) to (vi) above would be.

So we go on to list four additional obligations which are necessary elements of a Christian's subjection in a democratic state.

(vii) *Responsible participation in parliamentary and municipal elections, in the fear of Christ and in love to one's neighbour.* In normal circumstances to fail to register one's vote is to abandon one's share of responsibility for the maintenance of the state as a just state and therefore a dereliction of one's duty as a Christian. We should, however, allow for the possibility of exceptional circumstances arising, in which the only possibility open to a Christian might be to abstain from voting.

(viii) *A serious and sustained attempt to keep oneself as fully and reliably informed as possible concerning political issues* – since responsible voting in the fear of Christ and in love to one's neighbour is only possible on the basis of adequate knowledge. This will naturally involve a diligent reading of newspapers, and, unless we are going to read all the available papers, it will be important to choose some at least of those we are going to read for their reliability and not for less important reasons. Here obligations will vary according to the particular Christian's intellectual ability and education. Upon those who know that God has given them a more than average intellectual ability and who have had the advantage of a good education there rests a special responsibility in this matter. They may well often feel obliged to go farther afield than the newspaper and read books of background information and such things as reports of royal commissions.

(ix) *Criticism of the government, its policies and its agents, in the light of the gospel and law of God.* We have seen that even in an authoritarian state the Christian never owes the government an uncritical, unquestioning obedience. In a democracy, where the citizen's active co-operation is required and the scope of criticism is so much greater, the Christian owes the government in power a continuing criticism in the light of the Word of God. But, if he is to fulfil such an obligation, he will need not only the knowledge referred to under (viii) above, but also a real knowledge of Holy Scripture. He will not be able to render to the government the critical co-operation which he owes, unless he is a mature Christian who is ever striving himself to hear God's Word.

(x) Something which overlaps (ix) to some extent, but is not identical with it – *an unceasing, untiring endeavour to support just and humane policies and to oppose those policies and particular decisions which are unjust or inhumane, by helping to build up an enlightened public opinion and in the various other ways (besides voting in elections) which are constitutionally open to one.* The methods to be adopted will vary according to the situation and one's own personal circumstances. The obvious possibilities include such things as personal conversations, writing letters to one's M.P., to Cabinet Ministers, and to the Press, joining a political party (or resigning from one), canvassing in elections, organizing or attending mass meetings and demonstrations.

At this point it is, I think, probably right to list as a distinct element of the Christian's service of the state, whether under an authoritarian or a democratic system, something which, while it is not explicitly mentioned in the NT as a part of the Christian's obligation to the powers that be, is very obvious, has already been hinted at several times in this paper, and may be said to be the primary service owed by the Christian to the state, the service upon which the faithful rendering of all the other services depends, namely –

(xi) *A sustained endeavour to be a mature Christian, so transformed by the renewing of one's mind as to be able to 'prove what is the good and acceptable and perfect will of God'.* The first and fundamental service which the Christian owes the government and its agents is that he should himself be 'swift to hear' the Word of God, allowing himself to be continually engaged in conversation by the Lord of the Church through the medium of the written words of the Bible.

We must now mention two possible further elements of the subjection owed by the Christian, both of which are highly controversial. Each of them would require much more than a whole paper to itself for an adequate discussion. All I shall do is to indicate as briefly as possible my own present provisional opinion.

(xii) *Readiness, in certain circumstances and within certain limits, to join in military action at the command of the government.* The NT nowhere gives a direct answer to the question which has tormented so many in recent years, 'Should a Christian refuse to take part in military action?' This is not really surprising, since in the first century A.D. Jews were exempt from military service, and the Roman authorities, while they had the right to conscript non-Jewish males, seldom had any need to do so, there being generally an adequate supply of volunteers. We have therefore to try to discover what answer is implicit, and this is notoriously difficult. To state baldly my own opinion – it seems to me, so far as I can see at present, that the fact that the NT clearly affirms the state as a divine provision for men implies that its answer cannot be an absolute 'No'; for an absolute 'No' at this point is surely a 'No' to the institution of the state as such in the circumstances of this world as we know it. Paul himself seems in Rom 13.4 to be assuming that being in a position to use force is an integral part of the state's functioning. But I certainly do not think that there is any basis in the NT for the notion, common in the post-Constantinian Church, that war is a normal activity of a state which is to be accepted quite complacently, or for the assumption of the thirty-seventh Article of the Church of England that the mere fact that the government has decided to make war is in itself enough to make it lawful for the Christian to fight and kill. It seems to me very clear that the Christian is under obligation to refuse to participate in military action, if he is convinced either that it is being employed otherwise than in the last resort, or that it is being employed in an unjust cause. I should myself also have to say that I believe that there are some fairly clearly definable sorts of military action in which a Christian ought in no circumstances to be willing to take part.[1]

(xiii) *Readiness in certain extreme circumstances to engage in armed rebellion in order to overthrow a government that is intolerably unjust and to replace it.* Here again the NT gives us no direct guidance. Neither our Lord's attitude to the Zealots nor Rom 13.2 settles the matter. It does not follow from the fact that our Lord was opposed to the Zealots that He would necessarily have discountenanced on principle rebellion in all conceivable circumstances. It is easy enough to think of very good reasons for disapproving of the Zealots, quite apart from any disapproval of rebellion on principle. For one thing, the Roman government was certainly not so generally unjust as to warrant rebellion; for another, the Zealots were not merely thinking in terms of establishing a more just state but actually thinking to establish the kingdom of God; and, thirdly, it was obvious to the reasonably far-seeing that revolt would be hopeless. With regard to Rom 13.2, we should have to ask whether it is not possible for a government to be so unjust and so full of disorder as to

[1] See K. Barth, *Church Dogmatics*, III/4, §55, 2, for an extremely valuable discussion of the question of war, pacifism, etc.

[In 1983 I am bound to declare my conviction that the use of nuclear weapons, whether in a first strike or in retaliation, is, since it would necessarily be altogether indiscriminate, something which a Christian ought in no circumstances whatsoever to be willing to countenance.]

cease to have any claim to be regarded as an 'authority' (ἐξουσία, RV: 'power') in the sense of Rom 13.1 and 2, and whether a true and serious respect for God's ordinance may not in such extreme circumstances actually entail readiness to use force to overthrow a government that has become the direct opposite of what a government should be. For myself I cannot disapprove of those Christians in Germany who were involved in the attempt on Hitler's life in July 1944, and I am inclined to think that the Christian would be failing to take his government absolutely seriously – and so failing to render it the subjection which the NT enjoins – if, in the last resort, he were not ready even to use force against it, should it ever degenerate into mere tyranny.[1]

IV

In the fourth place, and finally, we ask, What guidance does the NT offer concerning *the spirit, the frame of mind, in which the Christian ought to try to fulfil his political responsibility?* It seems to me that there are at any rate three things to be said here.

(i) The Christian must, according to the NT, seek to fulfil his political responsibility *in all seriousness and earnestness*, as an obligation laid upon him by God and therefore inescapable, as a necessary part of his obedience to Jesus Christ, of his debt of love to his neighbour, of his evangelistic responsibility, a necessary part of that intelligent worship which he owes to God in gratitude for His mercy and goodness in Jesus Christ – in fact, because of all the things listed under II above. His right to think of

[1] On the subject of armed rebellion see, in addition to the section of the *Dogmatics* cited above, K. Barth, *The Knowledge of God and the Service of God*, London, 1938, pp. 229–232.

it as in any way an optional extra, in which he may or may not take an interest according to his personal temperament and inclination, is most decisively and emphatically denied.

(ii) He must seek to fulfil it *in sobriety and realism.* Under this heading there is a great deal to be said; but we only have time to mention a few points.

(*a*) The eschatological teaching of the NT makes clear the temporary nature of the state, and so warns against all absolutizing of it.

(*b*) The eschatological teaching of the NT makes it clear that we cannot establish the kingdom of God by our political (or, for that matter, by our ecclesiastical) actions, and so forbids 'zealotism' with its inherent tendencies to fanaticism and ruthlessness.

(*c*) The NT's disclosure of the grim reality of sin, of the fact that all men without exception are sinners, and that even the Christian remains a sinner until he dies, opens the way to a realistic apprehension of the human situation with which politics have to do. We have an instance of such proper realism in our Lord's words recorded in Mk 10.42: 'Ye know that they which are accounted to rule over the Gentiles lord it over them; and their great ones exercise authority over them.' The RV unfortunately conceals the fact that the two Greek words compounded with κατα- which are used here (RV: 'lord it over' and 'exercise authority over') denote the exercise of lordship and authority over people to one's own advantage and their disadvantage, in other words, the exploitation of those over whom one has power. The Christian must, in the light of the NT, reckon constantly with the fact that every member of the government, every official, and every member of the electorate, in his own as in other countries, is a sinner. If he does so, he will be very much aware of the need at all times for safeguards designed to limit as much

65

as possible the abuse of power, the need to scrutinize very carefully the claims and promises of politicians, the need to look beyond all high-sounding slogans to see how far they are but a mask disguising selfish purposes; and he will not be a party to any policy which involves handing over to any section of a community absolute power over the lives and destinies of another section.

(*d*) Both NT eschatology and the NT insistence on the fact of human sinfulness lead us to the realization that there are limits to what we can achieve in the sphere of politics, and that therefore limited goals are not to be despised. Often the only choice open to the Christian in a particular situation will be a choice between evils; but he will realize that it is not a matter of indifference whether the greatest possible, or the least possible, evil comes to pass, and that to help to bring about the greatest evil by refusing, out of a mistaken perfectionism, to choose the least is surely to be guilty of dereliction of duty. The Christian should be aware of the danger of being so preoccupied with the quest of the unattainable that one fails to achieve the limited goals which are within one's reach. Christian realism should enable us to see, that, while it is not given to us to establish a perfect society within the course of history, to build in our time a society, which contains such a measure of justice and compassion as may make it, in spite of all its human imperfections and frailty, a recognizable pointer to the justice and compassion of God, is not beyond the bounds of possibility, and is a goal worthy of our untiring efforts.

(*e*) Included in this sobriety and realism are: the recognition that the purpose of civil government and of the state in God's intention is a purpose of mercy toward men (1 Tim 2.1ff), that is, toward individual men and women and children; the recognition that every human being, not only in one's own country but also throughout the whole world, is a brother for whom Christ died (Rom 14.15; 1 Cor 8.11; 1 Tim 2.6), and therefore someone of inestimable worth; the recognition that in each of those who are wretched and needy, wherever they may be, the exalted Christ is present to be honoured or neglected (Mt 25.40, 45). Holding fast these truths, the Christian will not be able to forget that the state exists for the sake of men and women and children, not they for the sake of the state, and he will possess in them a standard by which to measure policies and legislation. He will know that he must at all times and in all circumstances loyally abide by the principle that persons are infinitely more precious than property. He will, for instance, allow himself to be guided by it, when he has to weigh the relative importance of the various issues in a general election. He will be more concerned that the starving and under-nourished throughout the world should have enough food than that his own countrymen should have more and more amenities; more concerned that the personal liberties and dignity of those who cannot defend themselves should be protected than that the income tax should be reduced. He will feel himself obliged to throw his weight on the side of generous and unselfish national policies, and in domestic affairs to take a special interest in the underprivileged, the misfits and the lame dogs of society. He will know that human life is always to be reverenced. In time of war he will never forget that even the lives of the enemy are not cheap.

(iii) The Christian should fulfil his political responsibility *in confidence and hope.* (*a*) He knows that the state and civil authority are God's ordinance, that God has ordained them for a merciful purpose, and that He who has ordained them has not lost control over them. He knows that governments are God's ministers, who cannot help but serve Him and further His gracious purposes, whether consciously or unconsciously, willingly or unwillingly, directly or indirectly. He is continually being reminded of one specially luminous instance, unique in its significance, that of Pontius Pilate, through whom, unworthy and unwilling servant though he was, God's perfect will for the redemption of mankind was accomplished. (*b*) The Christian knows that, when he passes from the ecclesiastical into the political sphere, he is not passing out of Christ's dominion into the dominion of some other lord, and that political affairs no less than the life of the Church are within the dominion of Christ. He knows that the same Lord who is confessed and acknowledged by the Church is also the Lord of the whole world, though not yet known as such by it. He knows that this Lord is already 'the ruler of the kings of the earth' (Rev 1.5), the 'Lord of lords, and King of kings' (Rev 17.14; 19.16), to whom 'all authority hath been given . . . in heaven and on earth' (Mt 28.18), and that the governments of the nations are the servants of His royal rule. How then can he do otherwise than fulfil his political responsibility in confidence and hope? (*c*) The Christian knows too that the end toward which history moves is the coming in glory of Jesus Christ, the decisive and unambiguous manifestation of the kingdom of God, the establishment of God's new order. In that event he sees not only the ultimate limitation but also the ultimate promise under which the states and governments of history stand; for he knows that the time must come when it can be said: 'The kingdom of the world is become the kingdom of our Lord, and of his Christ' (Rev 11.15) and when at last 'the nations shall walk amidst the light' of the 'new Jerusalem', and 'the kings of the earth . . . bring their glory into it' (Rev 21.24).

V
DIAKONIA IN THE NEW TESTAMENT[1]

1. THE USE OF DIAKONEIN AND ITS COGNATES[2]

In pagan Greek the verb *diakonein*[3] is used both in a narrow sense, with reference to waiting at table or attending to someone's bodily needs, and also in a broad sense, of service rendered to another person quite generally, while the cognates *diakonia* and *diakonos* are used to denote, respectively, the action of *diakonein* and the person who performs it. Further cognates, which are not found in the NT, also occur. In the eyes of the Greeks such service was undignified and menial (so, for example, in Plato's *Gorgias*[4] the adjective *diakonikos* appears in company with two other adjectives both of which mean 'servile'): the only *diakonia* regarded as honourable was that rendered to the state.

In the Septuagint *diakonein* never occurs, and *diakonia* and *diakonos* occur only a few times and then without any theological significance.

In the NT the word-group[5] is used non-theologically in both the narrow and the broad senses noted above for pagan Greek.[6] It is also used with theological significance

[1] First published in J. I. McCord and T. H. L. Parker (ed.), *Service in Christ: essays presented to Karl Barth on his 80th birthday*, London, 1966, pp. 37–48.

[2] In addition to the concordances, cf. Bauer, s.vv.; H. W. Beyer, in *TWNT* 2, pp. 81–93.

[3] Its earliest known occurrence is in Herodotus.

[4] 518 A.

[5] *Diakonein* occurs thirty-seven times in all in the NT, *diakonia* thirty-four times, and *diakonos* thirty times.

[6] e.g. in the narrowest sense, Lk 17.8; 22.27a; Jn 2.5, and, in the broad sense, Mk 10.45 = Mt 20.28 ('to be ministered unto'); Mt 22.13.

in a variety of ways. It is used with reference to Christ's service of men: *diakonein* in Mk 10.45 = Mt 20.28 ('the Son of man came . . . to minister') and Lk 22.27 ('I am in the midst of you as he that serveth'); *diakonos* in Rom 15.8 (Christ in His earthly life is the minister of the Jewish people). *Diakonos* is used generally in connexion with service rendered to God (Rom 13.4; 2 Cor 6.4; (1 Th 3.2)), to Christ (Jn 12.26; 2 Cor 11.23; Col 1.7; 1 Tim 4.6), to the new covenant (2 Cor 3.6), to the gospel (Eph 3.7; Col 1.23), to the fellow-disciple or to the Church as a whole (Mk 9.35; 10.43 = Mt 20.26; Mt 23.11; Col 1.25) – in this last connexion *diakonein* is also used in 1 Pet 1.12; 4.10, and *diakonia* in 2 Cor 11.8. *Diakonein* also occurs in Mk 1.31 = Mt 8.15 = Lk 4.39; Mk 15.41 = Mt 27.55; Lk 8.3; 10.40 (in this verse *diakonia* is used, too); Jn 12.2, where the reference is to such practical service as preparing a meal or waiting at table rendered to Jesus (or to Jesus and His disciples), and in Acts 19.22, where it denotes the assistance given to the apostle Paul by Timothy and Erastus. In the case of *diakonia* a technical use emerges, which we may call the *general technical use* – to denote a function or office within the Church or the activity of fulfilling it. Thus it is used of the ministry of apostles, evangelists, prophets, etc. (e.g. Acts 1.17, 25; 20.24; 21.19; Rom 11.13; 1 Cor 12.5; 2 Cor 4.1; 5.18: cf. the use of *diakonos* in 1 Cor 3.5). It is not without significance that the technical term for functions in the Church which necessarily involve some measure of leadership has from the first been a word which signifies not pre-eminence or power but simply humble service, and, further, that it is the same word that was used of Christ's own service of men and also of the service owed by every Christian to God, to Christ, to his fellows.

But, side by side with this general technical use, there is to be seen what may be called the *specialized technical use* of the word-group. Thus *diakonein* is used in Mt 25.44 as a term covering the various services to the needy mentioned in vv. 42 and 43. In Rom 15.25 it is used of the service Paul is rendering to the poor in Jerusalem by organizing the collection on their behalf. In Heb 6.10 the reference is probably to the relief of the bodily and material needs of fellow-Christians. In Acts 6.2 and 2 Cor 8.19f, while *diakonein* itself has some such sense as 'attend to', the combination of words of which it is a part refers, in each case, to service of the needy (in Acts 6.2 to the supervision of the communal meals, in 2 Cor 8.19f to the collection for Jerusalem). Especially instructive is 1 Pet 4.11; for, while in the previous verse *diakonein* was used quite generally of the service rendered to one's fellow-Christians by using to the full whatever spiritual gift one has received, it is here contrasted with *lalein* ('speak') and is most naturally understood to refer to the relief of physical and material needs contrasted with preaching, teaching, etc. In two other occurrences[1] it means 'discharge the duties pertaining to the office of a *diakonos*'.

Diakonia is used similarly of the daily distribution in the early days of the Jerusalem Church[2] and seven times[3] with reference to the collection for the brethren in Jerusalem. In Rom 12.7, where it occurs twice, while some scholars hold that it is used as a general term (our general technical use), which is then broken down into its various divisions ('he that teacheth', etc.), it is more probable that it is used in the specialized technical sense with reference to the practical service of the needy, since, if it were being used as a general term, it would more naturally have been placed before, rather than after, the reference to

---

[1] 1 Tim 3.10, 13.
[2] Acts 6.1.
[3] Acts 11.29; 12.25; Rom 15.31; 2 Cor 8.4; 9.1, 12. 13.

prophecy. It is likely that in 1 Cor 16.15 also the word has the specialized sense.

With regard to *diakonos*, there are three occurrences in which it quite clearly denotes the holder of a particular office: Phil 1.1; 1 Tim 3.8, 12. In Philippians the *diakonoi* are coupled with, though mentioned after, the *episkopoi*; and similarly in 1 Timothy the section on *diakonoi* follows immediately that on *episkopoi*. But in neither passage are the functions of a *diakonos* indicated – though there is possibly some force in the suggestion that the two groups are mentioned in Phil 1.1 because they have both had to do with the collection of the gifts for which Paul is thanking the Church, the *diakonoi* being mentioned after the *episkopoi*, as having acted as agents in the matter under their general supervision; and also in the suggestion that in 1 Timothy 3 the fact that, while aptness to teach (included in the section on *episkopoi*) is omitted from the requirements of a *diakonos*, the *diakonoi* are required to be 'not double-tongued, not given to much wine, not greedy of filthy lucre', might be a pointer to their office's having involved constant visitation of houses and the handling of material resources (though it is to be noted that the *episkopos* also is to be 'no lover of money'). The strongest argument – and it is a strong argument – in favour of the view that *diakonos* in these two passages denotes the holder of a particular office which had to do with the practical assistance of those who were in one way or another specially needy is the inherent probability that the specialized technical use of *diakonos* will have been parallel to the specialized technical use of its cognates *diakonein* and *diakonia*. What we know of the diaconate in the second century is, of course, further support.

There is one other occurrence of *diakonos* in the NT which must be mentioned. In Rom 16.1 Phoebe is described as '*diakonos* of the church that is at Cenchreae'.

It is possible to understand the word here as a quite general reference to her service of the congregation; but the form in which Paul expresses himself (οὖσαν διάκονον τῆς ἐκκλησίας . . .) makes it more natural to take it as referring to a definite office. The latter part of v. 2, if it may be connected with her office, suggests that it had to do with affording practical assistance to those who stood in need of it.

We have now seen that there is in the NT a specialized technical use of *diakonein* and *diakonia* to denote the practical service of those who are specially needy 'in body, or estate', and that it is highly probable that the specialized technical use of *diakonos* also has the same reference. It is with *diakonia* in this special sense that we are here concerned.

2. THE THEOLOGICAL NECESSITY OF DIAKONIA

The necessity of *diakonia* as an essential function both of the Church as a body and of its individual members severally is so clear that we need not labour it. It is a theological necessity having its ground in the gospel itself, in the grace of God in Jesus Christ. It will be sufficient here merely to indicate some of the ways in which the NT brings it home to us.

It is clearly implied by the divine commandment so frequently repeated in the NT, 'Thou shalt love thy neighbour as thyself';[1] for to love one's neighbour as oneself certainly involves assisting him when he is in need, as our Lord's exposition of the law[2] made clear. A love

[1] Lev 19.18; Mt 19.19; 22.39 = Mk 12.31; Lk 10.27; Rom 13.9; Gal 5.14; Jas 2.8.
[2] Mt 7.12; Lk 10.30–37.

which stopped short of such practical assistance could only be a love 'in word' or 'with the tongue' and not 'in deed and truth',[1] an empty and futile thing. A Church which was not zealous to succour the needy and afflicted would be a Church which flouted God's law.

It is brought home to us in the petition which Christ has placed on our lips: 'Give us this day our daily bread.'[2] For this is not just a petition for ourselves only, but intercession for others as well, prayer which embraces all who are our brothers in Christ, and not only those whom we can see and know to be such, but all men who are alive upon the earth.[3] And it is evident that to pray to God to give our fellow-men their daily bread would be an insolent mockery, were our prayer not accompanied by action aimed at doing all that is within our power to bring about the answer to our prayer. For the Church to pray these words and yet not do what it can to feed the hungry and the starving would be to condemn itself as hypocritical and to insult Him to whom its prayer is addressed.

It is set forth in the example of Jesus Christ, whose ministry is the pattern of the Church's continuing ministry. His service of men was not limited to preaching and teaching, but included His service of the sick, the hungry, the afflicted, in His healing and other miracles. He had compassion on human distress, and His compassion issued in action for its relief.[4]

It is implicit in the Church's duty to bear witness to Christ.[5] For the witness required of the Church is not a witness of words only: its actions as well as its words are to

[1] 1 Jn 3.18.
[2] Mt 6.11 (cf. Lk 11.3).
[3] Cf. Calvin, *Institutes of the Christian Religion* 3. 20. 38.
[4] Mt. 14.14; 15.32 = Mk 8.2; Mt 20.34; Lk 7.13.
[5] e.g. Lk 24.48; Jn 15.27; Acts 1.8; 4.33; 1 Cor 1.6; 2 Tim 1.8; 1 Jn 1.2; 4.14.

be pointers to the reality and the nature of the grace of God in Jesus Christ. The witness of a Church which did not concern itself with the humble service of the needy and suffering would be an altogether incredible witness.

It is, above all, made inescapably clear in the Discourse on the Final Judgment in Mt 25.31–46. For that discourse discloses a mystery – the mystery of the presence of the exalted Son of man in the persons of those who are needy and in distress. The theological necessity of *diakonia* as a function of the Church as a whole and of the individual Christian could not be more forcibly brought home to us; for when once it is apparent that 'Christ is either neglected or honoured in the persons of those who need our assistance',[1] there can be no question about the Church's obligation to minister to the needy with loving practical service. (On Mt 25.31ff see pp. 77–79; also *If God be for us*, 1985, pp. 97–111.)

3. THE NATURE OF TRUE DIAKONIA

What has been said above about its theological necessity suggests clues which we may follow in our attempt to gain a deeper insight into the nature of true *diakonia* and to draw out some of the characteristics which the Church's, and the individual Christian's, practical service will exhibit, in so far as it really is the *diakonia* which the gospel demands.

Our *diakonia* is part of our obedience to God's law. The NT makes it abundantly clear that the obedience God's law requires is not a legalistic obedience vainly aimed at putting God under an obligation but the true obedience which consists of faith and the attitudes and actions which

---

[1] Calvin, in his comment on Mt 25.40.

are the expression of faith.[1] As part of this obedience our *diakonia* is a part of God's establishment of His law.[2] It is an element of our calling God 'Father' in sincerity and truth which the Holy Spirit accomplishes.[3] As such it can only be an altogether free, grateful, and joyous activity.

It is the Church's enacted *amen* to its prayer of intercession for 'all those, who are any ways afflicted, or distressed, in mind, body, or estate', the deed which seals the sincerity of our words, the activity which marches side by side with our praying as its indispensable companion. But the indispensability is mutual; and *diakonia* in separation from prayer would as little be true Christian *diakonia* as would prayer in separation from *diakonia* be true Christian prayer. For Christian *diakonia* is not a self-reliant, self-sufficient human activity, but a human activity which is itself a humble waiting upon God's action. The Church remembers that the resources of its *diakonia* come not from its own independent generosity but from the generosity of God.[4]

It is a part of our following of Christ. His whole life was (in the general sense of the word) a *diakonia* of men, and the use in the NT of words of the *diakonein* group with reference to Christ[5] serves to indicate not only what His mission achieved but also the humble spirit in which He fulfilled it. True Christian *diakonia* (whether in the general or the special sense of the word) is always characterized by the meekness and humility of Christ. When those who give of their substance for the relief of the needy or those who organize and administer the Church's *diakonia* yield to the temptation to self-

[1] Cf. Rom 1.5 ('unto obedience of faith').
[2] This sentence has been revised (1983).
[3] Cf. Rom 8.15f; Gal 4.6.
[4] Cf. 1 Pet 4.11b.
[5] Mt 20.28 = Mk 10.45; Lk 22.27; Rom 15.8.

importance and lordliness, their service ceases to be authentic *diakonia.*

It is a part of our witness to Christ. It is action so genuinely consistent with the message which the Church has to proclaim that it serves to illustrate and to confirm it. By its simplicity, its directness, and its adequacy for the particular human distress in question, it points to the simplicity, the directness, the adequacy of the grace of God in Jesus Christ. It is of the nature of witness that it should point beyond, and away from, itself to something or someone else. So the Church's *diakonia* points beyond the Church and its actions to Him who is, in the last resort, man's only Helper and Healer. And since it is witness to Jesus Christ it will abhor as altogether unworthy all ostentation and boastfulness. In this connexion it is important at all times, but especially in a day of ecclesiastical public relations officers, when the danger of the Church's *diakonia*'s being preceded by a trumpet is specially great, for the Church to remember that true *diakonia* is under the discipline of Mt 6.1–4 as well as of Mt 5.14–16. At first sight the two passages might seem to be contradictory; for there seems to be little difference between 'before men, that they may see your good works' (5.16) and 'before men, to be seen of them' (6.1). But in each case the sequel makes the meaning plain. The Church is indeed to let its *diakonia* be seen so that men may have cause to glorify God; but that is something altogether different from every form of self-advertisement designed to make sure that the Church (or the individual Christian) 'may have glory of men'.

Finally, the mystery of the exalted Christ's presence in His suffering brothers and sisters means that *diakonia* is the Church's service of its Lord in person – the most intimate and personal service of Him that it is permitted to render. It is thus altogether free from the taint of patronizing. The Church knows well that, so far from there being any question of its being in a position to confer favours on the needy, it is the needy who are conferring a favour upon it, in that by their distress they present it with the opportunity to love and serve Him, to whom it owes more than it can ever repay. And, as the Church's *diakonia* is rendered without patronizing, so it can be accepted without any sense of humiliation. Moreover, it is unlimited, in the sense that the Church can never do enough, can never wish to set limits to the demands which the needy make upon it, can never be grudging in its service, because it knows that its indebtedness to Christ is infinite. So the Church, in so far as it is the true Church of Jesus Christ, delights to serve them unwearyingly and always to be patient with them, and does not resent the fact that they are often ungrateful and difficult to help. Even in the most unresponsive, sullen and embittered, it discerns by faith the presence of its Lord, and so is enabled to minister 'with cheerfulness'.[1] And true *diakonia* always treats the needy and the suffering as persons. The very use of the word carries with it some suggestion of personal service to a person. But it is the recognition that Christ Himself, in His freedom and lordship, is personally – though hiddenly and mysteriously – present in the needy which makes it impossible for the believing Church ever to regard or treat them as merely so many cases of poverty, malnutrition, or disease. For others they may perhaps be a problem to be solved, a political, social or economic untidiness to be cleared up, a potential danger to be neutralized: for the Christian Church they must always remain persons, whose status as persons is guaranteed by the mystery disclosed in Mt 25.31ff.

[1] Romans 12.8: ἐν ἱλαρότητι.

4. THE SCOPE OF DIAKONIA

The question we are here concerned with is the question whether, according to the NT, the Church is under obligation to seek to relieve human distress as such wherever it is to be found, or only to succour the needy and afflicted within its own fellowship.

As far as the Synoptic Gospels are concerned, the position seems clear. According to Mt 5.43–48 = Lk 6.27f, 32–36, the disciples of Jesus are to love their enemies, pray for their persecutors, and do good to them that hate them. In Mt 7.12 = Lk 6.31 it is perhaps significant that the general term 'men' is used, and not 'your brethren'. Again, when Jesus is asked by the lawyer, 'And who is my neighbour?', He tells a parable in which it is a Samaritan who is the example of neighbourliness.[1] The implication is that in the commandment of Lev 19.18, which the lawyer has just quoted, 'neighbour' is to be understood in the broadest possible sense. And, finally, in Mt 25.31–46, which is one of the most important NT passages for the theology of *diakonia*, it is hardly to be doubted – despite some opinions to the contrary – that 'these my brethren, even these least' in v. 40 and 'these least' in v. 45 denote the needy generally irrespective of whether they are disciples or not; for otherwise the having given help to them or withheld it could not be a universally applicable criterion, as v. 32 implies that it is (while all the individuals denoted by 'all the nations' would certainly have had an opportunity to assist a fellow-man in need, it obviously could not be assumed that they would all have had an opportunity to assist a needy disciple).

But what of the rest of the NT? There is certainly a preponderance of references to loving and succouring

[1] Lk 10.25–37.

fellow-Christians;[1] and, as has often been pointed out,[2] it is not easy to find outside the Synoptic Gospels absolutely clear examples of *agapan* or *agape* used of the love owed by Christians with a wider reference than the fellowship of the Church. Perhaps the most explicit passage is 1 Th 3.12 ('and the Lord make you to increase and abound in love one toward another, and toward all men . . .'). But there are others which make the wider obligation perfectly clear: Rom 12.14 ('Bless them that persecute you; bless, and curse not'); Rom 12.20 ('But if thine enemy hunger, feed him; if he thirst, give him to drink: for in so doing thou shalt heap coals of fire upon his head [i.e. inflict on him an inward sense of shame]'); Gal 6.10 ('So then, as we have opportunity, let us work that which is good toward all men, and especially toward them that are of the household of the faith'); 1 Th 5.15 ('. . . but alway follow after that which is good, one toward another, and toward all'); 1 Pet 2.17 ('Honour all men. Love the brotherhood . . .'). In the last of these, while a different word is used for the more intimate relationship within the Christian community and thus a distinction is made, the word 'honour' certainly implies that Christians are to assist all men as they have need. It is probable that in Rom 12.9 'love' has a general reference: there is then added point in the words, 'In love of the brethren be tenderly affectioned one to another', in the following verse. Love toward all men seems also to be intended by 'love' in 1 Cor 16.14 ('Let all that ye do be done in love').

These examples are enough to show that the second half of H. W. Montefiore's statement, 'It is probable

---

[1] e.g. Jn 13.34f; Acts 2.42, 44f; 4.32–37; Rom 12.10; 1 Cor 16.15; Gal 6.2; Col 1.4; 1 Th 4.9f; 2 Th 1.3; Heb 6.10; 10.33f; 13.1–3; Jas 2.15f; 1 Pet 4.8–10; 5.5; 1 Jn 3.10–18.

[2] e.g. in A. Richardson (ed.), *A Theological Word Book of the Bible*, London, 1950, p. 136.

(almost to the point of certainty) that Jesus had taught his disciples to show love to anyone in need, and that the early church narrowed the concept of neighbour until it was equivalent to church member',[1] is not justified by the NT evidence. There are a good many places in his article where NT passages are treated unfairly or where the argument is less than convincing. For instance, to infer from Paul's recognition that a fellow-Christian has a special claim on one's support (e.g. Gal 6.10) that 'Paul did not regard it as a Christian duty to go out of his way to love a non-Christian'[2] is surely unfair.

In connexion with the relative fewness of explicit references to Christians' assisting those outside the Church, it is important to remember the poverty of the primitive Church. In a situation in which it must have been difficult to support all the needy within the Church there will have been little opportunity for assistance on any large scale to the needy outside the household of faith. It was a situation altogether different from that of the Church in western Europe or the United States of America today.

There is, in any case, quite enough evidence in the NT – and it is not limited to the teaching of Jesus – to make it inescapably clear that churches and individual Christians, whether they are rich or poor, but especially when they are comparatively rich, are under an obligation to practise *diakonia* not only toward other Christians who are in need but toward the needy and afflicted wherever they are to be found.

[1] 'Thou shalt love the [*sic*] neighbour as thyself', in *Novum Testamentum* 5 (1962), p. 166.
[2] op. cit., p. 162.

5. THE DIAKONIA OF THE CONGREGATION AND OF ITS MEMBERS AND THE DIACONATE

We have now to ask what may be said, on the basis of the NT, about (i) the relation between the *diakonia* of the congregation as a whole and the *diakonia* of the individual members, and (ii) the relation of both to the diaconate.

With regard to (i) – while it is true that every act of *diakonia* performed by a member of the congregation is a contribution to the *diakonia* of the whole, and that the *diakonia* of the congregation as a whole must anyway be carried out by its members, it is of vital importance that we should neither dissolve away the responsibility of the individual member, as though there were no room for *diakonia* by individual members on their own initiative and responsibility, but only for the carrying out of what is initiated by, and is the responsibility of, the congregation as a whole; nor dissolve away the responsibility of the congregation, as though its *diakonia* were simply the sum total of the acts of service undertaken by the several members on their own initiative and responsibility. For the NT clearly envisages both a *diakonia* which is undertaken by the congregation as a whole (though it is necessarily carried out by particular members), as may be seen, for example, in Acts 6.1 and in passages referring to the collection for the poor in Jerusalem (Acts 11.28f; 24.17; Rom 15.25–27; 1 Cor 16.1–4; 2 Cor 8.1–15; 9.1–15) and also a *diakonia* which is a matter of the individual Christian's responsibility and initiative (though it is also, of course, a contribution to the *diakonia* of the congregation), as is clear from such passages as Mt 25.31–46; Rom 12.20; Gal 6.2. While the individual is loyally to join in the *diakonia* undertaken by the community, he is not thereby released from the responsibility to minister, on his own initiative and in his own name as a Christian man, as the opportunity for such ministering occurs; and, on the other hand, the congregation in its corporate life cannot escape its corporate responsibility on the pretext that *diakonia* is the private responsibility of its members. The responsibility for ministering to Christ, as He comes to us under the veil of the suffering humanity of His brothers and sisters whether inside or outside the fellowship of the Church, rests squarely both on the congregation as a whole and on every individual member severally.

With regard to (ii) – we have already seen that there are only two passages in the NT[1] which both use the word *diakonos* and make it absolutely clear that the reference is to the bearer of a specific office in the Church, and that, while it is very highly probable that the *diakonoi* referred to in these two passages had special responsibility in connexion with the *diakonia* of the congregation, like the deacons of the second century, this is not expressly stated in either passage. But the fact that there is thus some uncertainty in connexion with the diaconate in NT times is much less of an embarrassment than one might at first be inclined to expect. For the really important question is not whether there is absolutely clear evidence in the NT of the existence of a diaconate similar to that of the second century, but whether it affords unambiguous evidence of the perpetual necessity of *diakonia* as a function of the Church on earth. And of this there is no doubt at all. Even if there had been no mention of deacons in the NT, we should still have been obliged, in loyalty to the NT, to explore the possibility that the twentieth-century Church might fulfil its function of *diakonia* more effectively with an order of ministers having special responsibility in this field than without one.

[1] Phil 1.1; 1 Tim 3.8–13; Cf. pp. 72–73.

But the element of uncertainty which we have noticed ought not to be exaggerated. It is certainly the present writer's conviction that, when all the relevant NT material, and not just the two passages referred to above[1] (backed perhaps by the much more problematical evidence of Acts 6),[2] is considered, the image of a primitive diaconate becomes tolerably distinct. That the diaconate did not free either the congregation as a whole or the individual members severally from their responsibility for *diakonia* is clear from evidence already

---

[1] A verse, not yet mentioned, which is particularly interesting in this connexion, is Rom 12.8; for it seems very probable that in ὁ προϊστάμενος (RV: 'he that ruleth') and ὁ ἐλεῶν (RV: 'he that sheweth mercy') we catch a glimpse of the primitive diaconate at work, the former being probably either the person whose function it was to organize and preside over the congregation's charitable work or else someone to whom the congregation looked (perhaps partly on account of his social position) for support of those, such as widows and orphans, who were in a weak position in society, and the latter someone recognized by the congregation as having gifts which made him specially suited to concentrate on direct and personal contact with the needy, tending the sick, caring for the aged, relieving the poor, etc. (See, further, the present writer's *A Commentary on Romans 12–13*, Edinburgh, 1965, pp. 35–37; now I.C.C. *Romans*, pp. 623–628.)

[2] The difficulties of Acts 6.1–6 are well known. The word *diakonos* is not used here; after v. 3 nothing more is said of the involvement of the Seven in the Church's welfare work (it is noticeable that in 11.30 it is 'to the elders' that the gifts from Antioch are sent); one of them (Stephen) is depicted in the latter part of the same chapter as teaching and disputing, while another (Philip) is shown in chapter 8 proclaiming Christ and in 21.8 is referred to as 'the evangelist'; the others are never mentioned again in Acts. The questions raised by these verses are such that the proper discussion of them requires a whole paper to itself. But it may be said here that Acts 6.1–6 implies: (i) that the author regarded it as something to be taken for granted that the Church had an obligation to care for the poor among its members; (ii) that at the time when Acts was written it seemed natural to think of the Church's charitable work as a function separate from that of preaching and oversight; (iii) that, separated though they were in his own time, the author of Acts thought of these two functions as having been originally united in the ministry of the apostles.

considered. Rather it must have served to stimulate and to organize, to lead and to focus, the *diakonia* of the whole Christian community.

6. DIAKONIA AND CHURCH FINANCE

It is obvious that between the Church's *diakonia* and its finance, that vast ecclesiastical hinterland seldom explored theologically, there is an intimate and extensive mutual involvement. What light does the NT throw upon this complicated relationship?

The principle that those who are whole-time workers for the gospel are entitled to support from the Church's resources has good NT authority.[1] But, at the same time, the fact that the apostle Paul refused to claim this right for himself and preferred to work with his hands to support himself[2] – though he did apparently accept material help from the Church in Philippi[3] – is something which in this connexion should certainly not be entirely forgotten. And Mk 6.7–12 = Mt 10.1, 9–14 = Lk 9.1–6 and Lk 10.1–16, passages containing sayings-material which was no doubt specially preserved because of its relevance to the situation of later missionaries, should certainly be remembered. While full allowance must be made for changing conditions and circumstances (as a matter of fact, some modifications are already to be seen in Mk 6.8f as against Mt 10.10 and Lk 9.3), the Lord's instructions still hold in principle for the continuing ministry of the Church; and they certainly give no encouragement at all

---

[1] We may refer to 1 Cor 9.1–14; Gal 6.6; 1 Tim 5.17f, and also to Mt 10.10b; Lk 10.7.

[2] Acts 18.3; 20.34f; 1 Cor 9.12, 15–18; 2 Cor 11.7–12; 12.13f; 1 Th 2.6, 9; 2 Th 3.8f.

[3] 2 Cor 11.9; Phil 4.15f.

to the idea that the clergy have a right to be supported in luxury.There is no evidence in the NT to suggest that apostles normally travelled first class.

When we turn to the subject of church buildings and their maintenance, upon which such a large proportion of the modern Church's resources is spent, there is not unnaturally a sparsity of relevant material. It is probably not unfair to say that, since the need for the Church in a particular place to gather together regularly is clearly recognized,[1] and since the use of private houses could hardly be expected to continue indefinitely, the Church's possession of buildings for its own special purposes is justified in principle. According to Acts 19.9, Paul, when he was no longer able to use the synagogue in Ephesus, had resort to the lecture-room of Tyrannus for his teaching. On what terms he had the use of it we are not informed. But there is nothing in the NT to encourage the notion that God regards unnecessarily expensive buildings or furnishings as contributing in any way to His glory; and to appeal to the OT in this connexion is perhaps a questionable procedure. At any rate, Mk 13.1–4 may serve as a warning against assuming that the mere fact that multitudes of the curious come to admire an expensive new church is a proof that all the expenditure involved in its erection and adornment is justified.

But when we come to question the NT on the use of the Church's resources for the relief of human distress and need we get an altogether unambiguous answer. According to Mt 25.31–46, Christ has specially chosen the suffering humanity of His needy brothers and sisters as the place where He will receive our gratitude and service. To set against this Mk 14.3–9 and parallels is beside the

[1] e.g. 1 Cor 11.20; Heb 10.25.

point; for the circumstances of the incident there recorded were altogether unique.

We conclude that, while a large proportion of the Church's money is rightly spent on the training of the clergy and their support in modest comfort, on the erection and maintenance of necessary buildings, and on a good many other things which contribute to the efficient fulfilment of its mission, the relief of human suffering and wretchedness has a special claim upon the Church's material resources, and every proposed ecclesiastical expenditure ought to be responsibly and critically scrutinized in the light of this claim, lest the Church be guilty of using sacrilegiously for its own, and its ministers', worldly prestige and status, and for other selfish and frivolous purposes, that which by right belongs to Christ in the persons of His needy brethren.

VI
NEW CHURCH CONSTITUTIONS AND DIAKONIA[1]

In the course of his extremely valuable and stimulating study, 'Diakonia: Today's Task',[2] Dr Hans Christoph von Hase draws attention to the explicit reference to the Church's diaconal responsibility contained in the 1948 Constitution of the Evangelische Kirche in Deutschland, Article 15 of which declares:

> The Evangelische Kirche in Germany and member churches are called to proclaim Christ's love in word and deed. This love obliges all members of the Church to undertake service and takes form in a special way in the Diaconate of the Church. In accordance with this the Church's diaconal-missionary activities are part of its very being and life.[3]

Since it is likely that the next few years will see a number of new constitutions drafted and debated in various churches, it seems opportune to raise the question whether in this particular the German Evangelische Kirche has not set an example which other churches ought to follow. The purpose of this short article is to suggest that it is theologically appropriate and – in the NT sense of the word – expedient, that any new church constitution should have written into it in the most explicit and unambiguous terms a statement of the Church's perpetual obligation to give loving practical service to those who are specially needy or distressed,

[1] First published in *SJT* 20 (1967), pp. 338–341.
[2] In *SJT* 20, pp. 57–74.
[3] op. cit., p. 58.

whether within or without its own fellowship, both locally and wherever they are to be found.[1]

The question whether the inclusion of such a statement in a church constitution is theologically appropriate may be put in this way: Is it true that the Church's diakonia in this sense is 'part of its very being and life' as the Church of Jesus Christ? Is this an essential function of the Church, along with the preaching of the gospel and the celebration of the sacraments, a perpetual obligation which the Church can never shirk or shoulder only half-heartedly without being guilty of a radical rejection of the gospel and of the Lord Jesus Christ Himself? There can scarcely be any doubt that the answer to this question must be affirmative.

What recent theological work and ecumenical discussion on this subject[2] have done is not to discover something previously unknown or even something which had been for a number of years forgotten, but simply to bring out more clearly and sharply the true theological urgency and the true universal scope of an obligation which throughout the centuries the Church has always recognized – at least in theory. In this connexion it is

[1] I have already drawn attention in a letter to *The British Weekly* (30 March, 1967) to the absence of any such explicit statement from the *Proposed Basis for Union of The Congregational Church in England and Wales and The Presbyterian Church of England* (1967).

[2] Reference may be made to the following: H. W. Beyer's article in the Kittel-Friedrich *Theologisches Wörterbuch zum Neuen Testament* 2, pp. 81–93; K. Rahner and H. Vorgrimmler, *Diaconia in Christo*, Freiburg, 1962; H. Krimm, *Quellen zur Geschichte der Diakonie*, Stuttgart, 1960–63; L. Vischer, 'The Problem of the Diaconate', in *Encounter* 25 (1964–65), pp. 84–104; *The Ministry of Deacons* (World Council Studies 2), Geneva, 1965; H. Krimm (ed.), *Das Diakonische Amt der Kirche*, Stuttgart, 1965; C. E. B. Cranfield, *The Service of God*, London, 1965, pp. 23–34; J. I. McCord and T. H. L. Parker (eds.), *Service in Christ: Essays presented to Karl Barth on his 80th birthday*, London, 1966; and the study by H. C. von Hase already cited.

appropriate in a Scottish journal to recall chapter xxvi, section ii, of the Westminster Confession of Faith:

> Saints, by profession, are bound to maintain an holy fellowship and communion in the worship of God, . . . as also in relieving each other in outward things, according to their several abilities and necessities. Which communion, as God offereth opportunity, is to be extended unto all those who in every place call upon the name of the Lord Jesus

and also *The Form of Presbyterial Church-Government*, on deacons:

> The scripture doth hold out deacons as distinct officers in the Church. Whose office is perpetual. To whose office it belongs not to preach the word, or administer the sacraments, but to take special care in distributing to the necessities of the poor

and the section headed, 'Of the Officers of a particular Congregation', which includes the sentence:

> And likewise it is requisite that there be others to take special care for the relief of the poor.

The historic Westminster documents thus contain an unambiguous recognition of diakonia as an element of the Church's very being and life – though it is true that, while the Confession of Faith makes it clear that diakonia is not to be confined to the particular parish, it does not speak of its scope extending beyond the fellowship of believers. John Calvin, however, was well aware that Christian compassion is not to be confined within the bounds of the Church. So, for instance, he understands the first person plural of the Lord's Prayer as implying that the Christian is to embrace in his prayerful concern 'all who are his brothers in Christ, not only those whom he at present sees and recognises as such but all men who dwell on earth'.[1]

What then of expediency? We want to suggest that it is expedient – in the NT sense of συμφέρει, σύμφορος – that any church or combination of churches which has occasion to make a new constitution should include in it an explicit and unambiguous statement of the Church's diaconal responsibility, because such a solemn and public recognition of its duty will be a safeguard against its forgetting that duty – or else a witness against it, should it forget. That the mere inclusion of something in a constitution will necessarily mean that it will be effectively maintained in practice, no one with any familiarity with Church history would be likely to claim; but what can be said is that to neglect to write into the constitution a clear statement of an essential element of the Church's life and obedience is positively to invite the church concerned to forget that element – especially when what is in question is something costly which will require real self-sacrifice if it is to be worthily fulfilled.

Vague general phrases like 'to serve all men'[2] are not enough – they will be far too easily and lightly accepted. What is required is a perpetual reminder of the Church's obligation to succour the suffering and needy so explicit as to be a real embarrassment whenever their claims are being ignored. We would suggest that in a constitution which actually specifies the functions of the various courts

---

[1] *Institutes of the Christian Religion*, 3.20.38 (F. L. Battles' translation).

[2] This phrase occurs a number of times in the Congregational-Presbyterian *Proposed Basis for Union* (e.g. in paragraphs 11, 16, 19 and 21).

or councils of the Church the responsibility for seeing that the Church's diaconal task is being worthily fulfilled should be written into it in connexion with each court or council in turn.[1]

But there is something else which needs to be said – that there is a special feature of the present time which makes it particularly desirable that churches should thus solemnly and publicly acknowledge their diaconal responsibility. We live in a world in which the gap between the rich and the poor nations is growing rapidly wider.[2] Already the contrast between comfort and luxury on the one hand and abject misery on the other is a crying shame; but it is likely that hunger and starvation in the poor countries will in the next decade or so assume increasingly fearful proportions. There is a terrible danger that the governments and peoples of the rich countries may deliberately harden their hearts in the face of human misery on an unprecedented scale. The question arises whether the Christian churches in the wealthy countries are going to be parties to any such hardening of heart, and so fail even more spectacularly than they have done in the past to be worthy of the name of Church of Christ. The temptation even for Christians to harden their hearts in the face of unparalleled calamities suffered by people in distant parts of the world will be very strong; and it is a matter of the greatest urgency that they should be as effectively as possible forearmed against it.

[1] So, for example, we would suggest that it should be written into paragraphs 11, 32, 33, 34, 35 and 36 of the Congregational-Presbyterian *Proposed Basis for Union*.

[2] Cf. A. Biéler, *Calvin, prophète de l'ère industrielle*, Geneva, 1964; 'Report on the Biéler proposal', in *The Reformed and Presbyterian World* 29 (1966), pp. 113–119; W. A. Visser 't Hooft, 'World Conference on Church and Society', in *The Ecumenical Review* 18 (1966), pp. 417–425; and the Papal encyclical, *Populorum Progressio*, of March 1967.

Unfortunately, there are but few signs that the leaders of the churches are really fully aware of the critical significance for the churches of what is happening.[1] Perhaps too many of them are too preoccupied with the heady fascinations of reunion 'without tarrying for anie' to notice the fingers of a hand already beginning to write on the wall. But, unless the churches respond to the challenge of the hunger and starvation and abject misery of half the world with a compassion, imagination, energy and self-sacrifice far surpassing any they have so far shown, the judgment of God on the ecumenical movement of the twentieth century – despite all its glorious promise and real achievements – is likely to be: 'weighed in the balances, and ... found wanting'.

[1] Cardinal Heenan's call to his diocese (as reported in *The Observer* of 30 April, 1967) deserves honourable mention; but it scarcely goes far enough.

VII
THE CREATION'S PROMISED LIBERATION: SOME OBSERVATIONS ON ROMANS 8.19–21[1]

In Romans 8 (the fourth section of the main division of the epistle in which the life promised for the man who is righteous by faith is described) Paul is concerned with the fact that the life promised for the man who is righteous by faith is a life characterized by the indwelling of the Holy Spirit. In vv. 1–11 the basic statement of the section is made. Paul then goes on in vv. 12–16 to affirm that to be indwelt by God's Spirit is to be a child of God, having the freedom to call God 'Father'. The implication of v. 15 understood in its context would seem to be that it is in the believer's calling God 'Father' that God's holy law is established and its righteous requirement (v. 4) fulfilled. (To tell him that he has been given the freedom to call God 'Father' and to bid him exercise his freedom is to say *in principle* all that there is to be said in the way of Christian ethics; for nothing more is required of him than that he should do just this – should do it with full understanding of what it means, with full seriousness and with full sincerity. For to address the true God by the name of Father intelligently, seriously, sincerely, will, of course, involve seeking wholeheartedly to be and think and say and do what is pleasing to Him and to avoid being or thinking or saying or doing what displeases Him.) Verse 17 makes the transition from the subject of obedience (calling God 'Father') to that of Christian hope (that to be indwelt by the Holy Spirit is to be possessed of

[1] First published in R. J. Banks (ed.), *Reconciliation and Hope: New Testament essays on atonement and eschatology presented to L. L. Morris on his 60th birthday*, Exeter, 1974, pp. 224–230.

the gift of hope is the theme of vv. 17–30) by way of the connexion between sonship and heirship. The words εἴπερ, κ.τ.λ. (RV: 'if so be that', etc.) are added in confirmation of what has already been said in the earlier part of the verse, the sense being that the fact that believers are now suffering as a result of their loyalty to Christ, so far from calling the reality of their heirship in question, is in truth a pledge of their being glorified with Him hereafter. Verse 18 explains (hence the 'for') how the sufferings and the glory, to which v. 17 has referred, stand in relation to each other: in the light of his understanding of the gospel Paul can see that the sufferings of the present are but a very little thing compared with the transcendent greatness and splendour of that glory which is the object of the Christian hope.

Such is the context of the verses with which we are specially concerned. The first of them is introduced as support ('for') for what has been said in v. 18, and is then itself clarified by vv. 20 and 21.

About the meaning of ἡ κτίσις (RV: 'the creation') there has been much controversy. It has been variously interpreted down the centuries as signifying the whole creation including mankind, both believing and unbelieving, and also the angels; all mankind; unbelieving mankind only; believers only; the angels only; sub-human nature together with the angels; sub-human nature together with unbelieving mankind; sub-human nature only.[1] But believers must almost certainly be excluded, since in v. 23 they are contrasted with ἡ κτίσις. Moreover, οὐχ ἑκοῦσα (RV: 'not of its own will') in v. 20, if it is understood in the sense in which in the context it seems natural to understand it, namely, as indicating that it was

[1] For details of the history of exegesis reference may be made to volume 1 of my forthcoming commentary on Romans in The International Critical Commentary.

not as a result of its own choice that the κτίσις was subjected to vanity, would seem to exclude mankind generally; for, if Paul intended to include mankind, he could scarcely have meant to exclude Adam, the created man *par excellence*, and Adam clearly cannot be said to have been so subjected otherwise than as a result of his own choice. The suggestion that the reference is only to unbelieving mankind is unlikely, since, while it is true that κόσμος (RV: 'world') is sometimes used of unbelievers in contrast with believers, it is unlikely that a NT writer would use in this way a term which expresses a relation to God in which Christians stand equally with non-Christians and in which, moreover, they above all men must rejoice. That angels are referred to seems also unlikely, no really convincing suggestion being forthcoming as to what v. 20 could mean with reference to them. The only interpretation of ἡ κτίσις in these verses which is really probable is surely that which takes it to refer to the sum-total of sub-human nature both animate and inanimate.

The objection to this interpretation that it is inconsonant with Paul's use of personal language here is not to be sustained. Paul's use with reference to irrational nature of ἀποκαραδοκία, ἀπεκδέχεται, οὐχ ἑκοῦσα, ἐφ' ἐλπίδι, συστενάζει (RV: 'earnest expectation', 'waiteth for', 'not of its own will', 'in hope', 'groaneth ... together') is, as John Chrysostom recognized,[1] an example of personification such as is quite often to be found in the OT.[2] There is a poetic quality in parts of Romans 8, and especially in vv. 19–22, which must be recognized, if Paul's meaning is properly to be understood. What we refer to is not a matter of the things which belong to the outward form of poetry so much as of

[1] *PG* 60, col. 529.
[2] Cf., e.g., Ps 65.12f; Isa 24.4, 7; Jer 4.28; 12.4.

96

those things which belong to its inner essence – such things as imaginative power, feeling for the evocative word, deep sensitivity, universality of sympathy, and a true generosity of vision and conception. It is this poetic quality which is to be discerned in the personal language of these verses. With poetic boldness Paul speaks of the earnest anticipation, the neck-craning expectancy,[1] of the whole splendid theatre of the universe and of all the manifold sub-human life within it as eagerly awaiting the revelation of the sons of God. By 'the revealing of the sons of God' Paul means that revelation by which those who now are truly sons of God (cf. the present tenses of the verb 'to be' in vv. 14 and 16) but whose sonship is veiled and imperceptible except to faith, will at last be made manifest in their true glory, that public and open proclamation of their adoption which – rather than their adoption as such – is what is meant by υἱοθεσία (RV: '*our* adoption') in v. 23. Until that time, in the words of the Scottish paraphrase,

'Concealed as yet this honour lies,
By this dark world unknown'[2]

The 'For' at the beginning of v. 20 indicates that what follows explains why it is that the creation awaits so eagerly the manifestation of the sons of God. The explanation consists of vv. 20 and 21 together as a whole; but it is necessary to consider it piecemeal before we can hope to understand it as a whole.

---

[1] The basic idea expressed by ἀποκαραδοκία (also ἀποκαραδοκεῖν, καραδοκία, καραδοκεῖν) is that of stretching the neck, craning forward to see something which is approaching (κάρα is a poetical equivalent of κεφαλή): the ἀπο- is intensive, as also in ἀπεκδέχεσθαι.

[2] *The Church Hymnary*, rev. ed., Oxford, 1938, no. 483 [3rd ed., no. 396].

We take first the words τῇ ... ματαιότητι ἡ κτίσις ὑπετάγη (RV: 'the creation was subjected to vanity'). The aorist tense shows that the reference is to a particular event, and the passive voice is no doubt to be understood as an indirect reference to a divine action.[1] Paul probably had in mind the divine judgment recorded in Gen 3.17–19 (note especially the words in Gen 3.17: 'cursed is the ground for thy sake'). The position of τῇ ... ματαιότητι at the beginning of the sentence gives it special emphasis. In view of the parallelism between τῇ ... ματαιότητι ... ὑπετάγη and τῆς δουλείας τῆς φθορᾶς (RV: 'the bondage of corruption'), some interpreters have assumed that ματαιότης must here be used as a synonym of φθορά and others that the two words are intended to signify respectively the mutability and the mortality which characterize creaturely existence as we know it. Some have taken τῇ ματαιότητι to be an example of the abstract used for the concrete, and have understood Paul's meaning to be that the creation was subjected to vain men. Others have thought that the clue to the meaning of ματαιότης here was to be found in the way the cognate verb is used in 1.21 (RV: 'became vain'): they have therefore suggested that Paul had in mind the subjection of the creation to man's idolatry which exploits the sub-human creation for its own base and futile purposes (cf. 1.23, 25), and have gone on to explain φθορά as signifying the moral corruption resulting from idolatry (cf. 1.24, 26–32) and the δουλεία τῆς φθορᾶς as signifying the sub-human creation's bondage to man's corrupt and futile abuse of it. Others have suggested that, since ματαιότης could be used to denote a god of the heathen, Paul may have meant by subjection to ματαιότης subjection to various celestial powers, and Gal 4.9 with its reference to

---

[1] Cf. below on διὰ τὸν ὑποτάξαντα.

bondage to the weak and beggarly στοιχεῖα (RV: 'rudiments') has been adduced in support of this view. Yet others have maintained that it is along the lines of the sense which it has in Ecclesiastes, where the majority of its occurrences in the Septuagint are to be found and where it denotes the futility, the disorder, the sheer absurdity, of things, that ματαιότης is to be interpreted here. But the most natural and straightforward interpretation is surely that which understands it in its basic sense as denoting the ineffectiveness of that which fails to attain its goal (cf. the adverb μάτην which means 'in vain'), and so takes Paul's meaning to be that the sub-human creation has been subjected to the frustration of not being able properly to fulfil the purpose of its existence.

And, if the question is asked, 'What sense can there be in saying that the sub-human creation – the Jungfrau, for example, or the Matterhorn, or the planet Venus – suffers frustration by being prevented from properly fulfilling the purpose of its existence?', the answer must surely be that the whole magnificent theatre of the universe, together with all its splendid properties and all the varied chorus of sub-human life, created for God's glory, is cheated of its true fulfilment so long as man, the chief actor in the great drama of God's praise, fails to contribute his rational part. The Jungfrau and the Matterhorn and the planet Venus and all living things too, man alone excepted, do indeed glorify God in their own ways; but, since their praise is destined to be not a collection of independent offerings but part of a magnificent whole, the united praise of the whole creation, they are prevented from being fully that which they were created to be, so long as man's part is missing, just as all the other players in a concerto would be frustrated of their purpose if the soloist were to fail to play his part.

On the assumption that 'the creation' signifies the sub-human creation generally, οὐχ ἑκοῦσα (RV: 'not of its own will') is naturally understood as meaning 'not through its own fault'.[1] It is man, not the sub-human creation, which is to blame for the frustration of the latter. Contrasted (ἀλλά) with ἑκοῦσα is διὰ τὸν ὑποτάξαντα (RV: 'by reason of him who subjected it'). There is no doubt that ὁ ὑποτάξας must be God, not Adam, nor man in general, nor Satan; for it would be intolerably harsh to take the participle to refer to anyone other than the agent implied by the passive ὑπετάγη ('was subjected') in the earlier part of the verse, who must surely be God, since no one other than God could be said to have subjected the creation ἐφ' ἐλπίδι ('in hope'), and, moreover, 'subject' clearly denotes here an authoritative action such as neither Adam nor man in general nor Satan could have effected.[2] It is significant that Paul opposes to ἑκοῦσα not a mere reference to man's responsibility but a reference to the judicial decision pronounced by God on account of man's sin; for by keeping God's part firmly in view he preserves the thoroughly evangelical quality of what he is saying.

The words ἐφ' ἐλπίδι (RV: 'in hope') are more naturally connected with ὑπετάγη ('was subjected') than with ὑποτάξαντα ('who subjected it'). The sub-human creation was not subjected to frustration without any

[1] If 'the creation' were understood to mean or to include mankind, οὐχ ἑκοῦσα would have to be understood along the lines of Augustine's interpretation of it as referring to the involuntariness of the creation's submission to the penalty imposed upon it.

[2] Karl Barth's suggestion (*A Shorter Commentary on Romans*, London, 1959, pp. 99f) that Paul was thinking of Jesus Christ as having subjected 'man, and with him the whole creation, to vanity' by the judgment pronounced and executed on Golgotha, is surely a forced interpretation of τὸν ὑποτάξαντα – though it is, of course, thoroughly true that the Cross was the final revelation of the ματαιότης to which the creation was subjected on account of man's sin, just as it was the final revelation of the wrath of God (cf. Rom 1.18).

hope: on the contrary, the divine judgment consequent on man's disobedience included the promise of a better future, when at last the judgment would be removed. It is possible that Paul may have thought of the promise in Gen 3.15 that the woman's seed should bruise the serpent's head (cf. Rom 16.20: 'And the God of peace shall bruise Satan under your feet shortly'). Hope for the sub-human creation was included in the hope for man. The reading διότι is probably to be preferred to the variant ὅτι, and, in view of Pauline usage, διότι should probably be understood as meaning, not 'that', but 'because' or 'for' – that is, as introducing a statement explaining why the creation was subjected to frustration 'in hope' (the subjection was 'in hope', because the sub-human creation itself is going to be set free . . .). In καὶ αὐτὴ ἡ κτίσις (RV: 'the creation itself also') there is an implied contrast with the children of God (cf. vv. 16 and 17, and also the 'us' in v. 18 and 'of the sons of God' in v. 19). That Paul's main interest in these verses is in the certainty of the coming glory of believers is no doubt true (cf. the εἰς ἡμᾶς (RV: 'to us-ward') of v. 18); but to state categorically, as one commentator does, that Paul 'is not concerned with creation for its own sake'[1] is to do him a grave injustice (there is nothing in this context to warrant such a statement, and to cite 1 Cor 9.9 in support of it would surely be unfair). The implication of these verses is surely rather that, with a noble breadth and generosity of vision and sympathy such as may be expected of one who truly believes in God as Creator,[2] Paul sees the future

---

[1] C. K. Barrett, *A Commentary on the Epistle to the Romans*, London, 1957, p. 165.
[2] Suggestive in this connexion is the way in which in Genesis 1 God's approval of His whole creation including man (v. 31) is preceded by the often-repeated refrain of His approval of His sub-human creation (vv. 4, 10, 12, 18, 21, 25).

glory of believers not by itself but accompanied by the glorious liberation of the whole sub-human creation. This liberation (ἐλευθερωθήσεται is more accurately translated 'shall be set free' than, as in the RV, 'shall be delivered') is liberation from the condition of slavery to decay, death, corruption, transitoriness, into the condition of freedom (ἀπὸ τῆς δουλείας τῆς φθορᾶς εἰς τὴν ἐλευθερίαν). The words which follow, τῆς δόξης τῶν τέκνων τοῦ θεοῦ (RV: 'of the glory of the children of God'), define this condition of freedom. The first of the three genitives has often been taken to be adjectival to the preceding τὴν ἐλευθερίαν (so the AV has 'the glorious liberty'); but it is more consonant with the structure of the sentence and with the thought of the passage to take it to have a sense corresponding to that of τῆς φθορᾶς. As the δουλεία τῆς φθορᾶς is a bondage to corruption, the bondage which corruption may be said to impose, so the ἐλευθερία τῆς δόξης τῶν τέκνων τοῦ θεοῦ is the liberty which results from, is the necessary accompaniment of, the (revelation of the) glory of the children of God. (The meaning is, presumably, not that the creation will possess the same liberty resulting from glory as the children of God will possess, but that it will possess its own proper liberty as a result of the glorification of the children of God.) And this liberty which will come to the sub-human creation when at last the children of God are made manifest will surely be the liberty of each several part of that creation, whether animate or inanimate, fully and perfectly to fulfil its Creator's purpose for it – the liberty which it cannot have so long as man is unready to play his role in the great drama of God's praise.

What then may be said in conclusion about the significance of these three verses?

It is true that their function in their context is to underline the greatness of the believers' hope (the fulfilment of that hope is even longed for with eager anticipation by the sub-human creation, since it will mean its deliverance from its present bondage); but this does not mean that Paul was not interested in the sub-human creation for its own sake.

That the sub-human creation's subjection to ματαιότης is ἐφ' ἐλπίδι, that it is destined to be liberated in the way indicated in v. 21, this clearly has an important bearing on the Christian's relation to the sub-human creation and – more generally – on the whole subject of 'the environment' about which there is now such widely felt concern. It is of course true that the debt of love which we owe our fellow-men includes the obligation not to spoil or destroy their environment but to cherish it for their sake. We have an obligation to the sub-human creation for men's sake, for the sake of our living fellow-men and also for the sake of those not yet born. Of this truth we must not for a moment lose sight. But these verses indicate that this truth is by no means the whole truth of the matter and that to value the sub-human creation solely as man's habitat, man's environment, man's amenities – even if we do think of 'man's' as meaning 'our neighbour's' rather than 'our own' – is to be guilty of idolatry. If the sub-human creation is part of God's creation, if to it also He is faithful, and if He is going to bring it also (as well as believing men) to a goal which is worthy of Himself, then it too has a dignity of its own and an inalienable, since divinely-appointed, right to be treated by us with reverence and sensitiveness. And our duty to it is not only a part of our duty to love our neighbour as ourselves, but also an integral part of our duty to love God with all our heart, and with all our soul, and with all our mind, and with all our strength. Since God has not created the sub-human creation solely for man's use and comfort but also with the intention of bringing it in the end to that liberty of which v. 21 speaks, true love to Him must involve not only loving our fellow-men as ourselves but also treating with respect and with a proper sense of responsibility His humbler creation, whether animate or inanimate.

As well as indicating indirectly our obligation to the sub-human creation, these verses show us the hopefulness with which we should set about trying to fulfil that obligation; for they reveal to us the fact that over that groaning and travailing creation stands the promise: ἐλευθερωθήσεται ἀπὸ τῆς δουλείας τῆς φθορᾶς εἰς τὴν ἐλευθερίαν τῆς δόξης τῶν τέκνων τοῦ θεοῦ. And those who believe in God know that in the end, in spite of the worst that polluters, spoilers and destroyers, that insatiable greed and mindless cruelty, can do, God's word 'shall have its course'.

And these verses remind us too that the Christian hope is something far more wonderful and more generous than at most times our preoccupation with ourselves and the feebleness of our concern for God's glory allow us to conceive.

VIII
THOUGHTS ON NEW TESTAMENT ESCHATOLOGY[1]

To deal with NT eschatology in the time available to me, I should have either to be a vastly more competent NT scholar and theologian than I am or else to be prepared to state my own views dogmatically and treat differing views in a cavalier fashion, a procedure I regard as unscholarly and unacceptable. So what I am offering is something much more modest – just some thoughts on the subject.

Those of you who read detective stories will know that, if once you allow a particular suspicion to become firmly settled in your mind, various pieces of information, all of which are as a matter of fact consistent with a different solution of the mystery, will seem to combine to corroborate your suspicion convincingly. I want to suggest that the widespread confidence of NT scholars that the early Church believed that the end of the world would certainly occur within a very short period of time, and was then forced to revise its eschatology by the inescapable logic of this world's unexpected continuance, ought to be looked at critically in the light of this common experience of those who read detective novels.

It is certainly true that, if you begin by assuming that the primitive Church was sure that the Parousia was going to occur within at the most a few decades, then a great many features of the NT can be understood as corroborating your assumption. It is easy then to allow yourself to be convinced that the evidence for its truth is overwhelming, indeed completely conclusive, and that only a fool could think of doubting it. Many of today's

[1] A paper read to The Aberdeen University Theological Society on 4 May, 1981, first published in *SJT* 35 (1982), pp. 497–512.

NT scholars seem to be thus convinced, and in this situation it is difficult to obtain anything approaching an open-minded hearing for any view of NT eschatology which is not a variation of the commonly held view.

I cannot, of course, refer to anything like all the relevant evidence, but I should like to try to touch on enough of it to persuade you that it is *at least conceivable* that all those features of the NT which are usually seen as corroborating the widespread view may after all be consistent with a different view, and that it would therefore be wise to regard the question as not yet finally and decisively settled. If in what follows I refer rather frequently to my far-famed and extremely distinguished former colleague, Professor C. K. Barrett, it will not be out of any love of polemics but simply because his many works, which have ranged so widely and magisterially over so much of the NT, provide the most imposing and powerful presentation known to me of that view of NT eschatology from which, in spite of its being so confidently affirmed – in one or another of its variations – by so many scholars, my own study and reflection compel me to dissent.

I

I should like first to take a quick look at Luke, Acts and John. These three documents would seem to be a good place for a first testing of the commonly held view; for, if that view is correct, the Church must surely, by the time these documents were completed,[1] have had to come to

---

[1] I have not yet been convinced by J. A. T. Robinson's dates for Luke, Acts and John in his *Redating the New Testament*, London, 1976, but freely acknowledge that his arguments will need to be weighed with care.

terms with a difficult problem of disappointed hope. Scholars claim to see in them clear traces of this process. So, for example, Professor Barrett states in his *Jesus and the Gospel Tradition*[1] that the 'early dating of the end became a source of embarrassment, and, especially in the later gospels, traces appear of editorial and theological steps taken in view of the "delay of the *parousia*" '. But is the evidence really as clear as it has been claimed to be?

With regard to Luke an important contribution was made by H. Conzelmann in 1954.[2] According to him, Mark, though conscious of unexpected delay, was still confident that the Parousia would occur within the lifetime of some of Jesus' contemporaries, but Luke, since, when he was writing, its non-occurrence had become a pressing problem, deliberately revised the Marcan eschatology, eliminating altogether the primitive Church's near-expectation (or *Naherwartung*) of the end with thoroughness and consistency and replacing it by the idea of a salvation-history, in which the earthly ministry of Jesus was 'the middle of time' and the period of the Church stretched ahead into a quite extensive future. While Conzelmann certainly argued his case with much skill and with such patient exhaustiveness that nothing which could have been adduced in its support with any plausibility seems to have missed his eye, after a careful reading of his book I for one was left unconvinced. It seemed to me that again and again the cogency of his argumentation was open to question. But all I can do now is to call attention to one or two passages in Luke which seem to me quite clearly to express the thought that the end is near.

[1] London, 1967, p. 84.
[2] *Die Mitte der Zeit: Studien zur Theologie des Lukas*, Tübingen. I have used the 3rd ed., 1960. There is an English translation, *The Theology of St. Luke*, London, 1960.

I mention first Lk 18.1–8 (the parable of the unjust judge). If Luke was really intent on getting rid of the idea of the nearness of the Parousia, he has surely done his work with extraordinary maladroitness here; for, as the passage stands, it is natural for the reader to connect closely the coming of the Son of man referred to in v. 8b ('Howbeit when the Son of man cometh, shall he find faith on the earth?') with God's vindication of His elect which is promised in v. 8a as going to be accomplished ἐν τάχει (RV: 'speedily').[1] If, on the one hand, v. 8b is (as some think) Luke's editorial work, then he would seem to have gone out of his way to underline the eschatological significance of the parable and to bring out the applicability of the ἐν τάχει to the Parousia (Conzelmann's suggestion that v. 8b is meant to damp down the violent eschatological expectations of vv. 7 and 8a by means of the reference to the still-persisting deficiencies of the faithful is surely lame). If, on the other hand, v. 8b is part of what Luke took over, then why did he not remove the ἐν τάχει from v. 8a? Professor Marshall's concluding sentence on this section ('Thus an interval before the parousia is presupposed, but the sense of imminent expectation is not abandoned')[2] is surely justified. We may note in passing the reference in this passage to God's long-suffering or patience (μακροθυμεῖ in v. 7): the thought is present also in the next passage we shall look at, though no cognate of μακροθυμία is used.

---

[1] Attempts to explain ἐν τάχει here as meaning 'suddenly' or 'unexpectedly' seem to me unconvincing. See further C. E. B. Cranfield, 'The Parable of the Unjust Judge and the Eschatology of Luke-Acts', in *SJT* 16 (1963), p. 299. n. 1; I. H. Marshall, *The Gospel of Luke: A commentary on the Greek text*, Exeter, 1978, p. 676; and the new revised and augmented ed. of the W. F. Arndt-F. W. Gingrich translation of W. Bauer's dictionary, Chicago and London, 1979, pp. 806–807.

[2] op. cit., p. 677.

Conzelmann omitted Lk 13.6–9 (the parable of the fig-tree in the vineyard) from his discussion. But it is surely very relevant. As originally spoken by Jesus the parable was presumably an appeal to His fellow-Jews to repent while there was yet time. But we may, I think, assume that Luke meant his readers to re-apply it to their own situation. The time before the Parousia is to be recognized as time of God's undeserved patience, opportunity for the Christian disciple and those to whom he bears witness to repent, believe, bear fruit of obedience. In the words put into the mouth of the vinedresser, 'Lord, let it alone this year also, till I shall dig about it, and dung it: and if it bear fruit thenceforth, *well*; but if not, thou shalt cut it down', the thought of the nearness of the end would surely be heard by the Gospel's readers – and surely was intended by the evangelist to be heard by them – as well as the gracious significance of the time that remains before it.

The thought of the need to seize the opportunity of repentance while it lasts is surely to be recognized also in Lk 12.57–59 (the saying about giving diligence to be quit of one's adversary while one is still on the way with him to the magistrate – a saying Conzelmann does not discuss) and 13.25–26 (the saying about the closed door).

I shall refer to just one passage in Acts. According to E. Haenchen, the angels' question to the apostles in 1.11, 'Ye men of Galilee, why stand ye looking into heaven?', is intended by the author of Acts as a prohibition of near-expectation.[1] But the author of Acts, if he really expected his readers to recognize in the posture of the apostles, standing looking up to heaven, a picture of the early Church's near-expectation, as Haenchen apparently supposes, must have had an extraordinarily high opinion of their perceptiveness. The thought that the apostles

---

[1] *Die Apostelgeschichte*, Göttingen,[12] 1959, pp. 118–119.

were actually expecting Jesus to return while they were watching – like a boomerang! – would hardly have occurred to any reader. And the rest of the verse ('this Jesus, which was received up from you into heaven, shall so come in like manner as ye beheld him going into heaven') would surely be an inappropriate sequel if the point of the earlier part of the verse was to forbid near-expectation; but it is thoroughly appropriate as comfort to those whose posture expressed their forlornness at having been left, reminding them that they have not been left for ever. There is indeed no promise here that He will return soon, but the attempt to find in the first part of the verse a forbidding of near-expectation is surely altogether forced.

I turn now to the Fourth Gospel. Many see in it the climax of the development of the early Church's eschatological thinking, the climax in which a truly theological solution of the problem posed by the delay of the expected Parousia is at last found. I want to refer to just one particular passage and to one general feature.

The passage is Jn 16.16–20 (the passage beginning with the words of Jesus, 'A little while, and ye behold me no more; and again a little while, and ye shall see me'). Professor Barrett refers to the 'studied ambiguity' which marks the language of Jn 16.16ff, and notes that 'the sayings about going and coming can be interpreted throughout of the departure and return of Jesus in his death and resurrection; but they can equally well be interpreted of his departure to the Father at the ascension and his return at the *parousia*'.[1] With this I thoroughly agree. The natural meaning of the sayings in the context of the conversation between Jesus and the disciples is that in a little while they will see Him no longer because He will

---

[1] *The Gospel according to St. John: An introduction with commentary and notes on the Greek text*, London, 2nd (revised) ed., 1978, p. 491.

have gone from them in death and again in a little while they will see Him in His resurrection appearances. But for the evangelist and his readers there is another meaning: in a little while from when Jesus was speaking the disciples would see Him no more because He would have gone to the Father in His ascension, and again in a little while the Church will see Him in the Parousia. The second edition of Professor Barrett's commentary contains in his note on 16.16 a sentence which was not in the first edition: 'The short spaces of time referred to here create a tension comparable with that of the imminent eschatology of other parts of the NT'.[1] In so far as it indicates recognition of the fact that his interpretation of these verses involves acceptance of the applicability (in the evangelist's mind) of μικρόν to the time before the Parousia, it is – if I may be so bold as to say so – a significant step in the right direction. But, in my view, it does not go far enough. Surely the right conclusion to be drawn from the 'studied ambiguity' of these verses is that the evangelist intended his readers to pick up a confident affirmation of the near-expectation of the Church's traditional eschatology – not (*pace* Barrett, op. cit., pp. 139–140) a re-interpretation of a hope which had proved to be false. I suggest that these verses are evidence that the Fourth Evangelist shared the near-expectation of those who had gone before him, understanding it, and believing that they also had understood it, in a way which is quite different from that in which it is often taken for granted that the early Church must have understood it.

The general feature I wanted to refer to is the importance of the Holy Spirit in the theology of this Gospel. It is often assumed that this is closely connected with the evangelist's re-interpretation of the earlier

[1] ibid.

eschatology.[1] But I should like to place a question mark against this assumption. How much is there of significance in John concerning the Spirit which cannot (when allowance is made for differences of idiom between two theologians) be paralleled in the Pauline epistles?

All that I would claim to have done so far is to have shown that the assumption that there is a marked difference between the eschatology of Luke, Acts and John and that of Paul and Mark, due to 'the delay of the Parousia', is open to question and not an assured result. But, unless I am much mistaken, this assumption is a not unimportant element in the edifice of the commonly held view of NT eschatology.

II

I turn now to Mark. We may begin with Mk 13.30 ('Verily I say unto you, This generation shall not pass away, until all these things be accomplished'). In his *Jesus and the Gospel Tradition*, p. 83, Professor Barrett appeals to it in support of his statement, 'The early Church expected the *parousia* to take place within the first generation of Christians'. He goes on to say, 'It is impossible to make Mark 13 mean anything less than that Christians contemporary with Mark believed that they would see the whole story through up to the coming of the Son of man. Mk 13.30 alone is decisive, unless strained meanings are to be given to either γενεά (generation) or ταῦτα πάντα (all these things)'. But I am not at all convinced that the suggestion that Mark understood ταῦτα πάντα as referring to the various signs of the end mentioned in vv. 5–23 involves any strained meaning; for it seems to me

[1] See, e.g., Barrett, commentary on John, pp. 88 and 90 (especially what is said of the Spirit as 'the eschatological *continuum*'); and 'New Testament Eschatology I', in *SJT* 6 (1953), pp. 238–239.

natural to understand it to have the same reference as ταῦτα in v. 29, and, since to take ταῦτα there to include the coming of the Son of man mentioned in v. 26 would involve giving to v. 29 a sense tantamount to 'when you see the Son of man coming . . . , know that he is nigh', which would seem pointless, the further suggestion that ταῦτα in v. 29 refers only to the signs of vv. 5–23 and not to what is mentioned in vv. 24–27 seems to me not unreasonable. I therefore regard it as by no means forced to take the sense of v. 30 in its context to be that all the various unpleasant things mentioned in vv. 5–23 will be experienced by the contemporaries of Jesus, because these things are characteristic of the last times which have already begun.[1]

The other verse which is often adduced as clear proof that Mark was sure that the Parousia must occur within the lifetime of some of Jesus's contemporaries is of course Mk 9.1 ('And he said unto them, Verily I say unto you, There be some here of them that stand *by*, which shall in no wise taste of death, till they see the kingdom of God come with power'). Many regard the saying as Mark's own creation, assuming that it had its origin in the existence of disappointment at the non-occurrence of the Parousia and that Mark was writing to rally the disappointed by assuring them that the Parousia would certainly take place while some of the contemporaries of Jesus were still alive. But the suggestion – it goes back to the ancient Church – that Mark saw the saying as referring to the Transfiguration which he goes on to relate in the following verses still seems to me probable. It would

---

[1] The second person plural ὄψεσθε in Mk 14.62 is sometimes adduced as evidence that Mark (or Jesus) expected the Parousia in the lifetime of the High Priest and his associates; but the verb could equally well cover a seeing after resurrection to judgment as a seeing within their natural lifetime.

account for the careful note of time in 9.2. The expression 'the kingdom of God come with power' seems to me a not inappropriate description of the Transfiguration, if the Transfiguration really was a special brief disclosure to the three disciples (the mode of it I shall not attempt to explain) of that glory which Jesus possessed throughout His earthly life, though – to use Calvin's suggestive language – He steadfastly 'refrained from' it,[1] and which was later to be disclosed more definitively and to more persons in the Resurrection Appearances, and would finally be made manifest to all in the Parousia. I would assume that the point of the solemn language about not tasting death is that the persons referred to would have the privilege of seeing in the course of their natural life what others would see only at the final judgment. I am concerned just now not with Jesus but only with Mark; but I must say that I regard Professor Barrett's comment that 'if Jesus solemnly affirmed that some at least of his hearers would survive his prediction by one week he was uttering ridiculous bathos',[2] as rather perverse.

Mk 13.32 ('But of that day or that hour knoweth no one, not even the angels in heaven, neither the Son, but the Father'), if it had to be combined with Professor Barrett's interpretation of v. 30, would no doubt have to mean that 'within the general nearness of the end no one can name the precise moment of its arrival', as he explains it;[3] but so to interpret so solemnly formulated a statement seems to me to reduce it to the very sort of bathos which

---

[1] In commenting on Phil 2.7 he says, '... it is with right that Paul says that He who was the Son of God, in reality equal to God, nevertheless refrained from His glory when in the flesh He manifested Himself in the appearance of a servant' (*The Epistles of Paul the Apostle to the Galatians, Ephesians, Philippians and Colossians*, tr. by T. H. L. Parker, Edinburgh, 1965, p. 248).

[2] *Jesus and the Gospel Tradition*, p. 85.

[3] op. cit., p. 83.

Professor Barrett sees in 9.1 interpreted as referring to the Transfiguration. That the saying by itself is patient of the sense that only God knows at all when the end will be is of course clear. Mk 13.10 ('And the gospel must first be preached unto all the nations') seems to me to suggest that Mark reckoned with the possibility of a considerable period filled with the Church's preaching; but it will be convenient to reserve discussion of this to our consideration of Pauline eschatology.

That in Mk 13.29 ('even so ye also, when ye see these things coming to pass, know ye that he is nigh, *even* at the doors') we do have the thought of the nearness of the Parousia I accept as clear. I take the meaning to be that, whenever believers see any of those signs of the end referred to in vv. 5–23 which are characteristic features of all the last days (that is, of the whole period between the coming of the kingdom of God in hiddenness in the earthly ministry of Jesus and His final parousia), they are to allow themselves to be reminded that His parousia is in a real sense near, giving to the present moment its true significance. But at this point it will be convenient to turn to Paul.

III

In his presidential summing up of the colloquium on Romans 12 and 13 held in the Abbey of St. Paul Outside the Walls in 1974, Professor Barrett stated categorically: 'It [that is, the end of the world] was not near, in the sense in which Paul thought it was'.[1] He was assuming that it is an indisputable fact that, when Paul wrote Rom

[1] L. DeLorenzi (ed.), *Dimensions de la vie chrétienne (Rm 12–13)*, Rome, 1979, p. 233.

13.11–14, he was quite sure that the end would occur within a very few years and that history has proved him to have been mistaken. I have argued elsewhere[1] that the affirmation of the nearness of the end in Rom 13.12 is not the same thing as an affirmation that it must necessarily occur within at the most a few decades – and I want to say this also for the other NT passages (like the last verse from Mark we were considering) in which insistence on the nearness of the end is, I think, properly recognized – but is rather the expression of the recognition that history's most significant events have already taken place in the ministry, death, resurrection and ascension of Christ, so that all that remains between His ascension and His parousia can only be a sort of epilogue, during the whole of which, whether the actual length of time involved is short or long, the end presses upon the life and concerns of the believer as something urgently relevant to the present.

Professor Barrett understands Rom 15.19b ('so that from Jerusalem, and round about even unto Illyricum, I have fully preached the gospel of Christ') as asserting that Paul has completed, as far as the area indicated is concerned, all the preaching of the gospel that has to be done before the Parousia[2] (compare the saying attributed to Jesus in Mk 13.10 to which reference has already been made). It seems to me much more natural, in view of vv. 20 and 21, to take Paul to mean that he has completed, as far as the area indicated is concerned, that *pioneer preaching* which he believed it was his own special apostolic function to accomplish. The words 'having no more any place in these regions' in v. 23 should, I think, be explained along the same lines. To say, as Professor

---

[1] *A critical and exegetical commentary on the Epistle to the Romans* 2, Edinburgh, 1979, pp. 682–684.

[2] *A Commentary on the Epistle to the Romans*, London, 1957, p. 276.

Barrett does, that 'Since the eastern end of the Mediterranean had been dealt with and Paul had "no more scope in these parts" there remained for missionary work the north coast of Africa (from Alexandria to the province of Africa), Gaul, and Spain'[1] is surely to subject ancient geographical knowledge to a Procrustean bed treatment in support of one's view of NT eschatology.[2] If Paul took at all seriously the idea that before the end the gospel was to be preached to *all* nations, he can hardly have thought that he was going to finish the job in a few more years. (And this has a bearing also on Mark's understanding of Mk 13.10.)

It is widely assumed that Paul could have written 1 Corinthians 7 only if he was convinced at the time that the end would certainly occur within a decade or two. But I think that Karl Barth's discussion of this passage in *Church Dogmatics* III/4, pp. 144–148 (= *KD*, pp. 160–164) deserves very serious consideration. It points, I think, to the right interpretation. The statement in v. 29 that ὁ καιρὸς συνεσταλμένος ἐστίν I would interpret along the same lines as I suggested for Rom 13.12. The time has been shortened in the sense that the occurrence of the gospel events has rendered the remainder of history something which is only epilogue, subsequent to the last chapter. Nothing of independent significance lies ahead of mankind now except the Parousia itself and God's coming order. All intervening events of history have significance only in relation to the ministry, death, resurrection and ascension of Christ and His coming parousia. This means that this present world's affairs have been relativized (1 Cor 7.29b–31). Even marriage is something to which a Christian may say either

---

[1] op. cit., p. 277.
[2] Cf. my commentary on Romans 2, pp. 766–768.

'yes' or 'no', according to whether he has or has not a vocation for it from God: it is not something to which the answer can only be 'yes', as, almost without exception, the men of the OT felt it could only be. For Paul recognizes that marriage can take away from the fullness of a man's or a woman's commitment to Christ's service (vv. 32–35). The ἐνεστῶσα ἀνάγκη (RV: 'present distress') mentioned in v. 26 refers, I would think, either to the urgent relevance of the coming Parousia to the life of the present, the pressure which it already exercises, or to the sufferings and troubles which Christians must expect throughout the whole period between the gospel events and the end.

We turn next to 1 Th 4.15–17 and 1 Cor 15.51–52, two passages in which Paul uses the first person plural with reference to those who will still be alive when the Parousia occurs.[1] It is generally assumed that its use must imply that Paul was confident that he would be among them.[2] But it seems to me perfectly possible to take the 'we' to mean 'we Christians' (in 1 Th 4.17 – 'those of us [Christians] who are alive, who are left'). For this I would compare the use of the first person plural verb with regard to the past in Jn 1.14, concerning which Professor Barrett says: 'This first person plural does not necessarily imply that the gospel was written by an eye-witness. It is the apostolic church that speaks'[3] and 'It remains possible only that it should mean "we, the church", "we Christians" '.[4] I see no proof in these two passages that Paul was sure that he would himself live to the Parousia.

There are a good many other passages which it would be interesting to consider in connexion with Paul's

---

[1] For the view that there is a change of emphasis between these two passages see C. H. Dodd, *New Testament Studies*, Manchester, 1953, p. 110; Barrett, in *SJT* 6, p. 143.

[2] So, e.g., on the pages cited in the preceding footnote.

[3] p. 166 of his commentary on John already cited.

[4] op. cit., p. 143.

eschatological thought; but I must limit myself here to just two observations. The first is that in 2 Th 2.1–12, though it presents the exegete with some baffling puzzles, I see nothing which must imply that the end is thought of as certain to occur within a very short time. The second is that Rom 8.19–21 is specially interesting for its indication that Paul thought of the Parousia as effecting (to the eternal glory of God) not just the glorification of believers but the bringing of God's whole creation to a goal which is worthy of himself as the good, merciful, faithful, wise and almighty Creator (that in the Bible there is an intimate connexion between eschatology and the doctrine of creation should never be forgotten).[1]

IV

In the postscript of his *Jesus and the Gospel Tradition* Professor Barrett lists three 'major matters' in which Jesus was mistaken. First, 'He believed that his disciples would suffer with him, and they did not'; secondly, 'He believed that suffering would be immediately followed, or even interrupted, by a divine act of vindication that would establish the kingdom of God and bring world history to a close; but ... the world continued in the old way'; and, thirdly, 'since the things he looked for did not happen he died with the disillusioned avowal that God had forsaken him. But again he was mistaken: God had not forsaken him.'[2] In his next sentence Professor Barrett states: 'Christian theology has, understandably, been slow to

[1] See further my contribution, 'Some observations on Romans 8.19–21', in R. J. Banks (ed.), *Reconciliation and Hope: New Testament essays on Atonement and Eschatology presented to L. L. Morris on his 60th birthday* (in the present volume, pp. 94ff).

[2] p. 105.

acknowledge these errors, but they emerge clearly enough from historical study of the gospels'.[1] But do they? One very distinguished NT scholar's historical study of the Gospels has thoroughly convinced him that this is the correct interpretation of the evidence they afford: very probably a considerable number of other scholars agree with him. But to claim that 'these errors . . . emerge clearly enough from historical study of the gospels' is surely unwarranted while many other scholars reach quite different conclusions.

For – to pass over the point that, if what has been said above in I–III has some force, then the presuppositions of Professor Barrett's reconstruction of Jesus's eschatological expectations have already been considerably undermined[2] – many of those who take the view that the early Church, and Jesus Himself, thought that the end would certainly come within a few decades, are convinced that Jesus expected a significant interval between His resurrection and parousia. As outstanding representatives of such scholars Dr Barrett names Professor G. R. Beasley-Murray and Professor W. G. Kümmel. He then seeks to counter their arguments. But his argumentation in dealing with them (pp. 74ff), in the immediately preceding pages, and also in the previous chapter, entitled 'Christ Crucified', seems to me to include such a liberal disallowing of sayings material which conflicts with his thesis, either as being unauthentic or as having been radically changed in significance by the Church, and so much questionable exegesis (e.g., his ready acceptance of J. Jeremias's suggestion that the original reference of the sayings in Mk 13.10 and 14.9 was

[1] ibid.

[2] Note, e.g., his argument on p. 84 from the alleged later response to delay of the Parousia back to the probability that *Naherwartung* 'has deep roots in the tradition'.

not to the disciples', but to an angelic, proclamation), that it is far from convincing. Significantly, he never even mentions Mk 14.7 ('For ye have the poor always with you, and whensoever ye will ye can do them good; but me ye have not always'), a saying which has long seemed to me a particularly strong piece of evidence for Jesus's having envisaged a significant interval between His resurrection and parousia, since it surely implies that there will be a period during which disciples will be able to do good to the poor but will not be able to do good to Jesus Himself directly.

It is, I think, only fair to mention at this point the saying which can perhaps most plausibly be claimed as support for Professor Barrett's view, Mt 10.23b ('Ye shall not have gone through the cities of Israel, till the Son of man be come'). I freely admit I do not know how to explain it, though I might perhaps repeat the very tentative suggestion I have made elsewhere[1] that Rom 11.26a ('and so all Israel shall be saved') in its context and this logion might throw some light on each other. Could they both perhaps express the thought that the final conversion of Israel *as a whole* will be a strictly eschatological event?

The three mistakes in major matters attributed to Jesus by Professor Barrett, to which we referred above, taken together give us a very vivid picture of the eschatological thought of Jesus as understood by an eminent modern scholar. That this reconstruction is nearer to the historical truth than the accounts in our primary sources I remain – at the risk of seeming a theological ignoramus beyond all hope of enlightenment – totally unconvinced.[2]

[1] Commentary on Romans 2, p. 577.

[2] In support of his suggestion (p. 47), in connexion with the γρηγορεῖτε of Mk 14.34 and 38 and the sleeping of the three disciples, that 'The evangelists mistakenly turned into a command to remain physically awake an exhortation to look out for the long-expected

121

It seems to me – and I think my conclusions have been reached on the basis of historical study as serious, patient and objective as I could manage – that we can make the following statements about the eschatological thought of Jesus with a considerable degree of confidence:

(i) that He was convinced that in and through His ministry God's royal intervention to help and save men and to claim their trust and obedience was taking place;

(ii) that in His teaching He contrasted with the present hiddenness and apparent weakness of God's kingly activity in His ministry its certain future glorious manifestation;

(iii) that the manifestation of the kingdom which He expected was His own coming in glory and the end of history as we know it;

(iv) that He expected to die for men in obedience to God's purpose,[1] bearing the burden of their sins as the

---

fulfilment of the apocalyptic hope, and went on to draw the inference that those to whom the command was addressed were falling asleep', Professor Barrett argues that it is scarcely credible that the disciples could have fallen asleep, since they must have realized that they were in a situation of real peril and at least one or two of them were armed, and 'In these circumstances men may run away, but they do not normally fall asleep'. With regard to this argument I can only express my surprise that the author could have lived so long without ever having himself experienced or witnessed in another the irresistible power which sleepiness can have. The disciples had, after all, probably had a rather exhausting few days – or weeks. A further observation, relevant to the Gethsemane pericope but also more generally – as someone who in 1981 remembers much from the later 1920s and early 1930s, when I was at school, and from university days in the 1930s and from life in the army from 1942–46, I am inclined to make more allowance than many NT scholars seem to be for the part which human memory may have played in the production of the Gospel material. It does seem to me to require quite extraordinary resources of credulity to believe that the disciples did not remember as long as they lived with some measure of accuracy the most stirring months of their lives.

[1] The contention that the surprise of the disciples (Mark 14 and 15) at the suffering and death of Jesus makes it difficult to believe that Jesus

true servant of the Lord, and to be raised from the dead by God after a brief space of time;

(v) that He expected an interval between His resurrection and exaltation and His parousia, an interval in which His disciples would have the duty of bearing witness to Him among all the nations and suffering for His name's sake;

(vi) that He understood the whole period between His ministry and His parousia as the last days or end-time, a time, which, however long it might last, must be recognized as short time, interval-time, in which disciples have always to be ready for the coming of their Lord.

May I in conclusion try to draw together my thoughts on NT eschatology by making several points very rapidly?

1. Unlike those who are convinced that they can see in the NT three very different eschatologies sundered from each other by the intervention of two unexpected turns of events (first, the eschatology of Jesus; secondly, separated from it by the unexpected issue of Jesus's ministry in His death and resurrection and the continuing life of the disciples in this age, the eschatology of the primitive Church; and, thirdly, separated from the second by the failure of the Parousia to occur within the first generation of Christians, the eschatology which has been modified as a result of the delay of the Parousia),[1] I believe that there is an essential consistency of eschatological thought in the NT, an agreement which stands out all the more impressively in view of the undoubted differences of idiom, emphasis and circumstance.

---

had predicted His suffering and death fails to allow for the well known fact that men are extremely good at not believing what they do not want to believe.

[1] See Barrett, op. cit., p. 13, n. 26.

2. Insistence on the nearness of the end, on the shortness of the time which remains, is characteristic of the NT as a whole. (For some examples not mentioned above we may refer to Phil 4.5; Heb 10.25; Jas 5.8–9; 1 Pet 4.7; 1 Jn 2.18; Rev 22.20.) It was not a matter of Jesus's, or of the early Church's, confidently expecting that the end would necessarily occur within a very short time, but of the clear recognition of the ministry-death-resurrection-ascension of Jesus as the decisive event of history, between which and the end nothing of anything like comparable importance can take place in this world. What made it natural and necessary to see the intervening time as short, however long it might last, was the recognition of the decisiveness of what God had already wrought in Jesus and of the fact that the end which is still to come belongs together with it so closely that in a real sense the gospel events and the Parousia are one divine act. And this insistence on the nearness of the end is still surely an essential element of true Christian faith and life. It is by no means true, as far as I can see, that 'The mere extension of the interim in time' has 'given it a different valuation'.[1]

3. There is evidence in the NT (Jn 21.23; 2 Pet 3.3ff) that there were *some* people who *did* misunderstand this insistence on the nearness of the end as certainty that the end would. necessarily occur within at the most a few decades; but they appear in the NT as people whose views are being rejected as error, and there is no reason to suppose that their way of thinking was characteristic of the Church as a whole at any stage. It would indeed have

[1] Barrett, commentary on John, p. 140. At no stage in the Church's life was the interim 'almost insignificant'. The recognition of its shortness, while in some ways demoting the interval-time, also fills it with positive significance as time of opportunity for repentance, faith, witness.

been surprising if no members of the early Church had fallen to this particular error; for the Church of the first century must have had a goodly number of stupid members, just as the Church of the late twentieth century certainly has no shortage of such people. We know of course, from Galatians, 1 Corinthians, Colossians, 1 John, to mention only some of the documents which refer to them, of the existence of a number of groups of seriously misled Christians in NT times.

4. It is an essential feature of the end-time that men do not know how long it will last,[1] and believers have therefore always to watch for their coming Lord, to be ready for Him all the time. Like Paul and Mark and the others, from day to day we do not know at all how long history will continue. But there is between them and us this difference, that we – unlike them – actually *know* that the Parousia has *not* occurred within nineteen centuries.

5. Vitally important for the proper understanding of NT eschatology is the recognition of the connexion between the continuance of the end-time and the patience of God (see especially 2 Pet 3.9, 15). The interval is no meaningless, insignificant interim but the opportunity provided by the μακροθυμία of the gracious God, whose will it is 'that all men should be saved, and come to the knowledge of the truth' (1 Tim 2.4), for the gospel to be preached to all nations (Mk 13.10) and for men to have

---

[1] In this connexion it is important to see that what is said in Mark 13.5–23 about signs is not the sort of answer which the question ascribed to the disciples in v. 4 was seeking. Its function is not to enable the readers to predict the date of the end but to hold them faithful to their task of watching. For believers the events of history as they occur are to be reminders and pledges of their Lord's coming and of its nearness in the sense we have tried to suggest, and so an again and again recurring summons to faith and obedience. See further the author's *The Gospel according to Saint Mark*, Cambridge, [7]1979, pp. 387–412.

time and freedom to hear it, to repent, to believe and to glorify God. And the recognition of the reality of God's patience is no afterthought of a late NT writer trying to come to terms with an unexpected delay of the Parousia but an element of biblical faith characteristic of the OT as of the NT.

6. Because the interval is time of God's patience, the believer is held in a state of tension. On the one hand, he prays with earnest longing, 'Thy kingdom come' (Mt 6.10a); 'Marana tha' (Nestle-Aland 1 Cor 16.22b = 'Our Lord, come': RV has 'Maran atha'); 'Amen, come, Lord Jesus' (Rev 22.20b), living in hope (cf. Rom 8.23–25). On the other hand, he is grateful to God for every hour or year or century that He holds back Christ's glorious coming as so much more opportunity for repentance and for witness. Knowing the nature of his situation in the end-time, he will recognize that his whole duty is to watch for his coming Lord with mind alert[1] – with proper eagerness and proper urgency, and in all the resolute engagement in the work of faith and witness and love which these involve. The truth that the meaning of the command to watch in Mt 24.42 is drawn out in Matthew 25 with its parables of the ten virgins and of the talents and its discourse on the Final Judgment will not be lost on him.[2]

[1] Cf. J. Calvin, *The Epistle of Paul the Apostle to the Hebrews and the First and Second Epistles of St. Peter*, tr. by W. B. Johnston, Edinburgh, 1963, p. 303.

[2] Some bibliographical material on the subject of this paper will be found in my commentary on Romans (already cited) 2, p. 684, n. 3.

IX
DIVINE AND HUMAN ACTION: THE BIBLICAL CONCEPT OF WORSHIP[1]

We may distinguish three uses of the word 'worship': (i) to denote a particular element of what is generally referred to as worship, namely, adoration; (ii) to denote generally the public worship of the religious community gathered together and also the private religious exercises of the family and the individual; and (iii), in a still wider sense, to denote the whole life of the community or of the individual viewed as service of God. In the English versions of the Bible it is generally used in the first, the narrowest, sense; for it usually represents in the OT the Hebrew verb *hištaḥᵃwah*, which properly denotes bowing down, prostrating oneself, in homage, and in the NT προσκυνεῖν, which is the Greek equivalent of *hištaḥᵃwah*. But there is another Hebrew verb, *'abad* (the noun is *ᵃbodah*), nearly always represented in the English versions by 'serve' ('service'), which is more important for our present purpose, since it corresponds with use (ii) above. Its Greek equivalent is λατρεύειν (λατρεία). In the OT this word, when used in connexion with God, always refers to cultic service;[2] but there are passages like Deut 10.12; 1 Chr 28.9, where the use of the word to denote the service of God in sense (iii) above is not far off. In the NT, while λατρεύειν and λατρεία are sometimes used with reference to the cultus (for example, Rom 9.4), their use in sense (iii) is more characteristic (for example, Lk 1.74; Rom 1.9; Phil 3.3, and see especially Rom 12.1).

---

[1] First published in *Interpretation* 12 (1958), pp. 387–398, and reprinted (with slight alterations and an appended note) in C. E. B. Cranfield, *The Service of God*, London, 1965, pp. 9–22.

[2] Cf. H. Strathmann, in *TWNT* 4, p. 60.

We are primarily concerned in this short study with worship in sense (ii), but, in view of the NT use of λατρεύειν, λατρεία, we shall need to keep sense (iii) also in mind continually. Our intention is not to attempt to trace the history of the biblical concept of worship or to discuss the quite numerous contacts between the worship described in the Bible and the worship practised in other religions (though we recognize their existence is of theological as well as of historical importance), but to try to outline the main features of a biblical doctrine of Christian worship. The discussion may conveniently be arranged under two main heads: the divine action of worship and the human action of worship.

(1)   THE DIVINE ACTION OF WORSHIP

Throughout the Bible it is assumed that the initiative in true worship is God's. As far as the OT is concerned, reference may be made, in support of this statement, to the decisive part played by God's mighty acts in history (for example, the deliverance from Egypt) in determining Israel's worship, and to the assumption, characteristic of the OT, that all true worship must be an obedient response to definite divine commandments and promises (see, for instance, Exod 29.38–46) – must, in fact, be within the framework of God's covenant with His people – and that worship that is not thus determined by God's revealed will, but is invented by man (cf. 1 Kgs 12.33 – 'which he had devised of his own heart'), is to be condemned as false worship.

Of special significance for the understanding of the divine initiative in Israel's worship is the idea of the divine presence,[1] in connexion with which the following are

[1] See further L. H. Brockington, in A. Richardson (ed.), *A Theological Word Book of the Bible*, London, 1950, pp. 172–176.

128

particularly important: the ark and the mercy-seat[1] (e.g. Exod 25.22, Num 10.35f); the cloud (e.g. Exod 13.21f; 19.9, 16); the pillar of fire (e.g. Exod 13.21f); the tabernacle (e.g. Exod 40.34); the temple (e.g. Deut 12.5, 11, 21; 1 Kgs 8.11; 9.3; 2 Chr 7.15f); the glory (e.g. Exod 24.16; 29.43; 40.34f; Isa 6.3). The temptation to think of this presence of God as Israel's inalienable possession was a temptation to which Israel often fell; but the prophets were quick to denounce such ideas as false (Jer 7.1–15).[2] The gracious and at the same time solemn invitation of Isaiah 55.6 ('Seek ye the LORD while he may be found, call ye upon him while he is near') underlines both the freedom of God in being present to men and also the indispensableness of his presence if men's worship is to be of any avail.

What must be said about the divine initiative in Christian worship is closely parallel to what has just been stated with regard to the OT. Here too the initiative is God's. All Christian worship is a response to God's redemptive action in the past in Jesus Christ, and is determined by the commandments and promises of Christ. Moreover, in each particular act of worship the chief actor is not man, but God, the divine action consisting in the presence of Jesus Christ in fulfilment of His promise: 'Lo, I am with you alway, even unto the end of the world' (Mt 28.20). The Church's worship takes place in the period between Christ's ascension and His parousia, that is, in the time in which He is in a real sense absent from His Church (Mk 14.7: cf. 13.33–37). So His presence is an event, renewed again and again, not a continuing state. The risen and exalted Lord comes again

[1] See further A. Lelièvre, in J.-J. von Allmen (ed.), *Vocabulary of the Bible*, Eng. tr., London, 1958, pp. 23–25.
[2] Cf. E. Jacob, *Theology of the Old Testament*, Eng. tr., London, 1958, p. 53.

and again in fulfilment of His promise to be with His Church; but He comes always as the Lord, as the One who remains free, whose presence is not His Church's secure possession but His gracious gift. And His comings are indirect and veiled. He comes now not manifestly, as He will one day come in His parousia, but in a hidden way in the Word and the Sacraments and also in the flesh and blood of the least of His brethren.

He comes in the Word. He who is in His own person the living Word of God comes as the Word of God to His people in the Holy Scriptures which, as the written witness of prophets and apostles to Him, are also the Word of God. By the work of the Holy Spirit the human words of the Bible in all their brokenness and inadequacy become for the Church again and again the very Word of God, as the exalted Christ makes use of them, making them the medium of His conversation with His Church. He uses the ancient documents in all their historical particularity and concreteness as the vehicle of that which He wants to say to us in our actual situation and condition. In the lessons, the text, and also in the sermon, in so far as it is a humble and faithful exposition of Scripture, as also in our private study of the Bible, we deal with the real presence of Christ. (Cf. pp. 4ff.)

He comes in the Sacraments. The supreme gift that is given to us in the Eucharist is the real personal presence of the risen, glorified Lord.[1] The Supper is the Lord's appointed tryst with His own. So the early Church could pray *Marana tha*, 'Our Lord, come', and expect its prayer to be answered not only finally at the Parousia but also in the meantime in the Eucharist. So too in Baptism, Christ is present and active.

---

[1] Cf. Cranfield, *The Gospel according to Saint Mark*, Cambridge, [2]1963, pp. 425–427; and, for a fuller discussion of the meaning of the Lord's Supper, now *If God be for us*, Edinburgh, 1985, pp. 24–33.

In both Word and Sacraments He is present both in judgment and in mercy, bringing His criticism to bear upon the life of the Church and of its individual members, revealing sin in its true colours, summoning to repentance, healing, and forgiving.

He is present also as the One who lays his commands upon us and requires our obedience. His commands become concrete and particular in the course of His conversation with us through the Scriptures.

He is present not only for His Church but also for the world; for the Church's worship is indeed public in the fullest sense, taking place in the sight and in the hearing of the world. The Word read and preached and the Sacraments celebrated have significance for those outside as well as for those inside the Church. They are witness to Him before the world, witness in which He Himself is the main actor.

Christ's presence with us is not limited to the Word and Sacraments; He comes to us in a third way, as has already been indicated, namely in the persons of those whom he condescends to call his brethren (Mt 25.31–46). We must now try to see what significance this has for Christian worship. First, since Christ's brethren include our fellow-Christians, it means that Christian worship must be the worship of a community in which the members know that in each other Christ Himself is present to claim their love and service and concern. Secondly, since Christ's brethren are not limited to Christians but include all the needy and wretched,[1] it means that Christian worship cannot be oblivious of human wretchedness and need. It is the action of Christ Himself, His presence in the least of His brethren, which here again determines our worship and forbids us to make our attention to His presence in Word

[1] Cf. p. 79.

and Sacraments an excuse for turning our backs on human wretchedness – and so on Him. There is no place in truly Christian worship where the wretchedness and need of our fellow-men may be left behind and forgotten, since there is no place in Christian worship where Christ may be left behind and forgotten. And thirdly, this presence of Christ in His brethren is the divine action, the divine initiative, which determines our worship in the widest sense (sense (iii) above). By coming to us as our Lord in the persons of the despised and oppressed He gives us again and again the gracious opportunity to love and serve Him and so precedes and directs our obedience.

So far we have spoken of the presence or the comings of the exalted Christ in Word and Sacraments and in the persons of His brethren as the divine action in worship. But this is not all. There are three other things that must be mentioned briefly here as included in the divine action of Christian worship.

There is, first, the action of God the Father in foreknowing (Rom 8.29; 1 Pet 1.2), choosing (e.g. 1 Cor 1.27f; Eph 1.4; 1 Pet 1.1f; 2.9), calling (e.g. Rom 8.30; 9.24; 1 Cor 1.1f). Apart from this there could be no Christian worship.

There is, secondly, the action of the exalted Christ in heaven as our High Priest and Advocate with the Father. It is His presence before God on our behalf in the power of His accomplished work that gives us the right to approach God. It is through Him that we have our access unto the Father (Eph 2.18: cf. Rom 5.2; 1 Pet 3.18), through Him that we draw near unto God (Heb 7.25: cf. 10.19–22), through Him that we offer our prayers and praises to God (Jn 15.16; Eph 5.20; Heb 13.15), through Him that our obedience, our worship in the widest sense, in spite of all its falterings and inadequacies becomes a sacrifice acceptable to God (1 Pet 2.5). The efficacy of our worship as our action lies in His action on our behalf, His continual intercession (Rom 8.34; Heb 7.25; 1 Jn 2.1f).

And, thirdly, there is the action of the Holy Spirit, apart from which the true human action of worship, the proper response of man to God's action, would be impossible. His is the divine action within our human action of believing and responding, of hearing the Word of God, of understanding the things of God (1 Cor 2.10–16), of confessing Jesus as Lord (1 Cor 12.3), of knowing God as Father (Rom 8.15f). Since all our praying comes under the description, 'we know not how to pray as we ought', He 'maketh intercession for us with groanings which cannot be uttered; and he that searcheth the hearts knoweth what is the mind of the Spirit, because he maketh intercession for the saints according to the will of God' (Rom 8.26f). So too in the Church's worship in the widest sense, in the whole divine service of the Church's life and the life of its members, His action is the divine action within the human (e.g. Rom 8.1–14, Gal 5.16–26).

(2)   THE HUMAN ACTION OF WORSHIP

Christian worship is also human action. The human action is altogether secondary, being made possible by, and responding to, the action of God; but it is nonetheless – or rather for this reason – of immense significance. Barth's phrase, 'an action in which God acts and man serves,'[1] may be applied not only to the Sacraments but to Christian worship as a whole, including worship in the widest sense. The human action in worship is a humble and obedient service, a waiting upon, and responding to,

[1] *The Knowledge of God and the Service of God*, London, 1938, p. 191.

Him who comes as the Lord in Word and Sacraments and in the persons of His brethren.

In response to His previous comings and to His commandments and promises, the Church gathers about the Scriptures and about the table (or the font) to wait for Him to come to it again. It waits with expectancy, confident that He will keep His tryst with His people, yet respecting His freedom and recognizing that it cannot control His comings. So too in the wider sphere of our whole Christian obedience we have to wait upon His comings; but that waiting is no idle waiting with folded arms but a going forth to seek Him in the lost and afflicted. Such a waiting, that is also a seeking and a searching, stands under the divine promise: 'Ye shall seek me, and find me, when ye shall search for me with all your heart' (Jer 29.13).

Since the Church's waiting is not disappointed and He does come again and again, the human action in worship is a hearing and a receiving. The Church hears the Word of God which He is; it receives His gift of Himself. It enters into conversation with its present Lord – or, to put it better, allows Him to engage it in conversation. This hearing of the Word of God, hearing what the Lord of the Church wants to say to His Church in its actual situation, is the primary task of the Church, the basic human action in worship. It is the task not just of the clergy, but of the people of God as a whole (note the 'every man' in Jas 1.19); and, as a task of tremendous urgency, is meant to be engaged in eagerly, seriously, and resolutely. It is strenuous action; for the Bible is a difficult book and has to be wrestled with. The lessons and the reading of the sermon-text are not times for relaxation between the more serious activities of hymns and anthems, as is sometimes foolishly imagined, but times for the greatest attentiveness. We may add here in parenthesis that, if a congregation is serious about its business of hearing the Word of God, it will tend to prefer the lessons to represent a consecutive reading of the Bible rather than a selection of the minister's favourite passages, and the sermon-texts similarly to be determined by something other than the preacher's whim (for instance, the preacher might well preach through a book of the Bible, as was Calvin's practice, or preach on the liturgical epistles and gospels or on one of the lessons). The custom in some traditions, of the congregation standing during the reading of the sermon-text can be a salutary reminder of the fact that here above all the Church expects to hear the voice of its Lord and therefore here above all its full attention is required.

That the sermon, if it is to be a Christian sermon at all, must be an honest attempt to expound a passage of Scripture should go without saying. To by-pass Scripture at this point is like trying to celebrate the Holy Supper without bread or wine; it is to show that one is ignorant of the commandments and promises which determine Christian worship. But it is not enough just to take a text. To take a text and then proceed to use it as a peg on which to hang one's own thoughts is as bad as having no text at all: it is to handle the Word of God deceitfully and to insult the Lord who wills to speak to His people through the words of Scripture. But to say that preaching must be expository is not to say that it must not be topical in the sense of having direct relevance to contemporary events. On the contrary, the scriptural passage has not been properly heard and understood, until its relevance to the actual concrete situation of the congregation has been recognized; and the more patiently and honestly expository preaching is, the more relevant and contemporary does it become. Of course it is true that there is a sort of exposition that leaves everything in the air, but that is no proper exposition. A scriptural passage is not properly expounded until its relevance to the hearers becomes plain (cf. Nathan's 'Thou art the man' in 2 Sam 12.7!).

The notion (sometimes expressed in some quarters) that the sermon is to be contrasted with, and is inferior to, something else called 'worship' stems from misunderstanding – though, in view of the feeble discourses which often pass for sermons, it is not surprising – for the sermon, if it really is a sermon, is most certainly worship. For the faithful exposition of the Word of God is itself at the same time both Word of God (the divine action of worship) and also hearing of the Word of God (the primary human action of worship), the preacher leading the congregation in its work of hearing.

The hearing involves submission to Christ's criticism; for the One who uses the words of Scripture as the vehicle of His conversation with His Church is the Lord who has the right to criticize and to judge. Truly to hear is to lay open our whole life to His judgment and to accept it without resentment or evasion or reserve. Such hearing naturally issues in the response of confession of sin.

But Christ's coming is also in mercy. He comes as the One who died and was raised for the justification of sinners. To hear Him is to accept His mercy and forgiveness, and our response must therefore also be thanksgiving and praise. We shall praise and thank God in prayer and hymns for all His goodness and greatness, for all His gifts to us, and for all His care of us, but especially, and above all, for the grace of Jesus Christ our Lord, who, though He was rich, yet for our sakes became poor, that we through His poverty might become rich; who was crucified for us; whom God raised up and highly exalted; who now reigns and intercedes; who comes to us in Word and Sacraments and in the persons of His brethren; who shall come again in glory. If we are wise, we shall remember (especially in choosing hymns!) that, while it is good to thank God for streams and woods, it is not streams and woods, but Jesus Christ that is God's supreme Gift, and that it is perhaps one of the worst forms of ingratitude to be so occupied with thanking God for His innumerable lesser mercies that we have little time left for thanking Him for His supreme Gift. Our thanksgiving must naturally include the offering of ourselves to God, putting ourselves at His disposal, that He may use us according to His will for His glory and the good of our neighbours.

If we have really listened to Christ, our hearts will have been opened toward His brethren and their needs. So the human action of worship includes intercession for all men, for the Church throughout the world and also for those who still are outside the Church. In our intercession prayer for the civil authorities has a special place in accordance with 1 Tim 2.1–6. We pray for our own and other governments in the knowledge that the State was ordained by God to subserve His purpose of salvation (1 Tim 2.1–6) and that it is within the dominion of Christ (e.g. Mt 28.18; Rev 1.5), in the knowledge that 'rulers', whether Christian or not, are 'bound to render obedience to Christ in their own province' – to use the words of the Ordination Formula of the Presbyterian Church of England, words which, unfortunately, have recently been altered.

Our response to the Word of God includes also prayer for ourselves. Reminded once more of the goodness of God in Jesus Christ we confidently lay our needs before Him and cast our anxiety upon Him, in the knowledge that He cares for us and will answer our petitions according to His wisdom and mercy.

A further element in our response is the confession of

God's name, the confession of our faith, before God and before the world. While this is focused in the recital of the Creed,[1] it is by no means confined to it. The service as a whole is a declaration of our faith and allegiance addressed to God and also an act of witness to Him directed towards the world.

What has been said suggests to us that, normally, the more fitting position for the prayers of thanksgiving, intercession, and petition and also for the Lord's Prayer, in which we sum up all our prayers, is after the sermon, not before it. These prayers should normally, surely, be our response to what Christ has said to us, not just on some other occasion, but in the actual service in which they are offered; and in the sermon we are concerned with hearing what Christ has to say to us. The Creed, if recited, will also naturally follow the sermon. The confession of sin is traditionally placed near the beginning of the service, and it may well be left there; but it is fitting that some element of confession of sin should also find a place after the sermon, since the hearing of the Word of God involves, as we have seen, submitting to Christ's criticism.

In nearly all that we have said so far about worship as human action we have been thinking of the human action that answers to the presence of Christ in the Word; but much of what has been said is also applicable *mutatis mutandis* to the human action that answers to Christ's presence in the Sacraments. That which is received in the Sacraments is not something other than that which is received in the Word, though it is received in a different

---

[1] In 1983 I am more convinced than ever that the absence of the recited Creed from the great majority of our English Free Church services has meant a grievous impoverishment of our worship (*both* in sense (ii) and *also* in sense (iii)). That it is a sincere, intelligent and responsible, and not any merely formal and unthinking, recital of the Creed which is to be desired should, of course, go without saying.

way; for both in Word and Sacraments it is Jesus Christ Himself who comes to us. Ideally the main Sunday service should include both Word and Sacrament (Calvin was surely right in wanting the Lord's Supper to be celebrated every Sunday),[1] the presence of Christ in the Sacrament as it were sealing and confirming His presence in the Word. We catch a glimpse of this twofold pattern of the Christian service in the narrative contained in Luke 24.13–35, in which the risen Christ first opens the Scriptures to the two disciples in the way, interpreting 'to them in all the scriptures the things concerning himself' (v. 27) and afterwards takes bread, blesses the name of God, breaks the bread and gives to them (v. 30).

There remain three other points that must be made. The first is that any divorce between worship in the sense of Church services, private prayers, etc., and worship in the sense of the whole offering of our lives to God is intolerable. The very things which we have already considered as elements of the human action of worship direct us outward into the wider sphere of the Christian life as a whole. So, for example, the true hearing of the Word of God must, since God is God and since the Christ who engages us in conversation is the Lord who has the right to command us, involve obedience (cf. Jas 1.22–25); the confession of sin, if it be sincere, must lead to an honest attempt to forsake the sins we have confessed and to amend our lives; our prayers and hymns of thanksgiving point unmistakably to the obligation to express our gratitude in our daily living; and our intercession would be a mockery if we did not follow it up by serving in so far as we can those for whom we have prayed. For instance, it is surely a mockery for us who live

[1] See W. D. Maxwell, *John Knox's Genevan Service Book, 1556,* Edinburgh, 1931, pp. 201–205.

under a democratic form of government to pray for the civil authorities and then not try to play an active and responsible (and therefore well-informed and not uncritical) part in political life and to defend justice and truth with all our powers. Our response to Christ's presence in the Word and Sacraments, if it is sincere, must of necessity lead us on to respond to His presence in the persons of the least of His brethren. That is the point of the easily misunderstood verse in the Epistle of James: 'Pure religion and undefiled before our God and Father is this, to visit the fatherless and widows in their affliction, and to keep himself unspotted from the world' (1.27). It does not mean that participation in public worship is unimportant or optional, but that our participation in it is acceptable to God only when it is lived out in love to our neighbour. Acts of worship, however solemnly and beautifully executed, are not merely unacceptable to God, but actually an abomination to Him, if their reality is not demonstrated by just conduct and compassion toward the needy (cf. Isa 1.10–17; 58.1–11; Amos *passim*, but especially 5.21–24).

The second point is that the proper accomplishment of the human action of worship necessarily involves Church discipline. If the Church is truly and sincerely responding to Christ's presence in Word and Sacraments and in the persons of His brethren, it cannot help being concerned about the honour of Christ, the conversion of those outside, and the true welfare of its own members. Church discipline is the practical expression of those three concerns. It must certainly be admitted that often in the past the exercise of discipline has been misguided, its true purposes have been misunderstood or even lost sight of altogether, and things have been seen out of proportion, gnats strained out and camels swallowed. In insisting on the need for discipline we are not suggesting that the

Church should attempt to put the clock back and restore discipline as it was exercised in any particular period of the past. Attempts at reformation by simply putting the clock back are apt to be disastrous. But we are suggesting that the whole worship of the main churches of Christendom is today seriously impaired and disfigured by the widespread breakdown of church discipline.

In the first instance, church discipline, as the practical expression of the three concerns mentioned in the last paragraph, is simply a matter of the mutual encouragement, guidance, and frank admonishment that are proper within the fellowship of a Christian congregation. At the opposite extreme there are occasions when the name of Christ is being so grievously dishonoured, the church's witness so seriously impaired, and the offender's eternal salvation so evidently imperilled that the application of the church's ultimate sanction, exclusion from the Lord's table, is called for. When the members of a church court do exercise the right of excommunication, they should do so in fear and trembling, knowing the seriousness of what they are doing and how grievous it would be to excommunicate someone wrongly, knowing that they themselves are sinners who constantly bring dishonour upon Christ: they should do so in love, earnestly desiring to bring the offender to repentance, and certainly not in vindictiveness.

Perhaps the whole problem of church discipline and its relation to worship can best be high-lighted by reference to a notorious, controversial and – especially for the Reformed churches – extremely urgent matter, the support given by the Dutch Reformed churches in South Africa to the *apartheid* policy of the present South African Government. That the matter is complicated by many things – not least the fact that other churches are badly compromised – no informed person will deny; but the complications do not relieve other churches of their responsibility. By continuing to recognize the Dutch Reformed churches of South Africa as churches in good standing, the other Reformed churches are allowing it to appear to the whole non-Christian world that there is nothing absolutely incompatible between *apartheid* and its attendant injustices and brutalities and the gospel of Jesus Christ. May it not be that concern for the honour of Christ, the love we owe to those who are being wronged, the love we owe to those who are being hindered from accepting the gospel, and the love we owe to our Dutch Reformed brethren whose eternal salvation, is imperilled, alike require the breaking-off of communion until such time as those churches renounce their support of *apartheid*?[1]

The third and last point is that the final criterion by which the human action of worship must be judged is obedience to Christ. Throughout the Bible it is emphasized that true worship is obedient worship. It is not the costliness of the equipment or the majesty of the surroundings or the dignity of the ceremonial or the beauty of the music or the elegance of the language that commends our worship to God, but simply its obedience. That our ways of worship need to be subjected to continual reformation is certainly true; but the reformation required is not reformation according to the modern mind (cf. the question, recently asked by a

[1] In this connexion it is interesting to note in 1983 that the second general council of the World Alliance of Reformed Churches, met in Ottawa, Canada, in August 1982, declared apartheid heresy and voted to suspend two of its South African member denominations because of their refusal to condemn it. See *The Ecumenical Review* 35 (1983), p. 98; *Ecumenical Press Service* for 6–15 September, 1982 (item 82.09.25); *The Guardian*, 27 August, 1982; *The Observer*, 29 August, 1982.

minister in England in connexion with the Lord's Supper, 'Might it not be that a ritual that is based on ancient animal sacrifices is not altogether in harmony with the modern mind?') or according to aesthetic principles or popular taste, but reformation according to the Word of God. It is not our business here to be inventive. The example of 'Jeroboam the son of Nebat, who made Israel to sin' (2 Kgs 23.15, etc.; and see 1 Kgs 12.26–33 for what he did) should discourage us from trying to devise novelties in this field. If we were to set about the refashioning of our worship according to our own inventiveness, we might indeed conceivably succeed in producing a religious masterpiece; but, as Barth has pointed out: 'Religion with its masterpieces is one thing, Christian faith with its obedience another.'[1]

It would perhaps not be out of place to refer here to a matter which is certainly of relatively minor importance but may possibly be less insignificant than at first sight appears, namely the wearing of academic hoods by ministers when leading public worship. Since there may be a sound theological justification for this practice, although I have so far failed to discover it, I indicate my own personal misgivings only very tentatively. In the first place, I am unable to rid my mind of the suspicion that the time when one is leading public worship is about as unsuitable an occasion as there can be for displaying the insignia of one's personal scholastic attainments. While the minister's cassock and his preacher's gown and bands serve to remind both him and his congregation that he does not stand before them in his own name but as the servant of the Word of God, and to direct attention away from his person to the Word of which he is the minister, the academic hood seems to have precisely the opposite effect – to draw attention to the minister's person and to the details of his past career. In the second place, since in most, if not all, of the churches in which this custom prevails, there are at the present time a number of ministers who are not entitled to wear academic hoods, is there not a danger that the wearing of them in the conduct of worship by those who do have the right to wear them may cause those who do not to feel a certain sense of inferiority? If so, is this perhaps in itself a reason for questioning the seemliness of the practice?

[1] op. cit., p. 206.

143

X
HEBREWS 13.20–21[1]

These two verses, though formally (since God is not directly addressed but referred to in the third person) a wish or 'prayer-wish', are really tantamount to a prayer.[2] The structure of the sentence may be indicated as follows: (i) God is named ('the God of peace'); (ii) an adjectival clause follows (as very often in collects); (iii) the first part of v. 21 expresses the substance of the petition; (iv) the whole is concluded by a doxology. A most perceptive and stimulating commentary on these verses is afforded by Philip Doddridge's paraphrase, 'Father of peace, and God of love', to which we shall refer from time to time.[3]

I

Verse 20 may be said to set forth the grounds of the writer's confidence in God's ability and willingness to answer his prayer. It points to the objective reality of God and to the objective reality of His saving deeds. God is referred to as 'the God of peace', that is, the God who is the source of peace.[4] But 'peace' here (as often elsewhere in the Bible) means much more than we normally mean by the word: it signifies not merely peace as opposed to war, or peace and tranquillity of mind as opposed to disquiet and perturbation, but complete well-being, the sum of all

[1] First published in *SJT* 20 (1967), pp. 437–441.
[2] For this prayer-wish form cf. Rom 15.5–6; 2 Th 3.16a; 2 Tim 1.16, 18.
[3] This paraphrase is to be found in *The Church Hymnary*, 3rd ed., No. 395.
[4] The phrase 'the God of peace' is found also in Rom 15.33; 16.20; 2 Cor 13.11; Phil 4.9; 1 Th 5.23; and also in Testament of Dan 5.2. The expression 'the Lord of peace' is used in 2 Th 3.16.

true blessings, salvation.[1] By calling God 'the God of peace' the writer is indicating that God is the Source and Giver of all true blessings, the God who is able and willing to help and save. Unlike the god of some contemporary popular theology who is no more than the ground of our being, the principle of our more loving relationships, a god who has no real being outside and beyond and independent of the processes of our life and thought and so 'is unable by definition to stoop down to us and intervene creatively and redemptively in our need and condition',[2] the God of Holy Scripture is the living God, whose being is independent of us, beyond and outside our life, the transcendent God, who is able to condescend to us in mercy and to come to our help. Philip Doddridge brings out the meaning of the phrase well:

> *Father of peace, and God of love!*
> *We own Thy power to save.*

The author of Hebrews goes on to mention two of the mighty acts of God, in which His power and will to save are to be seen. One of those mighty acts is the raising of Jesus from the dead ('who brought again from the dead the great shepherd of the sheep . . . , *even* our Lord Jesus'). The language used is reminiscent of the LXX version of Isa 63.11, which speaks of God as ὁ ἀναβιβάσας ἐκ τῆς γῆς [so Rahlfs: B* has θαλάσσης] τὸν ποιμένα τῶν προβάτων. God's deliverance of Moses with his flock, the children of Israel, from the land of Egypt and from the Red Sea foreshadowed His deliverance of Jesus from the dead as the shepherd of the flock which consists of those 'many sons' whom God purposed to bring 'unto glory' by

[1] Cf. G. von Rad and W. Foerster, in G. Kittel and G. Friedrich (ed.), *Theologisches Wörterbuch zum Neuen Testament* 2, pp. 398–418.
[2] T. F. Torrance, *Theology in Reconstruction*, London, 1965, p. 277.

Him (Heb 2.10). The adjective μέγας is added by the writer to the Hebrews (cf. 'a great high priest' in 4.14 and 'a great priest' in 10.21). The implied comparison with Moses underlines the fact that the Resurrection is not thought of as a mere inward change in the thinking and attitude of the disciples but as an external event – God's decisive intervention by which He acknowledged, ratified, sealed, the cross of Christ as man's redemption. The fact of the Resurrection assures the writer that his prayer will be heard and answered.[1]

The other mighty act to which reference is made here is the Cross ('with the blood of the eternal covenant'). The Resurrection is thus defined as the resurrection of the Crucified. The language reflects the author's thought of Jesus as the great High Priest who takes His place in the innermost sanctuary of heaven. As the earthly high priest entered the holy of holies in Jerusalem on the Day of Atonement taking with him the sacrificial blood, so the risen Christ is thought of as having entered the heavenly holy of holies taking with Him the atoning efficacy of His death. His blood is called 'the blood of the . . . covenant', because the writer believes that, as the covenant of old was ratified by the sprinkling of the sacrificial blood (Exod 24.6–8), so the new covenant (Jer 31.31) has been established through the death of Jesus. And this new covenant is 'eternal' (for the phrase 'eternal covenant' cf.

---

[1] To conclude from the fact that this is the only direct reference to the Resurrection in Hebrews that the author of the epistle was probably not the original author of this prayer and/or that the Resurrection was not important to him, is surely unjustified. The absence of other references in Hebrews is probably adequately explained by the author's special concerns. His concern to show Jesus as the great High Priest, for example, makes it natural for him to concentrate attention on the sacrificial death on the one hand and on the entrance of Christ into the heavenly holy of holies on the other; the comparison he is making affords nothing to correspond to the actual Resurrection.

146

Isa 55.3; Jer 32 [LXX: 39].40; Ezek 37.26; and also the assurance expressed in Jer 31.35–37); for, since He who died on the cross is truly God as well as truly man, His death was *God's* mighty act for the redemption of the world, effective once for all, the one 'full, perfect, and sufficient sacrifice', and the forgiveness of the new covenant (Jer 31.34) is nothing provisional or temporary but God's final, costly forgiveness, which in no way glosses over or condones our sin, but is altogether worthy of the God, who in all His ways is holy, righteous and true. The essential meaning is brought out by the paraphrase:

> *Him from the dead Thou brought'st again,*
> *When, by His sacred blood,*
> *Confirmed and sealed for evermore*
> *The eternal covenant stood.*

II

Verse 21 contains the substance of the petition. It is that God may enable those whom the author is addressing to live the Christian life – a prayer for their sanctification.

The Christian life is here set under the sign of obedience, of doing God's will ('to do his will'). There is no Christianity worthy of the name which is not deeply concerned with the doing of God's will. And the will of God is neither capricious nor esoteric. Every book of the Bible attests the fact that God has graciously revealed His will. 'He hath shewed thee, O man, what is good . . .' (Mic 6.8). God's law is His revealed will for man. With true theological perceptiveness Doddridge has here made explicit the reference to the law:

> *But keep Thy precepts still.*

By His law God has claimed us wholly for Himself and for our neighbour, requiring – toward Himself – that love with the totality of our being which must include faith, gratitude, obedience, and – toward our neighbour – a love as sincere and real as that love which (sinners that we are) we all in fact have for ourselves (cf. Mk 12.29–31).

But the writer does not just speak of their doing God's will but of God's enabling them to do it and of His working in them ('make you perfect in every good thing to do his will, working in us that which is well-pleasing in his sight, through Jesus Christ'). Here the paraphrase rightly introduces an explicit reference to the Holy Spirit:

> *O may Thy Spirit seal our souls,*
> *And mould them to Thy will.*

For this divine work of restoring, repairing, equipping, enabling,[1] this 'working in us that which is well-pleasing in his sight', God accomplishes (according to the NT) by giving Himself to us in His Holy Spirit and thus Himself creating our response to His love in Christ. The gospel

---

[1] The verb καταρτίζειν was probably chosen, as C. Spicq suggests (*L'Epître aux Hébreux* 2, Paris, 3rd ed. 1953, p. 436) because of its very wide range of meaning. Its meanings include 'adjust', 'put in order', 'restore', 'mend', 'recommission', 'furnish', 'equip', 'make good', 'prepare'. It would, of course, be wrong to infer from the AV and RV rendering 'make perfect' that the writer to the Hebrews expected Christians to attain perfection in this life. It may be noticed that the lines of the paraphrase,

> *That to perfection's sacred height*
> *We nearer still may rise,*

while speaking of our approaching nearer and nearer to perfection, avoid implying that we should hope actually to attain it in this life.

148

would not be gospel – good news – at all, apart from this; for, of ourselves, we cannot respond, cannot love God or our neighbour, being held in bondage to self-love. Wherever a man begins to be turned in the direction of love to God and to his neighbour, there a miracle is taking place. Where this miracle is not taking place, there is no Church of Christ; for 'if any man hath not the Spirit of Christ, he is none of his' (Rom 8.9).

The Holy Spirit re-establishes God's law for us as no longer an irksome and resented burden or something we can try to use for our own ends by a legalistic perversion of it, but the gracious gift of the revelation of God's fatherly will for His children, and enables us to embrace it with gratitude and joy. And this He does 'through Jesus Christ', that is, by uniting us ever more and more closely with Him, enabling us to embrace again and again, in ever-deepening love and loyalty, Him to whom we already belong, and so moulding our lives more and more into conformity with Him.[1]

But this work of the Spirit, which is basic and primary (καταρτίσαι ὑμᾶς ... εἰς τὸ ποιῆσαι ... ποιῶν ἐν ἡμῖν), does not render our work superfluous or unimportant. On the contrary, it makes possible, and demands, a real working on our part (the divine καταρτίζειν and ποιεῖν claim us εἰς τὸ ποιῆσαι τὸ θέλημα αὐτοῦ), and gives to it its true dignity and worth. It is significant that this epistle contains a considerable amount of exhortation.[2]

Whether the concluding doxology is intended to refer

---

[1] The best sense is obtained by taking διὰ Ἰησοῦ Χριστοῦ with ποιῶν, as we have done above. It seems less satisfactory, though possible, to take it with τὸ εὐάρεστον ἐνώπιον αὐτοῦ. It is scarcely possible to take it as the end-formula of the prayer (a pleading of Christ's merits), since this is not a prayer directly addressed to God.

[2] The verb παρακαλεῖν is, as a matter of fact, used in both 13.19 and 13.22, though little weight can be put on this.

to Christ[1] or to God[2] it is probably impossible to decide for certain. In support of the former interpretation 2 Tim 4.18, 2 Pet 3.18 and Rev 1.6 may be cited, in support of the latter Phil 4.20 and 1 Tim 1.17. We prefer simply to leave this question open.[3]

These two verses are implicitly – though not explicitly – Trinitarian; for they lead us to the mystery of the triune God, who is the God of peace who raised Jesus from the dead, and who is the Son, in whom He has given Himself to us as our 'shepherd', priest and 'Lord', and who is the Holy Spirit, in whom He gives Himself to us into our very inmost being, to work within us our sanctification.

[1] So e.g. Spicq, op. cit., p. 437; F. F. Bruce, in M. Black and H. H. Rowley (ed.), *Peake's Commentary on the Bible*, London, 1962, p. 1019.

[2] So e.g. J. Moffatt, *A Critical and Exegetical Commentary on the Epistle to the Hebrews*, Edinburgh, 1924, p. 242; H. W. Montefiore, *The Epistle to the Hebrews*, London, 1964, p. 252.

[3] As does H. Strathmann, in *Das Neue Testament Deutsch* 9, Göttingen, 1949, p. 153.

XI
THE MESSAGE OF JAMES[1]

At least it may be said of the Epistle of James that it escapes the 'woe' of Luke 6.26 ('Woe *unto you*, when all men shall speak well of you!').

It was only slowly and in the face of some opposition that it came to be recognized as canonical by the early Church. Writing at the beginning of the fourth century, Eusebius of Caesarea (*c*. 260–*c*. 340) classed it among those books which are 'disputed, but familiar to the majority'.[2] Though from the time of Origen (*c*. 185–*c*. 255) it seems to have been widely accepted in the Greek part of the Church, there is no clear trace of acquaintance with it in any western author before the middle of the fourth century.

Luther's hostility to the epistle is well known. In his preface to the NT he describes it as 'a right strawy epistle in comparison with' certain other books, namely, John, 1 John, the Pauline epistles (especially, Romans, Galatians and Ephesians) and 1 Peter, and declares that it has 'no evangelical character'.[3] In his preface to the epistles of James and Jude, while commending it for its advocacy of God's law, he says that he does not regard it as an apostle's writing, since it teaches works-righteousness and does not mention the sufferings or resurrection of Christ.[4] In his commentary on Genesis he even speaks of James raving – *ut Jacobus delirat*.[5] And Luther's hostility

---

[1] Reprinted from *SJT* 18 (1965), pp. 182–193, 338–345. The Student Christian Movement kindly allowed me to make use in this article of some material from a study outline (*The Epistle of James: four studies*), which I had written for it in 1957.

[2] *H.E.* 3.25.3.

[3] 1522; in Weimar ed., *Die Deutsche Bibel* 6, p. 10.

[4] 1522 and 1546; op. cit., 7, p. 384f.

[5] In Erlangen ed., *Opera exegetica Latina* 5, p. 227.

151

has – not surprisingly – had a far-reaching effect on Protestant opinion.[1]

In modern times some scholars, seeing in the epistle little or nothing that they recognized as specifically Christian, apart from the two places where Jesus is named, have concluded that it was originally a Jewish writing which has been given a superficial Christian editing. Others, while accepting the view that the author must have been a Christian, have adopted a decidedly supercilious attitude. Martin Dibelius, for example, though he properly concedes that we have no right to assume that the author places no value on things he does not mention, sees here *Konventikel-Ethik*, the morality of the working-class conventicle, marked by resentment against the rich and suspicion of 'the world', a Christianity that is limited and narrow, with no understanding of Paul's missionary zeal or of the universal tendencies of primitive catholicism, the attitude of those who would rather witness the ruin of the rich man than welcome him into the congregation, for fear that his entry might undermine the conventicle's hostility to the

---

[1] It is perhaps only fair to Luther to mention the words which he wrote on a scrap of paper two days before he died: 'No one can understand Virgil in the Bucolics and Georgics unless he has been a shepherd and farmer for five years. No one understands Cicero's letters unless he has been engaged for twenty years in the affairs of some great state. No one should think he has sufficiently grasped the meaning of the Scriptures unless he has governed Churches for a century with the prophets. For mighty is the miracle (1) of John the Baptist, (2) of Christ, (3) of the Apostles. Do not then attempt this Divine Aeneid, rather bow down and humbly worship their footprints. We are beggars, that's certain!' (as quoted in W. Niesel, *Reformed Symbolics: a comparison of Catholicism, Orthodoxy, and Protestantism*, translated by A. D. Lewis, Edinburgh, 1962, p. 227). These words seem to indicate a humbler attitude toward Scripture, and perhaps Niesel is right in seeing in them something of a recantation of earlier too cocksure utterances (op. cit., p. 230).

world and its pride in its poverty. For Dibelius James represents the ethos of a lower middle-class and working-class Christianity, that cannot rise to the heights of a Paul or a John; and he justifies its inclusion in the NT on the ground that in a world-religion the humdrum persons (*die Alltagsmenschen*) of the lower classes (*die kleinen Leute*) and their needs must be allowed their place.[1] Another modern commentator, E. C. Blackman, damns the epistle with faint praise, summing it up as 'simple things for the ordinary member who is not interested in theology, has no deep religious experience, and yet feels called to be faithful in that which is least: who asks for no spiritual banquet, but is content with a diet of straw!'[2]

Very different, however, is the attitude of Calvin to the Epistle of James. According to him, 'it contains nothing unworthy of an Apostle of Christ. It is indeed full of instruction on various subjects, the benefit of which extends to every part of the Christian life . . .'[3] And Adolf Schlatter expressed the opinion that our churches have done themselves serious injury by giving to James only an altogether superficial hearing.[4] So, before we adopt a hostile, contemptuous or patronizing attitude toward this epistle, it will be as well to try to listen to what it has to say to us with as open a mind as possible. We shall find, I believe, that its message is extraordinarily relevant to the Church in Britain in the latter half of the twentieth century.

It may be suggested – at any rate as a working hypothesis – that the clue to the solution of the problem posed for us by the fact that Jesus Christ is mentioned by

[1] *Der Brief des Jakobus*, Göttingen, 3rd ed. 1957, pp. 47–50.

[2] *The Epistle of James*, London, 1957, p. 33.

[3] *Commentaries on the Catholic Epistles*, translated by J. Owen, reprinted Grand Rapids, 1948, p. 276.

[4] Quoted by E. Thurneysen, *Der Brief des Jakobus*, Basel, n.d., p. 6.

name only twice and by the absence of any direct reference to His life, death, resurrection or ascension, is to be found in the epistle's concentration upon the question of sincerity. When Christian people have become blind to, or unconcerned about, the contradictions between their practice and the gospel they preach and profess to believe, to keep on repeating the central truths of the gospel may not be the most effective way of penetrating their complacency. If it was to this particular spiritual condition that the writer was specially addressing himself, then the peculiarities of his tract are surely intelligible. We need not conclude that his own faith was not centred in Jesus Christ or that he was untheologically-minded or limited in capacity. There would be nothing surprising in his refraining deliberately (in this particular writing) from saying things which his readers would expect him to say, because he believed that, if he said them, they would only be received with complacent misapprehension. He may well have thought that to go on repeating the central gospel truths to those who were quite sure that they understood them well, while all the time they had misunderstood them altogether, was only likely to have the effect of making their gospel-hardened condition all the more obdurate. But when once we recognize that the epistle was written *ad hominem*[1] and that the author was addressing himself to the particular spiritual condition which we have tried to indicate, the feasibility of Thurneysen's statement becomes apparent: 'James preaches Jesus Christ, His cross and resurrection, the power of forgiveness and the obedience of faith, and nothing else; but he preaches this in his own peculiar way.'[2]

[1] Cf. K. Barth and E. Thurneysen, *Revolutionary Theology in the Making*, London, 1964, p. 127.

[2] *Der Brief des Jakobus*, p. 5.

It is wise then to reckon with the possibility that the author's description of himself as 'a servant of God and of the Lord Jesus Christ' (1.1) is sober truth, and that what we have here is no untheological moralism but a faithful – though, for a special purpose, oblique – proclamation of the gospel of Christ.[1]

For our present purpose there would be but little profit to be gained by entering into a discussion of the questions of authorship and date, since, on the one hand, it seems most unlikely that anything approaching certainty can be reached on either question, and, on the other hand, the peculiarly undated quality of the contents, which is so frustrating when one is trying to place the epistle historically, renders its interpretation independent, to a very large extent, of our ability to answer these questions at all decisively. It will be sufficient to note the existence of such views as that the author is James, the Lord's brother, that he is an otherwise unknown Christian called James, that an original nucleus, perhaps going back to the Lord's brother, was worked up into the present form by a later Christian well acquainted with Hellenistic culture, and that the epistle is pseudonymous; and that suggested dates vary from as early as A.D. 45 to as late as the first quarter of the second century.

That there is a looseness about the structure of James is obvious. In the first chapter several connexions are made by means of catchwords: between vv. 1 and 2 by χαίρειν ('greeting') and χαράν ('joy'), between vv. 4 and 5 by λειπόμενοι ('lacking'), and λείπεται ('lacketh'), between

---

[1] I regret that C. K. Barrett, 'The Centre of the New Testament and the Canon', in U. Luz and H. Weder (ed.), *Die Mitte des Neuen Testaments: Einheit und Vielfalt neutestamentlicher Theologie: Festschrift für Eduard Schweizer zum 70. Geburtstag*, Göttingen, 1983, p. 18, has ignored this possibility, characterizing the epistle by the single, uncompromising word 'moralism'.

vv. 12 and 13 by πειρασμόν ('temptation') and πειραζόμενος ('when he is tempted'). But looseness of connexion is also to be seen in the ethical teaching of Paul's most closely articulated epistle, in Rom 12.1–15.13 particularly in 12.9–21.

It is also apparent that the author has borrowed from various sources. Dibelius has called him, not without some justification, an eclectic.[1] We may trace his indebtedness to the OT, especially the Wisdom literature, to the sayings of Jesus and the Christian catechetical tradition, and to the Greek diatribe.

But, in spite of disconnectedness and in spite of borrowings, the epistle possesses a real unity derived from the persistence with which it puts the professions of Christians to the test.

We shall not attempt to expound the whole epistle in the following pages, but shall confine ourselves to the longer central sections.

We begin with 1.19–27, which may be entitled: *Of the right hearing of the Word of God.*

'Ye know [perhaps better: Know] *this*, my beloved brethren' introduces the new section. 'But let every man be swift to hear ....' The object of 'hear' is to be understood from v. 18 ('the word of truth': cf. 'the implanted word' in v. 21): the primary task of a Christian congregation as a whole and of the members of it severally ('every man') is to hear the Word of God. As a task of tremendous urgency it is to be engaged in eagerly, seriously and resolutely ('swift'). Where Christians are thus engaged in hearing the Word of God, they will be 'slow to speak'. It is not, of course, any reluctance to confess Christ that is meant, or any slackness in the work

[1] op. cit., p. 47: cf. p. 6f.

of mission, but rather patience to listen to God attentively before trying to speak in His name, and such a sense of the majesty and mystery of God and of the reverence due to His Word as kills cocksureness and glibness and makes men humble both in their theological activity and in their witness (cf. 3.1–12). Where the Word is really being heard, Christians will also be 'slow to wrath'; for they will not be able to forget that they themselves are not without sin. This does not mean that they will not call evil evil; but it does mean that they will not condemn hastily, and that, when they must condemn, they will not do so self-righteously. They will indeed protest against others' evil unambiguously, and without fear or favour, but always as fellow-sinners. The relevance of this today to, for example, the attitude of the respectable to rowdy and destructive youth, to those who get into prison, to those who belong to the opposite ideological camp, is obvious. There is here a liberating message for the modern world, in which the tendency to see all evil concentrated in the enemy and one's own side as uncompromised has in so many places led to the excusing of brutality and torture when inflicted upon enemies who are no longer recognized as *fellow*-sinners.

Verse 20 ('for the wrath of man worketh not the righteousness of God') states a reason for the last phrase of the previous verse. It is not to be assumed that the wrath of sinful men, even when they are Christians, is likely to fulfil the righteousness which God requires. Rather is it to be recognized that, when in fighting against evil men allow wrath against the wrongdoer to enter in, they are likely to be led into injustice. Those who hear the Word of God will in their crusading have as their motive the relief of the wronged rather than the infliction of retribution on the wrongdoer.

The section continues: 'Wherefore putting away all

157

filthiness and overflowing of wickedness, receive with meekness the implanted word, which is able to save your souls.' 'Meekness' here means 'humility and the readiness of a mind disposed to learn' (Calvin). The word translated 'implanted' (ἔμφυτον) has been variously explained. Ἔμφυτος (from ἐμφύειν, 'implant') can mean 'innate', but this is ruled out here by 'receive'. It can also mean 'deep-rooted' as opposed to 'superficial'. Calvin understood the sentence to mean: 'receive it, that it may be really implanted'; but the position of ἔμφυτον between the definite article and the noun makes this extremely difficult. The simplest and most satisfactory explanation is that 'the implanted word' means the Word of God that has been sown in their hearts (cf. Mk 4.3–20, and also 2 Esdras 9.31). To 'receive' it means to be such good soil as allows the seed to take root and establish itself (cf. 'accept' in Mk 4.20). The right hearing of the Word of God involves allowing it to do its work in one's heart and life unhindered.

It is in fact, as v. 22 ('But be ye doers of the word, and not hearers only, deluding your own selves') makes clear, not just to hear it but also to do it. We have not studied the Bible properly until we begin to live according to it. True theology is not just a matter of correct understanding; it involves deeds. To fail to see this is to deceive oneself. A commentary on this verse and on the rest of the section is to be found in Mt 7.21–27 and in the phrase ποιεῖν τὴν ἀλήθειαν ('do the truth') in Jn 3.21; 1 Jn 1.6.

Verses 23–25 underline what has been said in v. 22 by means of a homely illustration. One may look at one's face in a mirror, and then go away without doing anything about the untidinesses which it reveals. To be 'a hearer only' of the Word of God, 'and not a doer' also, is like that. But there is also a sensible way of using a mirror – and a right way of hearing the Word of God. In the last of these three verses ('But he that looketh into the perfect law, the *law* of liberty, and so continueth, being not a hearer that forgetteth, but a doer that worketh, this man shall be blessed in his doing') the writer still has his illustration in mind – hence the expression, 'looketh into'. To look into this mirror is to be shown ourselves as the objects of God's grace and forgiveness, and thereby to be shown our sin and need; it is also to be shown ourselves as the persons God wants us to be. The Word of God, which is at the same time both gospel and law in indissoluble unity, both judges us and sets us free. The demand which it lays upon us is nothing other than the liberty of the children of God. It is thus 'the perfect law, the *law* of liberty'. To look into this mirror steadily and persistently ('and so continueth'), not turning away in resentment at its criticism, and to respond to its gracious message in faith and penitence, in gratitude and obedience, is to 'be blessed' in one's 'doing'.

In the last two verses of the chapter the writer goes on to provide practical tests by which his readers may know whether they are doers of the Word or hearers only, tests by which they may assay the reality of their profession. Verse 26 ('If any man thinketh himself to be religious, while he bridleth not his tongue but deceiveth his heart, this man's religion is vain') is concerned with the test of speech. The right hearing of the Word of God is never without effect upon a man's speech. Verse 19 ('slow to speak') has already hinted at this. If our speaking is glib, arrogant, shuffling or uncharitable, if it is not at least beginning to be brought under the discipline of the gospel, this is a sure sign that our 'religion is vain'. The writer returns to this subject in 3.1–12.

The meaning of the first part of v. 27 ('Pure religion and undefiled before our God and Father is this, to visit the fatherless and widows in their affliction') is not that

159

participation in public worship is unimportant, but that it is only acceptable to God when it is accompanied by love to the neighbour. The most solemnly and beautifully executed act of worship is but an abomination to Him, unless it is lived out in justice and compassion (cf. Isa 1.10–17). Here is a test by which much church life is condemned, and churches which are worried by their inability to communicate the gospel to the contemporary world would do well to ask themselves whether it is not their failures here rather than any out-of-dateness of the gospel which are the main cause of the world's deafness to their words.

The latter part of the verse ('*and* to keep himself unspotted from the world') is neither to be explained as the expression of some strict Jewish-Christian abhorrence of intercourse with Gentiles nor yet as breathing the atmosphere of a narrow, pietistic conventicle-Christianity. The Epistle of James has no monopoly in the NT of this kind of use of κόσμος ('world'): we may compare, for example, Jn 14.30; 15.19; 16.33; 1 Cor 1.20; 2.12; 3.19; 7.31, 33; 2 Cor 7.10; Eph 2.2; Col 2.20; 1 Jn 2.15–17; 5.4, 19. There is no right hearing of the Word of God that does not include the recognition of the obligation to avoid being 'fashioned according to this world [αἰών, age]' (Rom 12.1). Though Christ would have His followers remain in the world (Jn 17.15), it is clear that He does not desire them to make the world's standards their own. There is a worldliness of thought and feeling and behaviour, which, in Christians, is an indication either of their having ceased, or of their never having begun, to look steadfastly into the mirror of God's Word.

We turn next to 2.1–13, to which we may give the title, *Of respect of persons*. Verse 1 is better taken as a prohibition, as in the RV text ('My brethren, hold not the faith of our Lord Jesus Christ, *the Lord* of glory, with respect of persons'), than as a question expecting a negative answer (as in the RV margin). The writer is exhorting his readers not to try to combine two incompatible things, faith in Christ and respect of persons. The Greek τοῦ Κυρίου ἡμῶν ᾽Ιησοῦ Χριστοῦ τῆς δόξης is difficult, but probably means 'in our glorious Lord Jesus Christ' (τῆς δόξης being a genitive of quality, equivalent to an adjective – cf. Lk 16.8: τὸν οἰκονόμον τῆς ἀδικίας, 16.9: τοῦ μαμωνᾶ τῆς ἀδικίας, 18.6: ὁ κριτὴς τῆς ἀδικίας – here qualifying the whole of the preceding phrase). The biblical term 'respect of persons' includes what we mean by 'snobbishness', but also much more (e.g. the failure to oppose injustice for fear of the powerful).[1]

The example set before the reader in vv. 2 and 3 might seem at first sight a fairly mild instance of snobbishness, but the writer goes on to expose its true significance. It is, in fact, a quite undated example of conduct incompatible with a sincere Christian faith. The same evil is seen today raised to a higher power, when within the Church discrimination between men on the ground of the colour of their skins is permitted.

The Greek, which is rendered in the RV 'are ye not divided in your own mind', should probably be translated 'have you not doubted in your own minds', that is, 'have you not fallen away from faith (in Christ) in your own hearts and minds'. (The Greek verb used here can have various meanings, and a variety of translations is possible; but to take it in the sense in which it is used in 1.6 seems to give the most likely meaning.) The point of the question is then that the conduct described in the two

[1] See further C. E. B. Cranfield, *The Gospel according to Saint Mark*, Cambridge, [8]1983, p. 370.

preceding verses is incompatible with faith in Christ. The second question, '[are ye not] become judges with evil thoughts?', is equivalent to an assertion that such conduct means passing a false judgment on the worth of the rich man and the poor man, a judgment based on wrong assumptions and revealing the unbelief of those who so act.

Verses 5–6a ('Hearken, my beloved brethren; did not God choose them that are poor *to be* rich in faith, and heirs of the kingdom which he hath promised to them that love him? But ye have dishonoured the poor man') go on to show that such conduct is opposition to what God has done in Christ, since it means dishonouring those whom God has chosen to honour. If the poor man believes in Jesus Christ, then he is the heir of God's promises and possessed of a dignity which cannot be dishonoured without dishonouring God. In other words, the conduct which has been described, so far from being a quite trivial matter, is, in fact, a radical denial of the gospel. We may compare the serious view taken by Paul in 1 Cor 11.20–22 of the behaviour of some members of the Corinthian church, who had put their poorer brethren to shame.

Verses 6b–7 make the point that the rich, to whom some Christians are so inclined to show obsequiousness, are often oppressors of the poor and blasphemers of the name of Christ. There is no need to see in these verses or in the preceding verse and a half an *Armenfrömmigkeit* or special poor men's piety with its accompanying hostility to the rich. It is not suggested that there is anything meritorious in poverty as such, nor is it denied that some rich men may be true Christians or affirmed that every poor man has been chosen.[1] Paul also recognized the fact that not many of the world's important ones were to be

---

[1] Cf. J. H. Ropes, *The Epistle of St. James*, Edinburgh, 1916, p. 193f.

found within the Church (1 Cor 1.26–29), and the tendency of the rich and powerful to exploit their position for selfish purposes and to take advantage of those who are less well placed is something which may be observed in every century and in all countries.

The section goes on: 'Howbeit if ye fulfil the royal law, according to the scripture, Thou shalt love thy neighbour as thyself, ye do well: but if ye have respect of persons, ye commit sin, being convicted by the law as transgressors. For whosoever shall keep the whole law, and yet stumble in one *point*, he is become guilty of all. For he that said, Do not commit adultery, said also, Do not kill. Now if thou dost not commit adultery, but killest, thou art become a transgressor of the law.' These four verses deal with a possible excuse. It is no use pleading that this attentiveness was shown to the rich man in obedience to the commandment to love one's neighbour. Respect of persons and the love which God commands us to show to our neighbour are two quite different and incompatible things. 'This word, "neighbour" ', says Calvin, 'includes all mankind: he then who says that a very few, according to his own fancy, ought to be honoured, and others passed by, does not keep the law of God, but yields to the depraved desires of his own heart. God expressly commends to us strangers and enemies and all, even the most contemptible. To this doctrine the respect of persons is wholly contrary. Hence, rightly does James assert that respect of persons is inconsistent with love.' In v. 8 it is better (with J. H. Ropes) to take 'the royal law' to mean the law as a whole than to limit it to the commandment of love to neighbour; for this avoids the necessity of positing an awkward change of meaning between 'law' in this verse and 'law' in vv. 9–12. The law is perhaps called 'royal' as deriving from God, 'the great King' (Mt 5.35), and therefore possessing royal majesty. The point of vv. 10

and 11 is that 'God will not be honoured with exceptions, nor will He allow us to cut off from His law what is less pleasing to us' (Calvin).

The relevance of these last four verses to the attitude reflected in these words addressed to Bishop (then Father) Huddleston by an acquaintance: 'You ought to try to be more Christian about these chaps [the South African government]. . . . Have you forgotten the commandment? Why don't you try a bit more love towards them, a bit more patience and understanding?'[1], is obvious. Perhaps they also have a bearing on the great tenderness which ecclesiastical leaders have often shown for the feelings of some white South Africans – the report which has recently appeared is evidence of a much more serious concern on the part of the British Council of Churches – and for white settlers in various other places.

Verse 12 ('So speak ye, and so do, as men that are to be judged by a law of liberty') bids the Christian remember in all his speaking and doing that he will one day have to give account to God. To assert the accountability to God of every individual man is to assert his inalienable dignity; and it would be difficult to think of any other single thing that has done as much in the last half-century to degrade human dignity as the weakening of Christian conviction at this point. How seriously have they misunderstood Scripture, who, failing to distinguish between the picture-language (necessarily to some extent historically conditioned), which the Bible often uses when speaking of God's judgment, and the reality itself, have allowed a perverse preoccupation with that picture-language to blind them to the reality which all the time it was meant to set forth!

[1] Quoted in T. Huddleston, *Naught for your Comfort*, London, 1956, p. 235.

The same verse asserts that God's judgment will be free from all caprice and in perfect accord with His own holy will which He has revealed to men. And this revealed will of God for men is here referred to (as in 1.25) as 'a law of liberty', because it is (as properly understood, and not abused by a legalistic misunderstanding) the holy, righteous and good law, of which Jesus Christ is the goal, the substance, and the meaning.

The last verse of the section is: 'For judgment is without mercy to him that hath shewed no mercy: mercy glorieth against judgment.' We may compare such passages as Mt 5.7; 6.12, 14f; 18.23–35, and 25.31–46. Here is no contradiction of the doctrine of justification by grace through faith by some theologically unperceptive person, but a salutary reminder that the absence of compassion for one's fellow-men is conclusive proof that one's professed faith is counterfeit, while mercy shown – though certainly not to be thought of as a meritorious work putting God under an obligation – may be an evidence of genuine faith.

To 2.14–26 we may give the title, *Of true faith*. The clue to the understanding of the section is the fact (very often ignored) that in v. 14 ('What doth it profit, my brethren, if a man say he hath faith, but have not works? can that faith save him?') the author has not said, 'if a man have faith', but 'if a man say he hath faith'.[1] This fact should be allowed to control our interpretation of the whole paragraph. The second 'faith' in the verse is to be taken as in inverted commas. By 'that faith' (ἡ πίστις) the writer means that thing which the man in question wrongly calls 'faith'; he does not imply that he himself regards it as faith. When this is recognized, it is clear that the burden of this section is not (as is often supposed) that we are saved

---

[1] Cf. Calvin, op. cit., p. 309f.

through faith plus works, but that we are saved through genuine, as opposed to counterfeit, faith.

Verses 15–17 assert that a faith which does not produce works, that is, good works, works of obedience tó God, is as futile as an almsgiving consisting merely of fine speeches. It is no more worthy of the name of faith than such an almsgiving is worthy of the name of almsgiving. Such a faith is dead; it is as ineffective as a corpse.[1]

Verse 18a ('Yea, a man will say, Thou hast faith, and I have works') introduces a possible objection, to the effect that faith and good works can exist separately and independently of each other (by 'Thou' and 'I' the objector means not James and himself respectively, but simply 'one' and 'another').[2] To this the author replies in v. 18b in the first place by challenging the objector to produce an example of faith existing by itself without works of obedience ('shew me thy faith apart from *thy* works'). The implication is that he does not think that such an example can be produced. The words are thus support for the view that the author does not regard the faith which is without works as really faith at all. The second part of the reply ('and I by my works will shew thee *my* faith') is the corresponding offer to demonstrate the existence of his own faith by the presence of the good works which are its fruit. The reply as a whole amounts to an emphatic denial that faith and works are separable.

---

[1] The meaning of καθ' ἑαυτήν (RV: 'in itself') in v. 17 is not certain. Does it mean 'by itself' (cf. the Old Latin codex Corbeiensis: *sola*) and so repeat the idea expressed by 'if it have not works' (so Dibelius)? Or does it mean 'in itself' (cf. Vulgate: *in semetipsa*) and so strengthen νεκρά – 'inwardly dead' (so Ropes)? But, in either case, the general meaning of the sentence will be as we have indicated.

[2] The second and first persons are equivalent to 'one' and 'another' (cf. Ropes, op. cit., p. 209; Dibelius, op. cit., p. 145 and Supplement, p. 16; F. Blass and A. Debrunner, *A Greek Grammar of the New Testament*, Cambridge, 1961, §281). The two statements are the opposite way round to what one would expect, if 'Thou' and 'I'

Verse 19 ('Thou believest that God is one; thou doest well: the devils also believe, and shudder') makes the point that orthodoxy, correctness of theological opinion, while it is an excellent thing so far as it goes, certainly does not by itself amount to saving faith. The devils may be said to have an intellectual grasp of theological truths, but this does not profit them.

At this point it will be as well to remind ourselves of certain linguistic facts. The Greek verb which is cognate with πίστις ('faith'), namely, πιστεύειν ('believe'), is used in the NT not only, with εἰς or ἐπί, of believing *in* (God, Christ) and, absolutely, of having faith, being a believer (i.e. a Christian) but also, with the dative, of giving credence to a person or a message, and, with ὅτι or the accusative and infinite, of believing *that*. . . . The noun πίστις is used to denote faithfulness or trustworthiness; faith (in God, Christ) or, absolutely, Christian faith, saving faith, that by the presence of which one is a Christian; and also faith in the sense of a special charisma possessed not by all, but only by some, Christians (as, for example, in 1 Cor 12.9; 13.2). For those whose language is English the situation is further complicated by the fact that, whereas in Greek we have to do with only one word-group, in English, as also in Latin, two distinct word-groups ('believe', etc., and 'faith', etc.: in Latin *credere* and *fidere*, etc.) are involved. That the possibilities, inherent in this linguistic situation, of Christians' being at cross-purposes with one another when talking about faith, both were and are considerable, is obvious.

It is probably a fair inference from v. 19 that those against whom the author is arguing were inclined to understand the faith, by the presence of which a man is a

referred to James and the objector respectively. For a full discussion of the difficulties and various suggested interpretations of this verse see Ropes, pp. 208–214.

Christian, too much in terms of belief *that*, though it would perhaps be pressing the evidence too far to conclude that they explicitly maintained that saving faith was purely an intellectual acceptance of certain doctrines. But it would be quite wrong to conclude from the author's use of πιστεύειν in v. 19 and from v. 20 ('But wilt thou know, O vain man, that faith apart from works is barren?') and its sequel that he himself thought of faith as being no more than belief *that*.

Verse 20 introduces the following argument from Scripture, in the course of which first the example of Abraham is adduced and then that of Rahab. Verse 21 (the rhetorical question, 'Was not Abraham our father justified by works, in that he offered up Isaac his son upon the altar?') might seem at first sight to be saying the exact opposite to what Paul says in Romans 4. But, in the light of the context, this can hardly be its meaning. For James, no less than for Paul, the words of Gen 15.6 quoted in v. 23 ('And Abraham believed God, and it was reckoned unto him for righteousness') are decisive. It was by his faith that Abraham was justified. His works (his readiness to offer up Isaac related in Genesis 22) did not earn his justification (about which we hear already in Genesis 15): they were simply the fruit and the outward evidence of his faith. It is true that James implies that, had there been no works, Abraham would not have been justified; but that would have been because the absence of works would have meant that he had no real faith. Here it is illuminating to compare Mt 25.31–46, where, though the division between men is made according to whether they have, or have not, shown mercy, it is not to be inferred that those who have shown mercy are thought of as having *earned* their reward.

It is probable that v. 22 ('Thou seest that faith wrought with his works, and by works was faith made perfect') should be interpreted in such a way that it also is an indication that v. 21 is not really contrary to what Paul says. What makes the verse perplexing is, of course, the difficulty of deciding the precise significance of συνήργει ('wrought with') and ἐτελειώθη ('was made perfect'). If we press the συν- of συνήργει and translate 'co-operated with', then the implication of the verse seems to be that faith and works are thought of as two quite separate things existing independently of each other. But the συν- need not be so pressed. We are probably justified in translating συνήργει, 'supported' or 'sustained', and understanding the verse to mean that Abraham's faith was the source and ground of his works, and his works the expression, the manifestation, of his faith. In view of the very close connexion between faith and works indicated by vv. 18b and 26, and also of the fact that faith without works is not only described as 'barren' (v. 20), but actually said to be 'dead' (vv. 17 and 26), this would seem to be the more natural interpretation. The verse is then tantamount to an emphasising of the inseparability of faith and works.

The false views which Paul and James are opposing, in Romans 4 and here respectively, are different. Paul is combating the idea that men can put God under an obligation to themselves: so he wants to show that not even Abraham, the father of all the people of God, earned his justification, and that, if he did not, then obviously no one else can do so. James is opposing the idea that a real faith can exist without producing works of obedience. The difference of aim accounts to a large extent for the differences of language. There is no need to infer any significant disagreement between their fundamental positions.

The clue to the understanding of v. 24 ('Ye see that by works a man is justified, and not only by faith'), which at first sight seems to contradict what is said by Paul (e.g. in Rom 3.28), is the recognition that here, as in v. 14, the author is making a concession to his opponents' use of terms.[1] He does not himself believe that a faith which does not produce works is really faith at all, but for the moment he accepts his opponents' way of speaking, and so is forced to deny that a man is justified by faith alone. 'By faith alone' is right, if what is called 'faith' is really faith; but, if something which can exist without producing works is meant, then the formula *sola fide* will not do.

After the example of Abraham that of Rahab is adduced: 'And in like manner was not also Rahab the harlot justified by works, in that she received the messengers, and sent them out another way?' Calvin suggests that the author 'designedly put together two persons so different in their character, in order more clearly to show, that no one, whatever may have been his or her condition, nation, or class in society, has ever been accounted righteous without good works'. Rahab (see Josh 2.1–22; 6.17, 22f, 25, and also Heb 11.31) recognized that Israel's God was the true God (Josh 2.9–11), and acted upon that recognition.

The purport of v. 26 ('For as the body apart from the spirit is dead, even so faith apart from works is dead') is not that works are to faith as the spirit is to the body – which would indeed be a strange thing to assert – but that a faith which does not produce good works is as dead as a body without spirit. It may seem like faith – especially to the person who has it – just as a dead body or a piece of sculpture may in certain circumstances be mistaken for a man; but it is no more faith than a corpse or a statue is a living person.

The next section (3.1–12) may be entitled, *Of right*

---

[1] Cf. Calvin, op. cit., p. 310.

speaking. We have already had hints of the author's concern about speech in 1.19 and 26.

'Do not all want to be teachers of the Church!' is the burden of the first verse of the chapter: 'Be not many teachers, my brethren. . . .' To be a teacher in the Church is to occupy a specially responsible position, in which, while one can do a vast amount of good, one can also very easily do a vast amount of harm. The writer realizes – what is sometimes forgotten – that to have a bad minister is a far worse evil for a parish than to have no minister at all.

Moreover, it is a dangerous position for the man who occupies it. He will have to give a particularly strict account. So James adds: 'knowing that we [that is, the teachers of the Church] shall receive heavier judgment.' 'Whosoever shall cause one of these little ones that believe on me to stumble', said Jesus, 'it were better for him if a great millstone were hanged about his neck, and he were cast into the sea' (Mk 9.42) – that is, his punishment will be so severe that it would have been better for him had he been drowned before he could do such wrong, and so been saved from the punishment that will be his. Others beside the official teachers of the Church can, of course, cause Christ's little ones to stumble; but it is they who can most easily do so. And if those who should feed them cause them to perish, their guilt is especially great.

The verse is a warning against entering upon the office of teacher in the Church unadvisedly, lightly or wantonly, a solemn reminder that to aspire to it, except under divine compulsion (which is not to be confused with the elation which anyone who loves the sound of his own voice experiences when he has a captive audience at his mercy), is the height of folly. It is also a warning to those who presume to 'recruit' for the ministry or for other teaching offices in the Church without fear and trembling and a due sense of the spiritual cost which others will have to meet.

Verse 2 ('For in many things we all stumble.[1] If any stumbleth not in word, the same is a perfect man, able to bridle the whole body also') underlines the warning just given. How perilous it is to be someone whose daily business is actually to speak about the Word of God is obvious when we remember how prone to err we all are, and especially to err in our speaking. To avoid erring in the matter of speech is so difficult that one might say without exaggeration that, if a man really could control his speech, really could be fully obedient to God in what he says (and also what he omits to say), he would be able to control himself altogether – would indeed be perfect.

In vv. 3–5 three examples of little things which have an effectiveness out of all proportion to their size are mentioned, the bit[2] in a horse's mouth, the rudder of a ship, and a spark. The point the writer wants to make is expressed in the sentence, 'So the tongue also is a little member, and boasteth great things', which is placed between the second and the third illustration. He is thinking specially of the tongue as the medium which the teacher uses; but what he says has also a more general relevance – to all speech whether spoken or written. Its power for good or evil is frighteningly great.

The last of the three illustrations (that of the spark which can destroy a mighty forest) is then taken up in v. 6. The verse in detail is extraordinarily difficult. The RV text ('And the tongue is a fire: the world of iniquity among our

---

[1] It is important to distinguish between 'stumble' in this verse, where it represents πταίειν = 'trip', 'take a false step', and in Mk 9.42 (quoted in the last paragraph but one), where 'cause to stumble' represents σκανδαλίζειν, which there is used of destroying someone's faith, causing him to fall away from God.

[2] There is a verbal link between vv. 2 and 3 formed by 'bridle' (χαλιναγωγῆσαι) and 'bridles' (χαλινούς).

members is the tongue, which defileth the whole body, and setteth on fire the wheel of nature, and is set on fire by hell') presupposes a full stop after ἀνάπτει at the end of v. 5, a colon after πῦρ, and no stop after ἀδικίας; and this would seem to give the best sense that can be got out of the Greek without having recourse to conjectural emendation. The RSV and the NEB offer substantially the same translation. (For other possible punctuations reference may be made to the 1958 British and Foreign Bible Society text and apparatus, and to the commentaries.) The phrase 'the wheel of nature' (τὸν τροχὸν τῆς γενέσεως) has a Greek background, but seems to be used here without reference to it, as a rhetorical expression suggesting the vast extent of the devastation. The general sense of the verse is tolerably clear. The tongue is indeed a fire! When it is set on fire by hell, it can set the whole world ablaze. While it may be used for far-reaching good, it possesses the most fearful potentialities for evil; and, since all men are sinners, the world is continually being subjected to its ravages. We may think, for example, of the confusion and ruin caused by false teachings in the Church (in view of v. 1 this is perhaps specially in the writer's mind), the blind hatreds and unreasoning prejudices produced by demagogy and propaganda, the moral havoc spread by corrupt suggestion.

Verses 7 and 8 ('For every kind of beasts and birds, of creeping things and things in the sea, is tamed, and hath been tamed by mankind: but the tongue can no man tame; *it is* a restless evil, *it is* full of deadly poison') express vividly man's inability to control the tongue. But in v. 8 the emphatic position of ἀνθρώπων ('of men'), at the end of the sentence and separated from οὐδείς '('no one'), is perhaps intended to suggest the thought that, though man cannot tame this 'restless evil', God can. At any rate, the confidence that God can, and from time to time does, make human tongues the bearers of His own Word is implicit in the very writing of the epistle, and is an essential presupposition of the next four verses which draw attention to the shameful inconsistencies of Christian speech.

Verses 9–10a ('Therewith bless we the Lord and Father; and therewith curse we men, which are made after the likeness of God: out of the same mouth cometh forth blessing and cursing') describe the compromised condition of the Christian speech of those for whom the epistle was intended. For readers today they open up the real nature of that 'problem of communication' about which so much is currently said with but little illumination resulting. They point us to the fact that our speech is so heavily compromised by being put to uses inconsistent with the gospel, that even the gospel itself is made incredible by being taken upon our lips; and invite us to ask ourselves whether our preoccupation with attempts at reforming the gospel by removing from it what we take to be intolerable to modern man is not really an escapism subconsciously motivated by our fear of having to face the painful truth that what most of all bedevils our proclamation of the gospel is our own lack of integrity.[1]

Verses 11 and 12 ('Doth the fountain send forth from the same opening sweet *water* and bitter? can a fig tree, my brethren, yield olives, or a vine figs? neither *can* salt water yield sweet') emphasise the unnaturalness, the absurdity, of the condition in which Christian speech so often finds itself, and thus underline the implicit command and

---

[1] It is surely time that we asked ourselves, for example, whether clergy who make solemn affirmations and promises with substantial mental reservations, and churches which condone such insincerity, have any reason to expect to be believed.

promise of v. 10b ('My brethren, these things ought not so to be'), that those who are thus solemnly addressed must, and can, do something – namely, seek His help who alone can tame their tongues and so bind them to His Word that a real measure of human dignity and integrity may be restored to their speech.

XII
THE INTERPRETATION OF 1 PETER 3.19 AND 4.6[1]

I

That 1 Pet 3.18–22 contains material taken from an early
Christian creed or hymn seems likely; but those who hold
this view differ as to the limits of the quotation. According
to H. Windisch[2] the whole passage is a baptismal hymn
consisting of four strophes, the exhortation contained in
vv. 13–17 being continued in 4.1. According to O.
Cullmann[3] we have in vv. 18, 19, 21c and 22 a confession
of faith dealing with the death of Jesus, His descent into
Hades, His resurrection, ascension and session at the
right hand of God, in the middle of which the author of
the Epistle has inserted a brief instruction on baptism

---

[1] First published in *ET* 69 (1957–58), pp. 369–372.

See further (in addition to the commentaries on 1 Peter): W. Bieder,
Die Vorstellung von der Höllenfahrt Jesu Christi, Zürich, 1949; R.
Bultmann, 'Bekenntnis- und Liedfragmente im ersten Petrusbrief', in
Coniectanea Neotestamentica 11, Lund, 1947; F. L. Cross, *1 Peter: A
Paschal Liturgy*, London, 1954; O. Cullmann, *The Earliest Christian
Confessions*, Eng. tr., London, 1949, pp. 18–21; G. Friedrich in *TWNT*
3, p. 705f (in article on κηρύσσω); J. Jeremias, 'Zwischen Karfreitag
und Ostern' in *ZNW* 42, (1949), pp. 194–201, and in *TWNT* 1, p. 149f
(in article on ᾅδης), and 5, p. 769f (in article on παράδεισος); J. N. D.
Kelly, *Early Christian Creeds*, London, 1950, pp. 378–383; B. Reicke,
The Disobedient Spirits and Christian Baptism, Lund, 1946; E.
Schweizer, '1 Petrus 4.6' in *Theologische Zeitschrift* 8 (1952),
pp. 152–154, and in *TWNT* 6, pp. 414, 446 (in article on πνεῦμα); E.
Stauffer, *Die Theologie des Neuen Testaments*, Stuttgart, 4th ed. 1948,
pp. 113–115. There is also a brief suggestive reference in K. Barth, *KD*
II/2, p. 561 [= *CD* II/2, p. 505].

[2] *Die Katholischen Briefe*, 3rd ed. rev. H. Preisker, Tübingen, 1951,
pp. 70, 73 – though see p. 71, lines 7ff, which perhaps implies that not
all these verses belong to the hymn.

[3] See note 1.

(vv. 20, 21ab). According to F. L. Cross,[1] the creed consists of vv. 18, 21c and 22. R. Bultmann[2] is more adventuresome and reconstructs a creed (in which he detects Gnostic influence) as follows:

> (? I believe in the Lord Jesus Christ,)
> who was foreknown indeed before the foundation of
> the world,
> but was manifested at the end of the times;
> who suffered for sins once,
> that He might bring us to God.
> Being put to death in the flesh,
> but quickened in the spirit,
> in which also He preached unto the spirits in prison,
> (and) having gone into heaven, He sat down on
> the right hand of God,
> angels and authorities and powers being made
> subject unto Him.

In this creed the preaching to the spirits is a preaching by the Risen Christ at the time of His ascension, addressed to departed souls which have been stopped in the course of their ascent to heaven and held captive by hostile spiritual powers (a Gnostic conception); but it has been misinterpreted by the author of the Epistle as a reference to a descent of Christ into Hades. But, in view of the large number of alterations of the text which are involved (the bringing of 1.20 into connexion with 3.18ff, the alteration of the order of words and the omission of several words in v. 18, the omission of πορευθείς in v. 19, the omission of ὅς, the substitution of ἐκάθισεν for ἐστιν, and the transposition of the first two clauses in v. 22) and of the

[1] See p. 176, n. 1.
[2] See p. 176, n. 1.

fact that the rhythmical form noticeable in vv. 18 and 22 is not discernible in v. 19, Bultmann's reconstruction seems extremely improbable. The conclusion of Jeremias,[1] that the most that can be said with any certainty is that in vv. 18 and 22 'older christological formulae are used' and that we cannot even be sure that vv. 18 and 22 formed originally a continuous text, would seem to be justified. We shall, therefore, not attempt to explain v. 19 as originally independent of v. 20, but shall consider it in the light of its immediate sequel.

In the exegesis of 3.19 there are three main questions to be answered.

1. *Who are meant by 'the spirits in prison'?* Calvin[2] understood the souls of the faithful of OT times to be meant. He explained φυλακή here as signifying not a prison but a watch-tower or else the act of watching ('the meaning would be very appropriate, that godly souls were watching in hope of the salvation promised them, as though they saw it afar off'), though he allowed the meaning 'prison' as a possible but less likely alternative ('as, while they lived, the Law, according to Paul (Gal 3.23), was a sort of prison in which they were kept, so after death they must have felt the same desire for Christ'). But Calvin's interpretation breaks down on v. 20; for his attempt to avoid taking ἀπειθήσασιν to refer to the spirits of the previous verse is unconvincing.

Since the publication of F. Spitta's *Christi Predigt an die Geister*, Göttingen, 1890, many scholars (e.g., R. Reitzenstein,[3] F. Hauck,[4] E. G. Selwyn,[5] B. Reicke,[6] J.

---

[1] In *ZNW* article: see p. 176, n. 1.

[2] *Commentaries on the Catholic Epistles*, Eng. tr. by J. Owen, reprinted Grand Rapids, USA, 1948, pp. 112–116.

[3] *Das mandäische Buch des Herrn der Grösse*, 1919, pp. 25ff, and *Das iranische Erlösungsmysterium*, 1921, pp. 111ff.

[4] *Die Kirchenbriefe*, Göttingen, 5th ed., 1949.

[5] *The First Epistle of St Peter*, London, 1946.   [6] See p. 176, n. 1.

Jeremias[1]) have accepted the identification of the spirits with the fallen angels of Genesis 6. In favour of this interpretation it is pointed out that πνεῦμα is occasionally used absolutely of supernatural beings elsewhere in the NT (e.g., Lk 10.20, Heb 1.14) as well as in the LXX (e.g., 1 Kgs 22.21) and the Pseudepigrapha; that a tradition based on Genesis 6 of an angelic disobedience was firmly established in Jewish thought (e.g., 1 Enoch 6 and 12–16, 2 Baruch 56.12); that this angelic disobedience was thought of as having occurred in the period immediately before the Flood; that according to Jewish tradition it was punished by imprisonment (e.g., 1 Enoch 10.11ff, 18.13ff); and that there are clear allusions to this tradition in the NT in 2 Pet 2.4 and Jude 6. According to Jeremias Christ's going and preaching (the possibility of deliverance) to the spirits in prison is intentionally contrasted with Enoch's going and proclaiming to them that their plea for forgiveness will never be granted.

Others (e.g., G. Friedrich,[2] E. Stauffer,[3] F. W. Beare,[4] E. Schweizer[5]) favour the older interpretation according to which the spirits referred to in v. 19 are the souls of those who perished in the Flood. The supporters of this view naturally appeal to v. 20 and to 4.6. There are others who, feeling the strength of the arguments on both sides, seek to combine both interpretations. So Windisch, while maintaining that the spirits in v. 19 must be the fallen angels of Genesis 6, thinks that in v. 20 the generation of Noah's contemporaries is referred to, and so suggests that the author has both groups in mind (cf. J. W. C. Wand[6]:

[1] In *ZNW* article: see p. 176, n. 1.
[2] See p. 176, n. 1.
[3] See p. 176, n. 1.
[4] *The First Epistle of Peter*, Oxford, 1947.
[5] In *TWNT* article: see p. 176, n. 1.
[6] *The General Epistles of St Peter and St Jude*, London, 1934.

E. G. Selwyn, mentioned above as supporting the fallen angels interpretation, admits that this explanation is possible). But in view of 3.20 and 4.6 the most probable interpretation is surely that which identifies the spirits in prison with the souls of the men who perished in the Flood. That πνεῦμα could be used to denote the soul of a dead person is clear from such examples as Heb 12.23 (πνεύμασι δικαίων τετελειωμένων) and Song of the Three Holy Children 63 (εὐλογεῖτε, πνεύματα καὶ ψυχαὶ δικαίων, τὸν κύριον) – though it is true that no exact parallel has so far been adduced for πνεῦμα used absolutely in this sense.

2. *When did this preaching of Christ to the spirits take place?* The suggestion (Augustine, Spitta, *et al.*) that it took place in the time of Noah and that the reference is to a preaching by the pre-existent Christ through the lips of Noah to those who at the time the Epistle was written were in prison in Hades, but at the time of the preaching were still alive, is far-fetched. That it took place after the Resurrection also seems, on the whole, unlikely, though this suggestion cannot be ruled out altogether (Calvin, who takes ᾧ to refer to πνεύματι, thinks of a going and preaching by the risen Christ through the Holy Spirit – and so not directly[1]). The most probable answer seems to be that this preaching took place in the interval between Christ's death and resurrection.[2] If we understand ζωοποιηθεὶς δὲ πνεύματι as indicating Christ's state during the period between Good Friday afternoon and Easter morning, when His spirit was alive but His body had not been raised, we may either explain ᾧ as referring to πνεύματι (the meaning of ἐν ᾧ being that it was 'in

[1] Op. cit., p. 113.

[2] Lk 23.43 ('Today shalt thou be with me in paradise') might seem to present a difficulty. But the descent into Hades and the fulfilment of the promise to the thief are surely not necessarily mutually exclusive. For a different explanation see Jeremias' *ZNW* article cited in p. 176, n. 1.

spirit,' i.e., as a bodiless spirit, that He went and preached to the spirits of the dead) or explain ἐν ᾧ as temporal (the meaning being that it was during this time, i.e., the time indicated by θανατωθεὶς μὲν σαρκὶ ζωοποιηθεὶς δὲ πνεύματι, that Christ went and preached). But it is perhaps rather more likely, in view of the use of ζωοποιέω elsewhere in the NT (cf. Jn 5.21; Rom 4.17; 8.11; 1 Cor 15.22, 36, 45), that ζωοποιηθείς refers to the resurrection of Christ. (For πνεύματι in this connexion, cf. Rom 1.3f and 1 Tim 3.16. It cannot be an instrumental dative, as we might at first be inclined to think; for the parallelism requires that it should have the same sort of meaning as σαρκί. It may perhaps be translated 'in the sphere of the Spirit [or, of spirit]' or 'in the spiritual sphere'.) If the reference of ζωοποιηθείς to the Resurrection is accepted, the preaching may still be understood to have taken place during the interval between Good Friday afternoon and Easter morning, if we take ἐν ᾧ in a temporal sense. It is possible that the writer added the words θανατωθεὶς μὲν σαρκὶ ζωοποιηθεὶς δὲ πνεύματι parenthetically on mentioning the death of Christ and intended ἐν ᾧ to refer back to the time indicated by καὶ Χριστὸς ἅπαξ περὶ ἁμαρτιῶν ἀπέθανεν, δίκαιος ὑπὲρ ἀδίκων, ἵνα ὑμᾶς προσαγάγῃ τῷ Θεῷ, or else that he intended ἐν ᾧ to refer to the whole of v. 18, since in a general way the time indicated by the whole verse (including the reference to the Resurrection) might be said to be the time of an event which took place between Christ's death and resurrection.[1]

3. *What was the content of this preaching?* It has been suggested by Selwyn that ἐκήρυξεν means not that Christ preached the gospel to the spirits in prison but that He

---

[1] The ingenious conjectural emendation by J. Rendel Harris, which makes Enoch the subject of ἐκήρυξεν, though accepted by Moffatt, may safely be rejected.

made proclamation to them of the approaching end of their power as a result of His victory. He compares the use of κηρύσσω in Rev 5.2, where the content of the κηρύσσειν is not the gospel but the challenge, 'Who is worthy to open the book, and to loose the seals thereof?' But it is much more likely that κηρύσσω has here its normal NT sense of preaching the gospel. That it does is confirmed by εὐηγγελίσθη in 4.6, if (as seems almost certain) that verse refers back to the preaching mentioned in 3.19. Whereas Enoch's message to the fallen angels in answer to their plea for forgiveness was the stark announcement of their irrevocable doom, 'You have no peace' (1 Enoch 16.4), Christ's message to the spirits in prison was the good news of the possibility of deliverance (cf. 4.6: ἵνα κριθῶσι μὲν κατὰ ἀνθρώπους σαρκί, ζῶσι δὲ κατὰ Θεὸν πνεύματι).

II

We turn now to the exegesis of 4.6. In the previous verse the writer has pointed out that those pagans who resent the changed manner of life of their former companions, now Christians, will have to answer before God who is ready to judge both the living and the dead. This mention of the dead (νεκρούς) apparently suggests to him another thought, to which he gives expression in this verse.

The suggestion that the νεκροί of v. 6 are the spiritually dead[1] is unlikely in view of the use of the word in v. 5. Hardly more probable is the view that by νεκροῖς are meant those Christians who, having heard the gospel (εὐηγγελίσθη) during their lifetime, have subsequently died.[2] By far the most likely explanation is that there is a

---

[1] So Clement of Alexandria; recently Bieder (see p. 176, n. 1).
[2] So Selwyn.

reference back to 3.19, and that the νεκροί of 4.6 are to be identified with the πνεύματα of 3.19 (or perhaps we should say 'include' rather than 'are to be identified with': 4.6 may represent a generalizing of the statement in 3.19) and that εὐηγγελίσθη refers to the preaching by Christ which is spoken of in 3.19.[1]

As to the latter half of the verse, the best explanation is that, although κριθῶσι κατὰ ἀνθρώπους σαρκί and ζῶσι κατὰ Θεὸν πνεύματι are grammatically co-ordinate, in thought the former is subordinate to the latter and is equivalent to a concessive clause[2] – 'in order that, although in the eyes of men they have been judged in the flesh, they might nevertheless live in God's sight in the spirit.' (It is interesting to compare Wisd 3.2, 4.) This involves taking κριθῶσι to refer to an action which had already taken place before the action of the main verb εὐηγγελίσθη (the reference in κριθῶσι being to their death): this is certainly difficult, but probably not impossible.[3]

III

That the doctrine of these verses is extremely perplexing cannot be denied. Here indeed, to use Bengel's apt phrase, is a *locus mysterii plenus*[4]. The idea 'that Christ's soul went' and preached to the dead obviously struck Calvin as fanciful, while the further idea that men who during their lifetime had never come to faith in Christ (not even

[1] So Beare, Schweizer, etc.

[2] Cf. Calvin, op. cit., p. 126.

[3] For the ingenious, but to the present writer unconvincing, suggestion that ἵνα in this verse has a causal sense with κριθῶσι and a final sense with ζῶσι, see Schweizer, *Theologische Zeitschrift* article (see p. 176, n. 1).

[4] *Gnomon Novi Testamenti*, on 1 Pet 3.19.

the faith which the men of the OT can be said to have had) could after their death be saved seemed to him to need 'no long refutation; for it is an indubitable doctrine of Scripture, that we obtain not salvation in Christ except by faith; then there is no hope left for those who continue to death unbelieving.'[1] So he was at pains to find another interpretation, as we have already seen; and in the *Institutes* 2.16.8–12, he explains the clause of the Creed, 'He descended into hell,' by reference to the Cry of Dereliction on the Cross. But – though for any one who knows how humble, sober and penetrating an exegete Calvin is, it is always a serious matter to disagree with him – we cannot follow Calvin in his interpretation of 1 Pet 3.19 and 4.6.

If then, unlike Calvin, we admit that these verses refer to a preaching by Christ to the souls of unbelievers during the interval between His death and His resurrection, what are we to make of this doctrine? We shall be wise, I think, to hesitate before brushing it aside as a 'fantastic dream,' as Beare does.[2] For one thing, the idea of a descent of Christ into Hades is not limited in the NT to these two verses: it occurs also in Acts 2.27, 31; Rom 10.6–8; Eph 4.8–10 (cf. Mt 12.40). For another thing, the restraint and sobriety of 1 Pet 3.19; 4.6 contrast significantly with the exuberance of the legends concerned with this theme. Moreover, it is quite unnecessary to see here (with Windisch, Beare, *et al.*) the influence of ancient pagan *Erlösermythologie* (e.g., Beare, op. cit., p. 145: 'It is nothing else than the appropriation, and the application to Christ, of a fragment of the redemption-mythology of the Oriental religions, best known to us in the ancient story of the Descent of Ishtar to the underworld, and reflected also in a number of Greek myths (Orpheus and

[1] Op. cit., p. 113.
[2] Op. cit., p. 145.

Eurydice, Heracles and Alcestis, the story of Persephone, etc.); it is rooted in old vegetation- and sun-myths'); for, given the fact of the interval between the death and the resurrection of Jesus, it was altogether natural for the earliest Christians, sharing contemporary Jewish ideas about the interim-state, to infer that the spirit of Jesus must have sojourned in Hades – an inference which Ps 16.8–11 (cf. Acts 2.25–28, 31; 13.25) was close at hand to encourage. Natural too for those who had come to know the grace and power of Christ was the further inference that even during this sojourn among the dead He must have been active to save. And the question whether there was hope for those who had died in unbelief was for many early Christians a poignant one, since it concerned their own parents and kinsfolk.[1]

Whether during the days between His resurrection and ascension Jesus ever gave His disciples any hint of what is asserted in these two verses we do not know. We cannot altogether rule out the possibility that He did. But, quite apart from such a possibility, what these verses say is, as an inference drawn by the faith of the Early Church[2] and finding a place within the NT witness to Christ, not without authority for us. It is a hint within the Canon of Scripture, puzzling indeed and obscure yet at the same time reassuringly restrained, that the mysterious interval between Good Friday afternoon and Easter morning was not empty of significance, but that in it too Jesus Christ was active as the Saviour of the world. It is a hint that the atoning efficacy of His death was available to those who had died in paganism in the generations before Christ. The generation of mankind which perished in the Flood is mentioned, not, we may assume, as being the sole

[1] Cf. Hauck, op. cit., p. 70.
[2] Of the first generation of the Early Church – if the Petrine authorship of 1 Peter is accepted.

recipients of this mysterious ministry, but because they were generally regarded as the most abandoned of sinners: if those whom Jewish opinion excluded altogether from hope (cf. Sanh 10.3: 'The generation of the Flood hath no share in the world to come, nor shall they stand in the judgment . . .'[1]) were not beyond the reach of Christ's saving work, then none could be. It is a hint, too, surely, that those who in subsequent ages have died without ever having had a real chance to believe in Christ are not outside the scope of His mercy and will not perish eternally without being given in some way that is beyond our knowledge an opportunity to hear the gospel and accept Him as their Saviour.

[1] H. Danby, *The Mishnah*, Oxford, 1933, p. 397.

XIII
AN INTERPRETATION OF THE BOOK OF JOB[1]

While the scene and characters are patriarchal and the style of the prose framework is that of the folk-story, the thought of the poem reflects the questions of a much later time. A certain awkwardness in the way the poem fits into the narrative gives the impression that part of the poet's material had been the vehicle of ideas quite different from those it is now being used to express. The natural inference is that the poet was using a story whose outline was already fixed. This is confirmed by Ezek 14.12–23, which proves that a tradition of a man of exemplary righteousness named Job was already well known. It seems reasonable to conclude that this tradition was our author's source. Both in Ezekiel and in the prose of our book Job is a notably righteous man. There is possibly a further point of contact. Ezekiel is saying that in the day of God's vengeance the righteous man's righteousness will *not* avail to save any but himself; the way he refers to the three typical righteous men gains point if they *had* actually saved others by their righteousness. We know this was related of Noah from Genesis 6. As in our book the three friends are saved for Job's sake in answer to his prayers, it seems plausible to conclude that they and their deliverance belong to the tradition known to Ezekiel. We may assume then with some confidence that there was, before our book of Job was written, a folk-story about a man called Job, whose outstanding goodness was rewarded by outstanding prosperity. One day Yahweh mentioned Job's goodness approvingly to Satan; he replied that it was not disinterested and would soon

[1] First published in *ET* 54 (1942–43), pp. 295–298.

vanish if his prosperity were taken away. Yahweh accepted the challenge and allowed Satan to test him. This Satan did; but through all Job was resigned and patient. In his adversity his friends came to visit him; but, being ignorant of the heavenly wager, they assumed that his sufferings must be the punishment for great sin. At last Yahweh vindicated Job, and rebuked his friends, though forgiving them for Job's sake. Job is restored to a prosperity twice as great as that he had formerly enjoyed. Underlying this tale and assumed by it was the *doctrine of retribution*, according to which suffering was always the punishment of sin, and good fortune the reward of virtue. To this law Job's adversity was a remarkable exception due to an extraordinary celestial event; but the exception is only temporary, the law being vindicated by Job's final reward. Job's friends are rebuked – apparently rather unfairly, since they could not know of the wager – for having counted this good man a sinner; but they are *not* blamed for their doctrine. Into this outline our poet has introduced the alien element of Job's conversion, and it becomes the decisive thing. From the point of view of the original saga Job needed no conversion; for our author he must repent in dust and ashes. In the saga Yahweh's intervention is simply to vindicate the hero; in our book, before He vindicates him, He rebukes him and makes him repent. Here, where our book diverges from the tradition, is to be sought the clue to its meaning.[1]

The Prologue follows the tradition faithfully; the righteous Job is submissive even after Satan's second onslaught. The friends are introduced. Overwhelmed with grief for him, they sit in silence with him seven days. At last Job speaks, and the poem begins. In a passionate outburst he directs the inevitable 'Why?' to God. There

[1] Cf. Sir Edwyn Hoskyns, *Cambridge Sermons*, London, 1938, pp. 66–69.

follows a series of speeches consisting of 'consolations' offered by the three friends in turn, each being answered by Job (chapters 4–31). Behind all looms the current doctrine of retribution, accepted by Job and his friends alike. It is this doctrine that barbs Job's sufferings; for in its light his troubles become the accusing hand of God.

We must not let the self-righteous brutality of the friends blind us to the fact that Job *is* proud. Bildad touches the root of the matter in 18.4; Job is utterly self-centred. He has to learn that he is not the centre of the world; its laws serve a purpose other than his convenience. On the other hand, we shall miss the whole point if we think Job is more self-centred than other men. We were warned against this error in the Prologue; Job *is* good, as Yahweh Himself acknowledges. He is no more self-centred than the friends in their priggishness; the difference is that he is under the microscope. A really good man is depicted in order than *nobody* can escape the judgment of Yahweh's answer. The sympathy shown by the poet to all his characters itself warns us against any superficial over-simplification. Let us not be too quick to feel ourselves superior either to the priggishness of the friends or the arrogance of Job.

Here is a really good man suffering the most ghastly calamity despite all his good works and religious life. It is not surprising that under such stress a conventional religion should break down. His religion had been self-centred. While his 'steps were washed with butter,' he had accepted happily the dogma that men's fortunes are God's reward for their deeds. He had the natural idea that God exists for the sake of man – of Job; God was *his* protector, *his* convenience. Suddenly plunged into disaster, without any consciousness of having deserved it, he felt betrayed. This was the reward of his piety. So the God who had been the guarantee of his security becomes to his fevered brain a cruel and deceitful Tormentor. To his horror he realizes his weakness, his Persecutor is stronger than he. He is the helpless target of His arrows (6.4; 7.20; 16.12f). Every throb of his pain and every spectre of his delirium he feels to be the work of God, an arrow from His deadly quiver or a cruel glance from His terrifying eyes. 7.17f is a resentful parody of Psalm 8 – shattering in its bitterness. The constant watchfulness of God, once his comfort, is now his torment, and makes him mad. But far worse for Job than the actual pain is the implication of dishonour which it brings; in the light of the doctrine of retribution, that he accepts, misfortune implies misdoing; it is God's accusing finger raised against him. God not only hurts him most savagely and unjustly, but He is casting a slur on Job's good name. Men will believe he is being punished for wrong-doing; of course, they will believe God rather than Job. It is this offence to his righteousness that torments him most. It is because his friends assume that, since he is suffering, he must have sinned, that he is so angry with them. He wanted them to confess that he was innocent, and his woe undeserved; that would have consoled his wounded pride.

It is Job's assertion of his righteousness that now becomes the theme of the poem. He may have been guilty of some misdemeanours in his youth (13.26), but he will not admit they were serious – nothing to deserve God's anger. In 7.20f he defies God: 'If I have sinned,' he says – for he will not admit that he really is a sinner or needs God's mercy in forgiveness. He is so puny that he could not hurt God, so God should not concern Himself with his sin. 'What do I unto thee?' – in other words, he takes forgiveness for granted. He does not see the seriousness of sin, because he does not take the holy God seriously. Sin *is* to do with God; therefore we dare not say, 'Why dost thou not pardon . . .?' When Bildad replies that God is always righteous, Job agrees; that he knows only too well. For it is God who is judge of righteousness, and He will make the innocent unrighteous, if it pleases Him. It is useless to contend with God. Who can bring Him to book? (9.2–12). He is irresponsible; though innocent, it is no use pleading with Him; seeing His might, it is better to throw oneself on the Tyrant's mercy. Why even if God were to offer to hear his case how could Job trust Him after all His cruelty? His strength would wring a false confession from the innocent (9.20). 'I am perfect . . .' but 'It is all one; therefore I say, He destroyeth the perfect and the wicked [alike]' (9.21f). 9.30f is no statement that, however good a man may be, when compared with God he is seen to be foul, but a declaration that God is flagrantly unjust and irresponsible, mocking all honest endeavours and plunging in the mire him who has kept himself unspotted. Job, having once lost confidence in his Maker's integrity, bitterly resents His undoubted might. The thought that there is no higher authority to whom to appeal is like a trap to Job (9.32f). God should appear as plaintiff and he as defendant, both on an equality. So he presumptuously couples himself with his Maker with 'we' and 'us'. Why does He contend with him? Has He some ulterior motive – does it profit Him? God is not unable to see clearly; yet, though He *must* know Job's innocence, He tortures him to get a confession, in the cruelty of omnipotence (10.4–7). Job turns to supplication. What pains has God taken in all the amazing process of forming him! Would not the thought soften Him? A darker thought crosses Job's mind. No, His care all along was treachery; these were the purposes hidden even then in His heart (10.9–13).

In a fresh onslaught Job rebukes the platitudinous friends. They were mere cringing flatterers of omnipotence, the Tyrant's yes-men; he will speak with

God, not them. He will declare his mind, come what may (13.13). Proudly he asserts his righteousness (13.18), and sneers at God – 'Who is he . . .?' (13.19). He demands that the contest be on *his* conditions, and patronizingly promises that, if God will agree to these terms, he (Job) will condescend to answer (13.20–22). Job begins his plea by asking to be told his sins! *Why ever* is God so against him? His thoughts return to the pity of mortality, which suggests a brief surrender to wishful thinking – the natural refuge of the self-centred man when crossed. For a moment he wishes that God might hide him in Sheol until His wrath be past; there he would wait patiently, and at last God would change His mood and bring him forth in kindness (14.13–15). But quickly he returns to reality. In his next speech he dwells on the cruelty of this God, whom he likens to a wild beast. As he faces the approach of death he will not let go of his righteousness. He asserts it again (16.16–18), and wants to ensure that God may never be able to bury the traces of His foul deed. Job's reputation must be saved at all costs. Then with a masterly stroke the poet makes him change his tone (16.19–21). Misunderstood and lectured by his friends he is driven to appeal to the God whom he has just charged with injustice and cruelty. There is none stronger to whom he can appeal against God or his friends. Despite His cruelty, God *is* all-seeing, and so knows the truth, even though at present He will not admit it. Therefore His knowledge is witness against His actions. God must know that He is being unjust, even His own divine conscience bears witness against Him.

In 19 Job brushes aside Bildad's rebukes; only in one thing is he interested – God has done him injustice (19.6f). God has taken away his righteousness, his 'glory' (19.9). If he must be despised by his contemporaries, surely posterity would be fairer, and would vindicate his name, if only it might read of his sufferings and innocence (19.23f). The one thing he cares for now is his good name; his actual pain is in the background. His seven sons and three daughters are less to him than his pride. But the thought of posterity gives him no peace of mind; so once more he turns to God. The passage that follows has been interpreted as a glorious example of faith in God, but it can hardly be that; we are still a long way from the turning-point. It is similar to 16.19–21 – very self-centred and very human wishful thinking (19.25–29). Because he is self-centred he cannot bring himself to face the thought that he must really let go of his righteousness *for ever*. God *must in the end* vindicate him. We all crave to believe that the world is meaningful. So Job cannot face the idea of its all being meaningless; but his pride will not admit that there could possibly be any goodness in a world in which *his* good name is not vindicated. The one absolutely real thing to him is his pride; so he builds upon its demands. There is here no thought of resurrection, but simply the contemporary belief in a shadowy existence after death. Job hopes that his bodiless ghost will see his reputation vindicated by God on earth.

With 23.3 we wonder whether perhaps he is at last softening, but no, the reason why he is so anxious to find God is only that he may pour his arguments about his righteousness into His ears (23.4), to satisfy his own pride, not in order to know God. In this passage the fear that God will be obstinate and the hope that He will heed him alternate (23.10, 13). It never once enters his head that he might be in the wrong, or that in a fair trial he might be condemned. Absolutely certain of his own righteousness, of God's justice he freely doubts. In 27 he is still as persistent, and with hammerlike blows asserts his righteousness against God's unrighteousness – 'my right . . . mine integrity . . . My righteousness' (27.2–6). His last speech before Yahweh's appearance is in chapters 29–31. This long speech sums up all he has said. In the first part – the reminiscences of his former prosperity – the pride is not hidden. 29.14 is very significant. The second part deals with his present sufferings, and makes clear that it is not the actual calamities, but the slur they cast on his honour that grieves him most. The last part of the speech is an oath of innocence. He has given up all hope of restoration, but he still clings to 'his right'. In 31.6 he charges God not to tamper with the scales; Job will not be judged except to be acquitted; if heaven's justice does not acclaim him as just, then so much the worse for heaven's justice! The possibility of his being in the wrong is ruled out of order from the start. But let us be fair to him. This is *not* the insolence of an extraordinarily self-important and petty man, but the mirror held up to the real self-centredness of the good and noble man. 31.1–34 is the statement of a rare character; note especially vv. 15, 29 – a very high standard. We shall understand the meaning of the author only if we heed his emphasis on Job's real goodness. The climax of the speech is the final challenge (31.35–37). It sums up all man's rebelliousness, his vexation that God and not he himself should be his judge. It is the attitude of the Pharisee of the Parable put into poetry. Thus man's righteousness would approach God – 'as a prince'! So proud are we in our blindness that we would fain turn even God's indictment into an ornament of distinction, boasting even in the Law!

Yahweh does not submit Himself to Job's conditions (9.34f; 13.20–22), but answers Job, as He Himself chooses, in majesty, out of the whirlwind. God deals with us on His terms, not ours. The distinction between God and man must not be blurred. There is a gentle irony throughout the speech, as in the question in 38.2 and as in 38.21. This loud-voiced, self-centred, ignorant little person Job – *man* – is rebuked. We see the world from the viewpoint of our own importance, judge everything by the standard of its usefulness to *us*. But nature's multitudinous life should warn us of our folly. The speech appeals to many things, that are *not* useful to men – and yet God is interested in them. Why, if the world exists for man, did nature lavish such care on things he does not see? (38.25–27). If the Creator's purpose was our comfort, He was not particularly successful; our pride would like very much 'to grasp this sorry Scheme of Things entire, ... shatter it to bits – and then re-mould it nearer to the Heart's Desire.' But the Bible proclaims that the world and man in it exist not for themselves, but for the glory of God. History and nature alike are the theatre of His glory.

With superb art the poet has sought to make us conscious of the unsearchable wisdom of God. The lesson of Yahweh's speech has its effect on Job – though it is rather the sight of Yahweh than His words that affects him. He had heard of Him in the past, now he sees Him, and, like Isaiah, he is broken and humbled (Isaiah 6); before the living God he knows himself a sinner, his arguments about his righteousness are gone, his mouth is shut, he repents in dust and ashes (40.3–5; 42.2f, 5f). This is Job's conversion. Really to know the true God is to be humbled and crushed; the cry of true faith is 'Have mercy upon me a sinner!'

After this repentance the final restoration is full of significance, not an anticlimax. In the saga Job had been vindicated for the sake of his own righteousness; in our book it is the penitent Job who is restored, not for the sake of his own merit but out of free grace. God's grace is vindicated as grace. In 42.7f Yahweh says that Job has spoken of Him the thing that is right; this does not mean that on the whole Job's sincerity despite its frequently blasphemous expression is preferred to the hypocritical flatteries of the friends, but refers simply to Job's confession in 40.3–5; 42.2f, 5f. But not only is Job restored; the friends are condemned; they have spoken wrongly of God, their doctrine of retribution has dishonoured Him. It was false because it took away the place of grace, and reduced religion to legalism. It made the initiative depend on man; man must be good and then God will be gracious; whereas grace means that the initiative is God's. Thus human piety was robbed of its sincerity, because it was given an ulterior motive; men were to love God in order to get prosperity, instead of out of gratitude for His undeserved love. Moreover, the doctrine led inevitably to self-righteousness. But the friends are forgiven – in answer to Job's prayer. The man whom God has forgiven must forgive his enemies – and his friends! – and pray for them.

The true nature of sin (man's attempt to make himself instead of God the centre) and the real sinfulness of man's goodness in its essential self-centredness are revealed. Man's religion, too, is self-centred; for he thinks of God as existing for his convenience – i.e., he worships an idol he himself has made. From this self-centredness only the true God's self-revelation (chapters 38ff) can save him. Disaster is God's hand shattering his false security in – mercy. Before the living God he knows himself a sinner, and repents. Only before an idol can man feel good. The contemporary doctrine of retribution is condemned, because it takes neither God nor sin seriously, and is a denial of grace. Because the book bears witness to the living God in His majesty and grace, it is a real answer to the problem of suffering. Job finds peace before and quite apart from his material restoration – in God's presence.

In all this the Book of Job is, surely, in its own special way an eloquent witness to Jesus Christ.

XIV
THE SIGNIFICANCE OF διὰ παντός IN ROMANS 11.10[1]

Both the AV and the RV render διὰ παντός in Rom 11.10 by 'alway' (the RV has: 'Let their eyes be darkened, that they may not see, And bow thou down their back alway'). The Twentieth Century New Testament[2] simply removed the archaism by adding an 's'. But J. Moffatt,[3] R. F. Weymouth,[4] the RSV, Professor C. K. Barrett (in the translation given in his commentary on Romans),[5] and now the NEB,[6] have all substituted 'for ever'. At first sight this may seem a not very significant alteration. But, while it is true that, on the one hand, 'alway(s)' can have the strong sense of 'world without end', 'eternally', and, on the other hand, 'for ever' can be used in a weak sense (as, for example, in the sentence, 'John Smith is for ever grumbling'), it would, I think, be generally agreed that the idea of endlessness, of something going on throughout eternity, is much more definitely suggested by 'for ever' (especially when it is placed in a position of emphasis in the sentence) than it is by 'alway(s)'. The intelligent but Greekless reader who compares the various translations will naturally conclude that, according to the best modern scholarship, St Paul is here quoting an OT prayer that God may bend down certain people's backs in an

[1] First published in F. L. Cross (ed.), *Studia Evangelica* II, 1, Berlin, 1964, pp. 546–550.

[2] London, 1904.

[3] James Moffatt, *A New Translation of the Bible*, London, 1926.

[4] R. F. Weymouth, *The New Testament in Modern Speech*, 5th ed. London, 1929.

[5] C. K. Barrett, *A Commentary on the Epistle to the Romans*, London, 1957.

[6] In the 2nd ed. of the NEB New Testament (1970) 'for ever' was replaced by 'unceasingly'.

197

everlasting bondage from which there is absolutely no hope of release. It is of considerable interest to know whether these modern translations have really represented the original more faithfully at this point than the AV and RV. Is 'for ever' a more accurate translation of διὰ παντός here than 'alway'?

As Rom 11.10 is a quotation from Ps 69 (it follows the LXX version of verse 23 exactly), we shall first consider the Hebrew word *tamid* which lies behind διὰ παντός here. In the second place, we must see how διὰ παντός is used in Greek generally and in the NT in particular. And, finally, we must ask whether the context of Rom 11.10 throws any light on the way in which Paul understands the psalm.

1. *What does tamid mean?* According to Brown, Driver and Briggs,[1] the noun *tamid* means 'continuity', and appears most often used as an adverb meaning '*continually: a.* of going on without interruption = *continuously*' and '*b.* of regular repetition'. Of these uses the former is the more common. It is seen in Jer 6.7, in which God is represented as complaining with reference to Jerusalem thus: 'As a well casteth forth her waters, so she casteth forth her wickedness: violence and spoil is heard in her; before me continually is sickness and wounds'. Very frequently the reference is to praising, or waiting upon, God continually (e.g. Ps 34.1; Hos 12.6); sometimes to ritual (e.g. Exod 27.20: the lamp to be kept burning continually). The latter use is illustrated by 2 Kgs 4.9 ('an holy man of God, which passeth by us continually' – i.e. repeatedly), and by various passages dealing with ritual to be regularly repeated. The word is also used as a substantive, almost always following

[1] F. Brown, S. R. Driver and C. A. Briggs, *A Hebrew and English Lexicon of the Old Testament*, Oxford, 1907; corrected imp. Oxford, 1952, p. 556.

another noun in the construct form: e.g. Ezek 39.14 ('men of continuity' – RV: 'men of continual employment', i.e. men continually employed for a particular purpose, namely, burying the dead); 2 Kgs 25.30 ('an allowance of continuity' – RV: 'a continual allowance' – of the allowance given by the king of Babylon to Jehoiachin 'every day a portion, all the days of his life'); and Exod 29.42 (of the 'continual burnt-offering' repeated every morning and evening).

The word *tamid* occurs more than a hundred times in the OT; but nowhere does it clearly have the strong sense which 'for ever' can have. Ps 119.44 might at first sight seem to be an example ('So shall I observe thy law continually For ever and ever'); but here *lᵉ'olam wa'ed* ('for ever and ever') is used in a weak sense – what is meant is surely 'all the days of my life'. When an OT writer wants to express the idea of 'world without end', he uses, not *tamid*, but such an expression as *lᵉ'olam* or *'ad 'olam* (though, as we have just seen, *lᵉ'olam* can also be used in a weak sense).

2. *What does* διὰ παντός *mean?* There is a slight inconsistency in Liddell and Scott[1] on the subject. Under διά, A.II.1, they give as the meaning of διὰ παντός simply 'continually'; but under πᾶς, D.IV, they give 'for ever, continually'. Altogether they mention only three examples (apart from one in Plato's *Republic* 407d in which διὰ παντός is not used temporally but means 'altogether'), though they indicate that the expression occurs more often. In Thucydides 1.38 it is used of the Corcyraeans' having been continually estranged from their mother-city Corinth; in Sophocles' *Ajax* 705 it might be translated 'for ever', but hardly has the strong sense; in Aeschylus' *Choephori* 862 it perhaps does mean 'for ever'

[1] H. G. Liddell and R. Scott, *A Greek-English Lexicon*, revised and augmented by H. Stuart Jones and R. McKenzie, Oxford, 1940.

in the strong sense. A few more examples of διὰ παντός in extra-biblical Greek may be gleaned from Arndt and Gingrich:[1] in *P. Lond.* 42.6 and *Berliner Griechische Urkunden* 1078.2 it clearly has a quite weak sense; and in the *Oracula Sibyllina* Fragment 1.17, while the context refers to God and the words εἰς αἰῶνα καὶ ἐξ αἰῶνος have just been used, διὰ παντός itself probably only has the sense of 'always', conveying the idea of continuousness rather than eternity (the actual phrase is ἄπαντα κρατῶν διὰ παντός). When we turn to the LXX, we find a large number of occurrences; but in the vast majority of them διὰ παντός represents *tamid* the significance of which we have already considered. In Isa 57.16 it renders *laneṣaḥ* (RV: 'always') which is parallel to *lᵉ'olam*. We may put this instance on the side of the strong meaning. The occurrences of διὰ παντός where there is no Hebrew text to compare add nothing of significance to what we have already seen.

In the NT διὰ παντός occurs ten times. It is used in Mk 5.5 (of the Gerasene demoniac who 'always, night and day, in the tombs and in the mountains, ... was crying out, and cutting himself with stones'); Lk 24.53 (the Eleven 'were continually in the temple, blessing God'); Acts 10.2 (of Cornelius 'who gave much alms to the people, and prayed to God alway'); Heb 9.6 ('the priests go in continually into the first tabernacle' [i.e. the Holy Place] in the course of their duties, in contrast with the High Priest going into the second tabernacle [i.e. the Holy of Holies] only once in the year); Heb 13.15 ('Through him then let us offer up a sacrifice of praise to God continually, that is, the fruit of lips which make confession to his name'). In none of these instances is there any question of διὰ παντός having the strong sense.

[1] W. F. Arndt and F. W. Gingrich, *A Greek-English Lexicon of the New Testament and other Early Christian Literature*, Cambridge, 1957.

There remain four occurrences (apart from the one which is the subject of this paper), which are perhaps not quite so clear. The first is Mt 18.10: 'See that ye despise not one of these little ones; for I say unto you, that in heaven their angels do always behold the face of my Father, which is in heaven.' But here the point is not that the little ones' angels will behold God's face for ever, but that now, in the time when the little ones are liable to be despised, they are continually doing so. The second is Acts 2.25, where Peter says: 'For David saith concerning him, I beheld the Lord always before my face; for he is on my right hand, that I should not be moved.' It is a quotation from Ps 16, and the διὰ παντός (RV: 'always') represents *tamid*. The passage is being applied to Jesus and to His resurrection. The thought of surviving death is, of course, prominent in the context, and so some suggestion of everlastingness may be said to be present; but the thought actually expressed by διὰ παντός is that of continuousness, not of going on throughout eternity. The third is Acts 24.16, where Paul says to Felix, 'Herein do I also exercise myself to have a conscience void of offence toward God and men alway'. If the RSV is right in taking διὰ παντός with ἀσκῶ, there is obviously no question of its having the strong sense: it is scarcely any more likely if διὰ παντός is taken (as it probably should be) with ἔχειν. The fourth occurrence is 2 Th 3.16: 'Now the Lord of peace himself give you peace at all times in all ways. The Lord be with you all.' There can be little doubt that the RV translation 'at all times' gives the right sense here. The thought is of all the various times and circumstances of the Thessalonian Christians' lives.

It is clear that, while in a very few cases διὰ παντός may have the strong sense of 'for ever', in the overwhelming majority it certainly does not. We may add that, when a NT writer wished to express the idea of 'for ever', 'world without end', he had other terms ready to hand, namely, εἰς τὸν αἰῶνα, εἰς τοὺς αἰῶνας, εἰς τοὺς αἰῶνας τῶν αἰώνων.

3. *What light, if any, does the context throw on the meaning of* διὰ παντός *in Rom 11.10?* Paul is applying to those Jews who are at present disobedient to the gospel words which in their original context in Ps 69 refer to those whom the psalmist speaks of as 'enemies', 'adversaries', 'them that hate me'. But Paul writes immediately after his quotation (in the RSV): 'So I ask, have they stumbled so as to fall? By no means! But through their trespass salvation has come to the Gentiles, so as to make Israel jealous. Now if their trespass means riches for the world, and if their failure means riches for the Gentiles, how much more will their full inclusion mean!' In view of this, to suggest that Paul understood the διὰ παντός in Ps 69.23 in the strong sense of 'for ever' is to do his powers of argumentation an injustice. The context of Rom 11.10 is conclusive evidence that Paul meant by διὰ παντός not 'for ever' in the sense of 'world without end', but 'continually'. He is thinking of a temporary exclusion of the majority of Jews which gives the Gentiles their chance. The bending down of the backs is not to go on for ever, but so long as it lasts it is to be continuous and sustained, not spasmodic.

We conclude, then, that the substitution of 'for ever' for the 'alway' of the AV and RV, so far from being an improvement, has obscured Paul's meaning. The older translation here is better. But better still is the late Mgr. Knox's rendering[1] – 'continually' – which is to be found also in the French versions of Segond[2] and Ostervald,[3] both of which have 'continuellement'.

[1] R. A. Knox, *The New Testament of our Lord and Saviour Jesus Christ newly translated from the Vulgate Latin*, London, 1944.
[2] L. Segond (trans.), *La Sainte Bible*, rev. ed. Geneva, 1942.
[3] J. F. Ostervald (trans.), *La Sainte Bible*, rev. ed. Paris, 1931.

XV
Μέτρον πίστεως IN ROMANS 12.3[1]

Three basic questions confront us in the phrase μέτρον πίστεως in Rom 12.3: (i) In what sense is μέτρον used? (ii) In what sense is πίστις used? (iii) What kind of genitive is πίστεως? While there has been a good deal of discussion and considerable disagreement among commentators about the second of these and about the meaning of the clause as a whole, with regard to the first there has been very widespread agreement that μέτρον here means *measure* in the sense of *measured quantity*, and this has carried with it agreement concerning the third question (the nature of the genitive). Μέτρον is understood in this sense by, for example, Origen,[2] Chrysostom,[3] Theodoret,[4] Oecumenius[5] (tenth century), Theophylact[6] (eleventh century), Luther,[7] Calvin,[8] Matthew Poole[9] (the seventeenth-century English Puritan commentator), Bengel,[10] and in more modern times – to mention just a few names – Beet,[11] H. C. G. Moule,[12] Sanday and

[1] A short study read at the St Andrews meeting of Studiorum Novi Testamenti Societas on 7 September, 1961, first published in *NTS* 8 (1961–62), pp. 345–351.

[2] J.-P. Migne, *Patrologia Graeca*, 14, col. 1211.

[3] Migne, *PG* 60, col. 599.   [4] *PG* 82, col. 188.

[5] *PG* 118, col. 565.   [6] *PG* 124, col 501.

[7] *D. Martin Luthers Werke: Kritische Gesamtausgabe* (Weimar) 57, 103. (I was unable to consult the previous volume which contains the *Vorlesung* on Romans.)

[8] *Corpus Reformatorum*, 77, col. 237.

[9] *Synopsis Criticorum aliorumque S. Scripturae Interpretum* 4, Pars Posterior, London, 1676, cols. 267–268.

[10] *Gnomon Novi Testamenti*, 1742; 3rd ed. reprinted London, 1862, p. 553.

[11] J. A. Beet, *A Commentary on St Paul's Epistle to the Romans*, 1877; 10th ed. London, 1902, pp. 318f.

[12] *The Epistle of St Paul to the Romans* (The Expositor's Bible), London, 1894, pp. 329f.

Headlam,[1] Denney,[2] Lagrange,[3] Pallis,[4] Schlatter,[5] Althaus,[6] Brunner,[7] Gaugler,[8] Michel,[9] Leenhardt,[10] Barrett,[11] and Huby-Lyonnet.[12] Neither Lietzmann[13] nor Dodd[14] comments on the phrase; but Lietzmann's translation is probably intended to be understood in this sense and Moffatt, whose translation Dodd is using, certainly takes μέτρον in this way. Of all these commentators only Michel gives any indication that μέτρον could be understood differently. Such agreement across the centuries is certainly impressive. But, in spite of it, I find it difficult to regard the question of the meaning of μέτρον here as closed. I propose, therefore: (I) to set out severally the various possible answers to these three questions; (II) to set out some, at least, of the possible combinations of these possibilities; and (III) to consider which of these combinations is the most probable interpretation of the phrase.

[1] W. Sanday and A. C. Headlam, *A Critical and Exegetical Commentary on the Epistle to the Romans*, Edinburgh, 1895; 3rd ed. 1898, p. 355.

[2] J. Denney in *The Expositor's Greek Testament* 2, London, 3rd ed. 1904, p. 689.

[3] M.-J. Lagrange, *Épître aux Romains*, Paris, 1916; reprinted 1950, p. 296.

[4] A. Pallis, *To the Romans: A Commentary*, Liverpool, 1920, p. 134.

[5] A Schlatter, *Gottes Gerechtigkeit: Ein Kommentar zum Römerbrief*, 1935; 3rd ed. Stuttgart, 1959, pp. 336f.

[6] P. Althaus, *Der Brief an die Römer*, 1935; 6th ed. Göttingen, 1949, pp. 107f.

[7] E. Brunner, *The Letter to the Romans* (1938), Eng. tr. of 1956 ed., London, 1959, pp. 103f.

[8] E. Gaugler, *Der Brief an die Römer* 2, Zurich, 1952, pp. 240f.

[9] O. Michel, *Der Brief an die Römer*, Göttingen, 1955, p. 265.

[10] F.-J. Leenhardt, *L'Épître de Saint Paul aux Romains*, Neuchâtel, 1957, pp. 173f.

[11] C. K. Barrett, *The Epistle to the Romans*, London, 1957, p. 235.

[12] J. Huby, *Saint Paul: Épître aux Romains* (new ed. by S. Lyonnet), Paris, 1957, pp. 415f.

[13] H. Lietzmann, *An die Römer*, 4th ed. Tübingen, 1933.

[14] C. H. Dodd, *The Epistle to the Romans*, London, 1932.

I

The noun μέτρον can denote (1) *a means of measurement*: (*a*) literally, *a measuring-rod* or *-line, vessel for measuring capacity*, etc.: for example, in Mk 4.24, ἐν ᾧ μέτρῳ μετρεῖτε μετρηθήσεται ὑμῖν . . .; (*b*) metaphorically, *a standard, norm*: for example, according to Protagoras,[1] man, and according to Plato,[2] God, is 'the measure of all things' (πάντων χρημάτων μέτρον); and in Xenophon's *Cyropaedia*[3] Mandane tells her young son Cyrus that his father's standard is not his own will but the law (μέτρον αὐτῷ οὐχ ἡ ψυχή, ἀλλ' ὁ νόμος); (2) *the result of measuring*: (*a*) *measurement, dimensions*, the *size, quantity, length*, of anything: for example, in Ezek 43.13, 'These are the measures (i.e. measurements) of the altar' (καὶ ταῦτα τὰ μέτρα τοῦ θυσιαστηρίου); (*b*) *that which has been measured, a measured quantity, length*, of anything: for example, in Homer's *Iliad* 7.471, 'a thousand measures' (χίλια μέτρα) of wine; (3) *due measure* or *limit, proportion*: so (*a*) *full measure, goal*: for example, in Hesiod's *Works and Days* 438, 'the full measure of youthful vigour' (ἥβης μέτρον); and in Eph 4.13, εἰς μέτρον ἡλικίας τοῦ πληρώματος τοῦ Χριστοῦ; (*b*) *limit*: for example, Aristotle asks whether there is a limit to the number of friends one can have (ἔστι τι μέτρον καὶ φιλικοῦ πλήθους);[4] (4) *metre, verse*.[5]

[1] Fr. 1 (in H. Diels, *Die Fragmente der Vorsokratiker* 2).
[2] *Leges* 4. 716c.
[3] 1.3.18.
[4] *Ethica Nicomachea*, 1170b, 30.
[5] On μέτρον cf. LSJ, p. 1123; W. F. Arndt and F. W. Gingrich, *A Greek–English Lexicon of the New Testament and other Early Christian Literature*, Cambridge, 1957, p. 516; K. Deissner in *TWNT* 4, pp. 635–638. It is interesting to compare M. Jastrow, *A Dictionary of the Targumim, etc.*, New York, 1950, p. 732, on *middah*; and also K. G. Kuhn, *Konkordanz zu den Qumrantexten*, Göttingen, 1960, p. 115, where seven occurrences of *middah* in the Dead Sea Scrolls are listed.

With regard to πίστις, we note the following meanings: (1) *faithfulness, trustworthiness*; (2) *faith* in the sense of Christian faith (*fides qua*); (3) *faith* in the sense of a special *charisma* possessed not by all, but only by some, Christians; (4) *faith* in the sense of 'the faith', the body of truth believed by Christians (*fides quae*); (5) *that which is entrusted, a trust*.

With regard to the genitive πίστεως, there would seem to be four possibilities to be considered; (1) a partitive genitive; (2) a genitive of apposition; (3) a subjective genitive; and (4) an objective genitive.

II

We may now tabulate, not all the various possible combinations, but those which seem to have some claim to consideration, as follows:

(*a*) Taking μέτρον in the sense of *standard*, πίστις in the sense of (Christian) *faith* or *fides qua*, and the genitive as a genitive of apposition (i.e. μέτρον 1(*b*); πίστις 2; genitive 2) – 'a standard (by which to measure, estimate, himself), namely (his) Christian faith'.

(*b*) Taking μέτρον and the genitive as in (*a*), and πίστις in the sense of *the faith*, the body of truth believed, *fides quae* (i.e. μέτρον 1(*b*); πίστις 4; genitive 2) – 'a standard (by which to measure himself), namely the faith'.

(*c*) Taking μέτρον in the sense of *measured quantity*, πίστις in the sense of (Christian) *faith, fides qua*, and the genitive as partitive (i.e. μέτρον 2(*b*); πίστις 2; genitive 1) – 'a measure (i.e. measured quantity) of faith'.

(*d*) Taking μέτρον and the genitive as in (*c*), and πίστις in the sense of (special miracle-working) *faith* (i.e. μέτρον 2(*b*); πίστις 3; genitive 1) – 'a measure (i.e. measured quantity) of (special miracle-working) faith'.

(*e*) Again taking μέτρον and the genitive as in (*c*), but πίστις in the sense of *that which is entrusted* (i.e. μέτρον 2 (*b*); πίστις 5; genitive 1) – 'a measure (i.e. measured quantity) of trust'.

(*f*) Taking μέτρον in the sense of *limit*, πίστις in the sense of (Christian) *faith, fides qua,* and the genitive as subjective (i.e. μέτρον 3 (*b*); πίστις 2; genitive 3) – 'a limit set by (his) faith'.

(*g*) Taking μέτρον and πίστις as in (*f*), and the genitive as objective (i.e. μέτρον 3 (*b*); πίστις 2; genitive 4) – 'a limit to his faith'.

(*h*) Taking μέτρον and the genitive as in (*g*), and πίστις in the sense of (special miracle-working) *faith* (i.e. μέτρον 3 (*b*); πίστις 3; genitive 4) – 'a limit to his (special miracle-working) faith'.

III

We have now to consider these various combinations with a view to determining which of them is the most probable. We may, I think, tentatively set (*b*) aside as not very likely. The fact that there is considerable doubt whether Paul anywhere else uses πίστις in the sense of *fides quae* should make us hesitate to accept this interpretation here, when other interpretations which are at least equally suitable to the context are possible. Moreover, even if we agree with Professor Bultmann[1] that Paul does sometimes use πίστις with this meaning, an examination of those passages in the NT where πίστις either has, or may plausibly be taken to have, this meaning, would, I think, lead us to expect that, had Paul here meant πίστις in the sense of *fides quae*, he would have written τὸ μέτρον τῆς πίστεως.

[1] *TWNT* 6, p. 214.

(*e*), which is the interpretation favoured by Pallis, who renders the whole clause 'each man according to the measure of trust apportioned to him by God' and takes the reference to be to 'office in the Church', should also, I think, be regarded as not very likely. It is true that LSJ gives some examples of πίστις used in this sense;[1] but they are very few, and, while πιστεύειν τινί τι is used in Lk 16.11; Jn 2.24, of entrusting something to someone, and the passive πιστεύεσθαί τι in Rom 3.2; Gal 2.7, etc., of receiving something as a trust, the noun πίστις is nowhere else used in the NT in this sense.

In spite of the considerable weight of support for taking πίστις to mean a special miracle-working faith (for example, Oecumenius, Theophylact, Lagrange, Barrett, Huby-Lyonnet), both (*d*) and (*h*) should, in my opinion, also be set aside as improbable, on the ground that Paul is here explicitly addressing *all*[2] the members of the Roman Church (λέγω γὰρ ... παντὶ τῷ ὄντι ἐν ὑμῖν ... ἑκάστῳ ὡς ὁ θεὸς ἐμέρισεν ...), while he clearly regards the special miracle-working faith as something possessed not by all, but only by some, Christians (cf. 1 Cor 12.8–11).

With regard to (*f*) and (*g*), while (*f*), particularly, makes excellent sense and suits the context admirably (a man's faith in Christ certainly does set a limit to his self-estimation), the fact that μέτρον does not seem to be used anywhere else in the NT in the sense 3 (*b*) (though the idea of limitation is sometimes prominent in contexts in which it is used, as, for example in 2 Cor 10.13–16) should perhaps, since μέτρον does occur quite a number of times in the NT, make us hesitate to accept either of these

---

[1] op. cit., p. 1408, under πίστις, III.

[2] Unless we are going to accept Venema's conjecture that τι has fallen out after ὄντι – a course which it would be extremely hard to justify.

interpretations. (This applies, of course, equally to (*h*), which we have already set aside on another ground.) Nevertheless, I am inclined to regard (*f*) as a stronger claimant than any other of the combinations we have so far considered.

A possible reason for hesitation with regard to (*c*) (though I do not want to put much weight on this) is the fact that, while πίστις occurs very frequently in Paul (in the thirteen epistles 146 times, excluding the Pastorals 110 times, excluding Ephesians also 102 times), there appears to be only one other place where the genitive πίστεως could be explained as partitive, Philem 6, which is very probably to be explained otherwise. This might suggest that the use of the genitive of πίστις partitively did not come readily to Paul.

It is a much more serious objection to (*c*), that, if it is accepted and if the usual interpretation of μὴ ὑπερφρονεῖν παρ' ὃ δεῖ φρονεῖν, ἀλλὰ φρονεῖν εἰς τὸ σωφρονεῖν is correct, the implication of the verse would seem to be that a Christian is to think of himself more highly than he thinks of his fellow-Christian who has a smaller quantity of faith[1] – an implication which it is very difficult to believe that St Paul intended.

But is the usual interpretation of μὴ ὑπερφρονεῖν, κ.τ.λ. correct? (By 'the usual interpretation' I mean that which takes φρονεῖν here to refer to a man's estimation of

[1] Chrysostom might seem to avoid this difficulty by putting the emphasis on ὁ θεὸς ἐμέρισεν; but, after the idea of μετρεῖν has been so much emphasized in the earlier part of the sentence (μὴ ὑπερ-, παρ' ὃ δεῖ, and, in this context, σωφρονεῖν), μέτρον can hardly be used unemphatically. A different way out of the difficulty would be to assume that Paul was thinking of all the μέτρα as being equal; but this must be rejected, since Paul clearly recognized that some Christians have more, and some less, faith (cf., for example, Rom 14.1 [though see on this now my I.C.C. *Romans*, pp. 697ff]; 2 Cor 10.15).

himself.) There is, of course, a very reputable body of opinion which interprets it differently, a body of opinion which includes Origen, Calvin, Schlatter and Michel, among others. Calvin, for example, takes Paul's meaning to be that we are not to range in our thinking beyond the limits of the amount of faith God has given to us. 'Praeceptum deinde sequitur', he says, 'quo et nos retrahit ab earum rerum investigatione, quae nihil quam tormentum ingeniis afferre queant, nullam vero aedificationem ...' and a bit later, 'Atque hic quidem exprimitur ratio illius sobriae sapientiae quam commemorat. Quando enim distributio gratiarum varia est, ita sibi optimum quisque sapiendi modum statuit dum se intra collatam sibi a Domino fidei gratiam continet.' But here I think we must agree with Erasmus rather than with Calvin, and, along with AV, RV, RSV, Moffatt, NEB, Barrett, Huby-Lyonnet, etc., accept what I have called 'the usual interpretation' of μὴ ὑπερφρονεῖν, κ.τ.λ.; for the philological evidence tells heavily in its favour, as does also, I think, the context in Romans 12.

If, then, μὴ ὑπερφρονεῖν, κ.τ.λ. is to be understood as referring to the Christian's estimation of himself, it seems to me that (c) must be regarded as improbable.[1] (This objection to (c) is also, of course, *mutatis mutandis* a further objection to (d) and (e).)

I turn now to (a), according to which μέτρον is used in

[1] Equally improbable is the variation of (c), according to which πίστεως stands for χάριτος by metonymy (so Theodoret: τὴν χάριν ἐνταῦθα πίστιν ἐκάλεσε. διὰ γὰρ πίστεως ἡ τῆς χάριτος δόσις, καὶ πρὸς τὸ μέτρον τῆς πίστεως χορηγεῖται τὰ δῶρα τῆς χάριτος. κελεύει δὲ τῇ δοθείσῃ χάριτι μετρεῖν τὸ φρόνημα τῆς ψυχῆς. Cf. Origen: '... hoc est, ut sciat unusquisque et intelligat quae in eo sit mensura gratiae Dei, quam consequi meruit per fidem'). On the variant reading χάριτος for πίστεως here in Rom 12.3 see G. Zuntz, *The Text of the Epistles*, London, 1953, p. 76.

the sense of *standard*,[1] πίστις in the sense of (Christian) *faith* (*fides qua*), and the genitive πίστεως is a genitive of apposition (for which we may compare Rom 4.11 (σημεῖον ... περιτομῆς), Jn 2.21 (περὶ τοῦ ναοῦ τοῦ σώματος αὐτοῦ) and perhaps 2 Cor 10.13 (τὸ μέτρον τοῦ κανόνος)). I can see no serious objection to this interpretation. The presence of μερίζειν in the clause, which might seem to suggest that the genitive should rather be taken as partitive, is not a serious objection; for 1 Cor 7.17 is clear evidence that Paul could use μερίζειν without having any strictly partitive idea in mind. On the other hand, there is much to be said in favour of this interpretation.

It should perhaps first be pointed out that *means of measurement* is actually the primary meaning of μέτρον. In the NT μέτρον is used in this sense quite often (for example, Mt 7.2; Mk 4.24; Rev 21.15). It occurs only five times in the Pauline Epistles apart from Rom 12.3. While in Eph 4.7 it should probably be understood in sense 2 (*b*) and in Eph 4.13 and probably also in 16 it is used in sense 3, in 2 Cor 10.13 (where it occurs twice) it probably both times has the sense *means of measurement, standard* (cf. H. W. Beyer in *TWNT* 3, pp. 603f.: *contra* K. Deissner in *TWNT* 4, p. 637). It is interesting to note that in Aristotle's *Nicomachean Ethics* it occurs (according to Bywater's index)[2] ten times – nine times in the sense of *means of measurement* and once in the sense of *limit*. In Greek philosophy, as Deissner points out,[3] the concept of the μέτρον/*means of measurement* played a significant

---

[1] Abelard's comment (Migne, *Patrologia Latina* 178, col. 939: '*Sicut Deus divisit mensuram fidei*, id est prout credit faciendum esse, ita hoc impleat') might suggest that he understood *mensura* in this sense, but the sequel makes this doubtful.

[2] I. Bywater, *Aristotelis Ethica Nicomachea*, Oxford, 1890, p. 249.

[3] op. cit., p. 635.

part (Protagoras, Plato, Neo-Platonism).[1]

But the strongest support for interpretation (*a*) comes from the context and the excellence of the sense which results. To begin with the most immediate context, v. 3 itself, this interpretation agrees well with the words παντὶ τῷ ὄντι ἐν ὑμῖν and ἑκάστῳ (for every Christian has been given μέτρον πίστεως in this sense) and with μὴ ὑπερφρονεῖν παρ' ὃ δεῖ φρονεῖν, ἀλλὰ φρονεῖν εἰς τὸ σωφρονεῖν. Every member of the Church, instead of thinking of himself more highly than he ought, is so to think of himself as to think soberly, measuring himself by the standard which God has given him in his faith. When Christians measure themselves by themselves (or by their fellow-Christians or their pagan neighbours), they display their lack of understanding (cf. 2 Cor 10.12), and are sure to have too high (or else too low) an opinion of themselves; but, when they measure themselves by the standard which God has given them in their faith, they then – and only then – achieve a sober and true estimate of themselves as, equally with their fellows, both sinners revealed in their true colours by the judgment of the Cross and also the objects of God's undeserved and triumphant mercy in Jesus Christ.

Verses 4 and 5 are, I think, best understood as explaining (note the γάρ in v. 4) what measuring oneself by this standard means for one's estimation of oneself in relation to one's fellow-Christians. Those who do measure themselves by the standard which God has provided for them in their faith will not fail to discern the one body; they will recognize that they do not exist for themselves but are ἀλλήλων μέλη, and that their fellow-

[1] There is an interesting occurrence of *middah* apparently meaning 'standard' in the Dead Sea Scrolls, 1QS viii.4: ... *uᵏhithallek 'im kol bᵉmiddat ha'ᵉmet ubᵉtikkun ha'et* ... (An original *bysdt* has been corrected to *bmdt*.)

Christians, whether their gifts are more, or less, impressive than their own, are equally with themselves members of the one body.

The sequel (vv. 6–8) indicates the unselfconscious, businesslike, sober way in which such Christians will give themselves to the fulfilment of the tasks apportioned to them by the χαρίσματα they have received, using their particular χαρίσματα to the full in the service of God and of one another, undistracted by futile calculations about precedence. In v. 6 κατὰ τὴν ἀναλογίαν τῆς πίστεως has a special interest for us in view of the close correspondence between it and ἑκάστῳ ὡς ὁ θεὸς ἐμέρισεν μέτρον πίστεως[1] – a correspondence underlined in the Peshitta Syriac by the use of the same word to translate both μέτρον and ἀναλογία. If κατὰ τὴν ἀναλογίαν τῆς πίστεως means, as I think (*pace* G. Kittel[2] *et al.*) it does, 'according to the standard which he has in his faith' (i.e. the prophet is to test what he says by his faith to see whether it agrees with it), then it supports interpretation (*a*).

And when we look back to vv. 1 and 2, which set forth the theme of the whole division 12.1–15.13, what else does the ἀνακαίνωσις τοῦ νοός mean but ever more and more consistently to measure oneself and all things by the standard which God has given one in one's faith and so to become ever more and more able δοκιμάζειν ... τί τὸ θέλημα τοῦ θεοῦ, τὸ ἀγαθὸν καὶ εὐάρεστον καὶ τέλειον?

My tentative conclusion, then, is that μέτρον πίστεως in Rom 12.3 means 'a standard (by which to measure himself), namely (his) Christian faith'. But, since the all-important thing in Christian faith is not the activity of the believer but the Object believed in, to say that the

---

[1] ἑκάστῳ, κ.τ.λ. would seem to be equivalent to ἕκαστος κατὰ τὸ μέτρον τῆς πίστεως, ὃ ἐμέρισεν αὐτῷ ὁ θεός.

[2] *TWNT* 1, p. 350f.

Christian is to measure himself and all things by his faith is really to say that he is to measure himself and all things by Jesus Christ. The μέτρον πίστεως is really Jesus Christ Himself[1] as the Standard and Norm. For the Christian Jesus Christ Himself – and He alone – is the true πάντων χρημάτων μέτρον.

---

[1] K. Barth, *Der Römerbrief*, 2nd ed. reprinted Munich, 1929, p. 429, allows for an identification of the μέτρον πίστεως with Jesus Christ, but he translates μέτρον *Ziel* ('Ist der gekreuzigte Christus das "Ziel des Glaubens, das Gott einem Jeden (und zwar Jedem gerade in seiner Einzelnheit!) zugewiesen hat" ...'). In his *Kurze Erklärung des Römerbriefes*, Munich, 1956, p. 186, he has: '... dass er darauf sinne, besonnen zu sein, was dann sofort damit erklärt wird: dass er den ihm von Gott bestimmten Lauf seines christlichen Glaubens antrete und vollende (v. 3).' But in neither commentary does he anywhere, as far as I can see, make absolutely clear exactly how he understands the phrase μέτρον πίστεως.

XVI
CHANGES OF PERSON AND
NUMBER IN PAUL'S EPISTLES[1]

A good many of the problems connected with Paul's
varying uses of the first, second and third persons singular
and plural and the apparent suddenness of his changes
from one person to another have, of course, often been
noted and studied; but the whole subject strikes us as
fascinating, and we cannot help wondering whether a
careful, systematic and comprehensive study of it might
not make some modest but worthwhile contribution to
the exegesis of the epistles – though any one engaging in
such a piece of research would be well advised not to take
himself too seriously or to try to claim for his 'findings' a
greater reliability than could properly be ascribed to
them. Such a study is quite beyond the range of a brief
paper. All that can be undertaken here is to note just a few
of the things which have interested us in this area.

I

It will be convenient to start with Paul's use of the second
person plural and his transitions to it from other persons,
because the occurrence of the second person plural in
itself clearly requires no explanation in letters addressed
to communities. Its frequent occurrence is only to be
expected. We may notice that Paul occasionally uses it
with reference not to the community, to which his letter is
addressed, as a whole, but just to a particular section of it.
Thus in Rom 11.13, 25, 28, 30f, the second person plural

[1] First published in M. D. Hooker and S. G. Wilson (ed.), *Paul and Paulinism: essays in honour of C. K. Barrett*, London, 1982, pp. 280–289.

refers to the Gentiles in the Christian community in Rome, not to the whole community. But what interests us particularly is the question whether it is possible to detect any special significance in Paul's transitions to the second person plural when he has been using another person.[1] We may look at a few examples.

An interesting one is to be seen in 1 Cor 15.58. In the preceding verse the first person plural has been used ('but thanks be to God, which giveth us the victory through our Lord Jesus Christ').[2] The second person plural has occurred only once (in v. 51: 'Behold, I tell you a mystery') since v. 34 ('Awake up righteously, and sin not; ... I speak *this* to move you to shame'). Then in v. 58 we have 'Therefore, my beloved brethren, be ye stedfast, unmoveable, always abounding in the work of the Lord, forasmuch as ye know that your labour is not vain in the Lord'. In this situation the second person plural imperative seems to us to be a good deal more forceful than an exhortation in the first person plural would have been. The effect of the sudden change to the second person plural imperative seems to be to recall the Corinthian Christians with a certain peremptoriness from thoughts of future glory, on which they may well have been too ready to dwell, to the urgent demands of the present for resolute obedience to the Lord Jesus Christ.

In 1 Cor 10.13 the effect of the return to the second person plural is rather different. The verse is the conclusion of a paragraph which began with this person

---

[1] The possibility that some of these changes were motivated by nothing more serious than a desire for variety or are merely accidental is not to be ruled out. Textual variants often occur where there are changes of person; but, since the tendency to assimilate was strong, readings which involve a change of person are, other things being equal, probably to be preferred to those which do not.

[2] We shall quote the English Revised Version unless we indicate otherwise.

(v. 1: 'For I would not, brethren, have you ignorant . . .') but is more strongly characterized by the use of the first person plural (vv. 6, 8f, 11) than by use of the second person plural (vv. 7 and 10). After the warning note sounded by the third person singular imperative of v. 12 ('Wherefore let him that thinketh he standeth take heed lest he fall') the return to the second person plural in v. 13 ('There hath no temptation taken you but such as man can bear: but God is faithful, who will not suffer you to be tempted above that ye are able; but will with the temptation make also the way of escape, that ye may be able to endure it') seems to give additional emphasis to the comfort and encouragement which are being offered.

In Rom 8.9a there is an interesting change from the third persons plural and singular of vv. 5–8 to the second person plural, which is then continued (after the third person singular in the parenthetic v. 9b) in vv. 10 and 11. We suggest that by introducing the second person plural at this point, when it has not been used since 7.4 (though the second person singular was, it is true, used in 8.2, which will be discussed below), Paul is emphasizing the contrast between those whom he thus addresses directly ('But ye are not in the flesh, but in the spirit [RV: but "Spirit" is surely to be preferred], if so be that the Spirit of God dwelleth in you') and those about whom he says in v. 8, 'they that are in the flesh cannot please God'. The continuation of this direct address in vv. 10 and 11 is natural enough. The extraordinary series of changes of person which follow in vv. 12–18 will be more appropriately discussed under III. It is interesting that in Romans the use of the second person plural, while it is frequent in 1.1–15 and 15.14–16.27, is in the rest of the epistle – apart from the passages in chapter 8 already mentioned in this paragraph – confined to 2.24; 6.3, 11–14, 16–22; 7.1, 4; 11.13ff (the occurrences mentioned above in which the reference is to the Gentile Christians alone); 12.1–3, 9–19; 13.6–8, 11, 14; 14.1, 16; 15.5–7, 13.

II

We turn next to the use of the second person singular. One reason for the relative scarcity of occurrences of the second person plural in Romans is the frequency of the use of the second person singular (see 2.1, 3–5, 17–23, 25, 27; 8.2; 9.19f; 10.6, 8f; 11.17–22, 24; 12.20f; 13.3b–4; 14.4, 10, 15, 20–22). In chapter 2 Paul apostrophizes those who set themselves up to judge others. That from v. 17 to the end of the chapter he has the Jews in mind is clear, but we agree with those who think that Paul has them in mind right from v. 1. It is for the sake of greater forcefulness that the individual is addressed. The use of the second person singular in chapter 11 is not quite the same; for, whereas in chapter 2 Paul is apostrophizing the typical individual member of a group which is neither the community to which the letter as a whole is addressed nor yet a section of that community, so that the use of the second person singular is a somewhat artificial rhetorical device, in 11.17–22, 24, he uses the second person singular as a means of bringing home what he has to say as vividly as possible to each individual in the particular section of the Roman church which he is specially addressing in this passage of his letter (see 11.13).

In Rom 12.20 ('But if thine enemy hunger . . .') the second person singular belongs to the OT quotation, and the use of the same person in v. 21 ('Be not overcome of evil, but overcome evil with good') is natural enough. The individual Roman Christian is directly addressed. In Rom 10.6, 8f also Paul is using OT passages, and the second person singular comes with what he takes over

('Say not in thy heart, . . . The word is nigh thee, in thy mouth, and in thy heart: . . . with thy mouth . . . in thy heart'), and again he continues with the same person in his own 'thou shalt be saved' at the end of v. 9. In Rom 13.3f the individual believer is addressed for the sake of vividness and forcefulness; and in chapter 14 the force of the appeal is greatly strengthened when in vv. 4 and 10a the individual 'weak' Christian is addressed and in vv. 10b, 15 and 20–22 the individual 'strong' Christian. The second person singular in 9.19f is directed to an objector (cf. 1 Cor 15.35–37).

The most interesting occurrence of the second person singular in Romans is surely that in 8.2, which is altogether unexpected and isolated. The best explanation of the σε[1] would seem to be that Paul, being very conscious of the amazing and momentous nature of the affirmation he was making and of its apparent incompatibility with what he had just said in the latter part of chapter 7, and fearing that its significance would be likely to be missed, hoped to compel the most alert attention possible by thus suddenly addressing the individual Roman Christian: 'the law of the Spirit of life has in Christ Jesus set thee free from the law of sin and of death' (our translation).

There is an interesting and significant variation between the second person singular and the second person plural in the Epistle to Philemon. In vv. 2, 4–22a and 23, the second person singular is used, the reference being to Philemon himself; but in vv. 3, 22b and 25, where Paul is associating with Philemon the other people mentioned in v. 2 (Apphia, Archippus and the church meeting in Philemon's house), the second person plural is

---

[1] On the textual question reference may be made to C. E. B. Cranfield, *A Critical and Exegetical Commentary on the Epistle to the Romans* I, Edinburgh, [3]1980, pp. 376f.

used. The distinction disappears in the modern English versions – without trace.

The disastrously flattening effect of the abandonment of the second person singular in translation may be vividly illustrated by setting side by side the 1611 rendering of 1 Cor 15.35f ('But some *man* will say, How are the dead raised up? . . . *Thou* fool, that which thou sowest . . .') and the 1881 rendering ('But some one will say, How are the dead raised? . . . Thou foolish one, that which thou thyself sowest . . .'), on the one hand, and the translation in the NEB ('But, you may ask, how are the dead raised? . . . How foolish! The seed you sow . . .'), on the other.[1]

[1] Perhaps it would not be out of place to record here our conviction that the jettisoning of the second person singular in recent English versions has not just resulted in a lessening of accuracy in detail and a considerable literary impoverishment, but has also effected a much more serious and substantial loss. By obliterating what we would call 'the evangelical second person singular', that use of the second person singular which so often, both in the OT and in the NT, expresses with pointed directness and haunting appeal the truth that God's grace and judgment concern not just men in general but each individual man in particular, it has obscured something utterly essential to the gospel, which it is always the Church's duty to try to declare as unambiguously as possible. In a day when the individual, unless he happens to belong to a privileged élite of power, wealth or ability, tends to count for less and less, and is often oppressed by his consciousness of the fact, one might have expected the Church to cherish every resource at its disposal for emphasizing the direct appeal of the gospel to the individual. It is, in our view, an extraordinary ineptitude hastily to throw away the means our language possesses for expressing directly that gospel truth which cannot be so readily or effectively expressed without it, on the ground that it seems archaic to our bourgeois taste (it is still to be heard in ordinary use in some parts of the country among manual workers), and to insist on preferring to it the plural of politeness which originated as a servile plural in the rigid class distinctions of a feudal society (the serf addressing his manor lord in the plural while the lord addressed his serf in the singular). (That we also regard the deferential plural as a thoroughly inappropriate form of address to the God whose oneness is fundamental to the faith of Christians, Jews and Moslems alike need hardly be said!)

III

We turn now to the first person plural. A number of different uses may be distinguished.

The most obvious is that which joins together Paul and those to whom the particular epistle is addressed – though it should be noted from the start that it is often difficult, or maybe impossible, to be sure whether in a particular occurrence of the first person plural the 'we' is thus limited or includes Christians quite generally. This use is frequently alternated with that of the second person plural. Thus in Rom 8.9–17 we have the second person plural in vv. 9a and 10f (in the parenthetic v. 9b the third person singular is used) followed by the first person plural in v. 12, with which a new paragraph begins. The vocative 'brethren' makes it natural to understand the 'we' to mean just Paul and those addressed (though it does not necessitate it). By using the first person plural Paul takes his place alongside the Roman Christians rather than bringing out the contrast between himself and them. We might perhaps term this 'the first person plural of humility'. While the statement of obligation is not less authoritative, the fact that the authority is the authority of the gospel, to which Paul just as much as those he addresses is bound to submit, is emphasized rather than his own special position as an apostle. But in v. 13 he reverts to the second person plural with the warning and promise, 'for if ye live after the flesh, ye must die; but if by the spirit [RV: better "Spirit"?] ye mortify the deeds of the body, ye shall live'. We then get a statement in the third person plural (the general statement, 'For as many as are led by the Spirit of God, these are sons of God'). Verse 15 then starts off in the second person plural, but in the middle of v. 15b Paul changes to the first person plural: 'whereby we cry, Abba, Father'. This use of the first person plural is then continued in vv. 16 and 17. While in v. 12 Paul's motive in using the 'we' form was probably (as we suggested above) to get alongside his readers in a brotherly way, it may be suggested that in vv. 15b–17 its use was motivated rather by the desire to acknowledge his own personal involvement – we might perhaps call it a 'confessional first person plural'. In the rest of the chapter the first person plural is predominant. It may well be that the more inclusive 'we Christians' use should be recognized here.

For further examples of the use of the first person plural in which something of a confessional significance is perhaps to be discerned we may compare Rom 4.24f (in v. 25 a traditional formula is probably present); 5.1–11, 21; 6.1–8; 9.24 (the 'us', which is inserted rather awkwardly as far as the grammar is concerned, seems to have the effect of giving to the statement something of the character of a confession of faith); 15.4 and 7 (if Nestle 25th ed. is right as against 26th in reading ἡμᾶς: RV has 'you').

Rom 13.11–14 shows an interesting alternation between the second and first persons plural. Paul changes from the second person to the first person plural in the middle of v. 11. Then in vv. 12b–13 we have a hortatory use of the first person plural, Paul taking his place alongside the Christians of Rome in the consciousness that he himself too needs to try to do the things indicated. In v. 14 we have a crisp second person plural imperative. The three instances of the first person plural in Rom 14.10c, 12 and 13a ('for we shall all stand before the judgement-seat of God', 'So then each one of us shall give account of himself to God', and 'Let us not therefore judge one another any more', respectively) may all perhaps, like those in 13.12b–13, be regarded as examples of what we called above 'the first person plural of humility'.

In Rom 14.7f the first person plural is used in what would seem to be general doctrinal statements concerning all Christians. For some further instances of this usage, in which the 'we' most probably means Christians generally, reference may be made to 1 Cor 15.19, 49, 51f, 57; Phil 3.3, 20f; 1 Th 4.14f (though here the 'we' of the λέγομεν is different), and 17.

Another use of the first person plural is that to be found in Rom 15.1, where 'we that are strong' refers to Paul together with one particular section of the Christians to whom the letter is addressed.

Elsewhere Paul uses the same person to associate himself with his fellow-Jews (e.g. Rom 3.9; 4.1; 9.10).

Two other uses may be mentioned together: first, the special use of οἴδαμεν δέ in Rom 2.2; 3.19; 8.28; and 1 Tim 1.8 and of οἴδαμεν γάρ in Rom 7.14; 8.22; 2 Cor 5.1, to introduce a statement which the writer can assume will be generally acceptable to those whom he is addressing or whom he has in mind (the use of οἴδαμεν in 1 Cor 8.1 and 4 may also be compared, though it is somewhat different); and, secondly, the formula τί ἐροῦμεν, which is employed in Rom 3.5; 6.1; 7.7 and 9.14 to introduce an indication of a possible false inference from what Paul has been saying before rejecting it, in Rom 8.31 and 9.30 to introduce his own conclusion, and in Rom 4.1 to introduce the case of Abraham to clinch his argument.

The fact that the superscriptions of a number of the epistles include one or two other names alongside that of Paul[1] raises the question whether some of the first person plurals refer to Paul and persons associated with him in the composition of his letters. But this question cannot be isolated from another question, namely, that of the possible presence in the Pauline epistles of instances of an

[1] In Gal 1.1–2 we have 'Paul . . . and all the brethren which are with me'.

223

author's or literary plural with reference simply to Paul himself. So we shall consider the two together. In the case of 1 Thessalonians, which is written in the names of Paul, Silvanus and Timothy, it seems fairly natural to understand the first person plurals as far as 2.16 to refer to the three colleagues (apart from the double 'our' in 1.3 which is more naturally understood to refer to Christians generally or to the three colleagues and the people addressed). The use of the plural 'apostles' in 2.6 [RV: in Nestle 2.7] would seem to be some support for this interpretation. But, when 2.17–3.13 is taken into consideration, doubts arise. Does 'I Paul once and again' in 2.18 just emphasize Paul's own eagerness which was part of the common eagerness of the three colleagues or does it interpret the first person plurals 'we would fain' and 'us' in the same verse? And are we to understand the first person plural 'sent' (ἐπέμψαμεν) in 3.2 as referring to Paul and Silvanus or are we, in view of the use of the first person singular in 3.5 ('For this cause I also, when I could no longer forbear, sent') to take it to refer to Paul alone? And, when we turn to the end of the epistle, what are we to make of 'I adjure' in 5.27? Does it stand in contrast with 'we exhort' in 4.10, 'we would' in 4.13, 'we say' in 4.15, 'we beseech' in 5.12 and 'we exhort' in 5.14, or does it rather interpret these occurrences of the first person plural? In 2 Cor 1.19, at any rate, it is clear that 'us' refers to Paul, Silvanus and Timothy, since it is explicitly so interpreted; and it seems likely that the first person plural pronouns in the following three verses have the same reference. Another clear instance of a first person plural referring to Paul and a colleague is to be seen in 1 Cor 4.6 ('Now these things, brethren, I have in a figure transferred to myself and Apollos for your sakes; that in us ye might learn . . .'), and the first person plurals in vv. 1 and 8 may best be explained as having the same reference. Compare 1 Cor

9.6 ('Or I only and Barnabas, have we not a right to forbear working?') and the possibility that some other first person plurals in the context may also refer to Paul and Barnabas. The expression 'us the apostles' in 1 Cor 4.9 probably has a wider reference than Paul and Apollos.

That Paul did sometimes use the first person plural with reference simply to himself we regard as almost certain. It has been claimed that no such author's plural is to be found in those epistles of the Pauline corpus the superscriptions of which do not associate one or more persons with Paul.[1] But 'we received' in Rom 1.5 ('through whom we received grace and apostleship, unto obedience of faith among all the nations') is, we think, most probably to be explained as such a plural;[2] and βλασφημούμεθα and ἡμᾶς in 3.8 and προῃτιασάμεθα in 3.9 of the same epistle are surely also most naturally so explained. In 1 and 2 Corinthians (both of which do have more than one name in the superscription) there are quite a number of first person plurals which it seems most natural to take as referring simply to Paul: for example, those in 1 Cor 9.11f (in view of the use of the first person singular in the sequel); those in 2 Cor 1.4–14 and 18 (compare vv. 15–17) and 24 (compare v. 23); 7.5–7 (note the combination of the plural and singular of the first person pronoun in v. 7 and the continuation in the first person singular in vv. 8ff); 7.12–8.8 (note the occurrences of the first person singular in 7.12, 14, 16; 8.3 and 8) and 9.3 ('our glorying on your behalf': cf. 'your readiness, of which I glory on your behalf' in the previous verse).

From what has been said above it is clear, we think, that there is scope for a good deal of further, and more careful,

---

[1] So, for example, in F. Blass and A. Debrunner, *A Greek Grammar of the New Testament and other early Christian literature*, Eng. tr. by R. W. Funk, Cambridge, 1961, §280.
[2] See further Cranfield, op. cit., p. 65.

investigation of the occurrences of the first person plural in Paul's epistles.

IV

We must look now briefly at Paul's use of the first person singular. We refer, first, to two points in connexion with Rom 1.8–16. One is the use of the genitive of the first person singular pronoun with 'God' in v. 8. It is something which is not common in Paul's letters, being limited otherwise to Phil 1.3 and Philem 4, which are similar contexts to this, and 2 Cor 12.21 and Phil 4.19 (it occurs also in some authorities in 1 Cor 1.4). It strikes a strongly personal note reminiscent of some passages in the Psalms. Compare 'Jesus Christ my Lord' in Phil 3.8 and 'who loved me, and gave himself up for me' in Gal 2.20. The other point is just that the contrast between the ordinary use of the first person singular in these verses and the – if we were right about 'we received' – perhaps somewhat formal and official tone of v. 5 may be noted.

A number of places where there is a specially emphatic use may be noted: Rom 9.3 (ηὐχόμην γὰρ ἀνάθεμα εἶναι αὐτὸς ἐγὼ ἀπὸ τοῦ Χριστοῦ ὑπὲρ τῶν ἀδελφῶν μου τῶν συγγενῶν μου κατὰ σάρκα); 2 Cor 10.1 (Αὐτὸς δὲ ἐγὼ Παῦλος παρακαλῶ ὑμᾶς ... ὃς κατὰ πρόσωπον μὲν ταπεινὸς ἐν ὑμῖν, ἀπὼν δὲ θαρρῶ εἰς ὑμᾶς); 1 Th 2.18 (διότι ἠθελήσαμεν ἐλθεῖν πρὸς ὑμᾶς, ἐγὼ μὲν Παῦλος καὶ ἅπαξ καὶ δίς ...). There is a special emphasis also in the first person singular perfect passive (πέπεισμαι) in Rom 8.38 following the use of the first person plural (referring to Christians generally) in v. 37: it was surely intended to emphasize the character of personal testimony possessed by vv. 38 and 39. Emphatic also are the instances of the first person singular in Rom 14.14 ('I know, and am persuaded in the Lord Jesus . . .') and 15.14 ('And I myself also am persuaded of you, my brethren, . . .'). Mention may also be made of Rom 11.1 ('. . . for I also am an Israelite . . .'), where Paul appeals to the evidence afforded by the fact that the chosen apostle of the Gentiles is himself a Jew. We may notice here that, while sometimes Paul seems to use a first person plural with a certain authoritative formality and solemnity (so, we think, in Rom 1.5), he seems also on occasion to employ the first person singular with a specially solemn effect (e.g. λέγω in Rom 12.3 and 15.8; παρακαλῶ in Rom 12.1).

There seems also to be a generalizing use of the first person singular in a number of places in the Pauline epistles. We mention as probable examples Rom 3.7 ('But if the truth of God through my lie abounded unto his glory, why am I also still judged as a sinner?'); 1 Cor 6.15b (cf. v. 12); 10.29f; 13.1–3, 11f; 14.11 (cf. vv. 14f); Gal 2.18. The most discussed passage in this connexion is Rom 7.7–25; but, as we have recently discussed it at some length elsewhere,[1] we refrain from treating it here.

V

The third person singular and plural in Paul's epistles we can do no more here than just touch on. That the occurrences are very numerous goes without saying; but there are some things in particular which we should want to consider, if space permitted, as, for example, the passages of some length which are prevailingly in the third person plural; the characteristics and functions of short third person singular or plural statements introduced in

[1] op cit., pp. 340–370 (especially 342–347).

the course of passages marked by the use of another person; and Paul's apparent reference to himself in the third person (2 Cor 12.2–5).

Perhaps what has been said above may be, in spite of its cursoriness and other very obvious defects, enough to suggest that Paul's uses of the different persons and his sometimes remarkably rapid transitions from one to another (which surely contribute a good deal to the general impression of vivacity which one gets from his epistles) may deserve rather closer attention than they usually receive.

XVII
THE CHURCH AND DIVORCE AND THE RE-MARRIAGE OF DIVORCED PERSONS IN THE LIGHT OF MARK 10.1–12[1]

The clue to the understanding of this passage is the statement of Jesus in v. 5: 'For your hardness of heart he [that is, Moses] wrote you this commandment'. Emphasis falls on 'for your hardness of heart'. The commandment referred to is the provision of Deut 24.1 that a man divorcing his wife must give her a written certificate of divorce. The Pharisees had referred to this as though it meant that God had no objection to divorce and that one might divorce one's wife with complacent assurance of God's full approval provided one gave the required certificate (v. 4). Jesus, by referring to the hardness of heart which necessitated the provision, by reminding His questioners of the Genesis account of God's original institution of marriage (vv. 6–8), and by His clear prohibition, 'What therefore God hath joined together, let not man put asunder' (v. 9), was not (as is often alleged) brushing aside Deut 24.1 and taking a rigorist stance, but was drawing attention to something extremely important which the Pharisees were inclined to ignore, namely, the need to distinguish clearly between those elements of the OT law which set forth the perfect will of God (what we may call – in one sense of the word – His

[1] An earlier version of this was included in a collection of papers, *Marriage, divorce and remarriage*, published by the United Reformed Church in 1978. For detailed exegesis of the passage reference may be made to my *The Gospel according to Saint Mark*, Cambridge, [8]1983, pp. 317–322.

absolute will, that is, His will in itself, not affected by the fact and the results of human sin), on the one hand, and, on the other hand, those elements which, taking into account the fact of men's sinfulness, indicate not God's perfect, absolute will, but His will in response to the circumstances brought about by human sin.

Whereas Exod 20.14 and the passages from Genesis quoted in Mk 10.6–8 represent God's will in itself, Deut 24.1 is of the other sort, an expression of God's will in response to the consequences of human sin, a merciful provision intended to protect, in some measure at least, those who in the circumstances of a particular society would be likely to suffer most from them. Jesus is seeking to make His questioners face this distinction and realize that it is by the perfect will of God, that is, by His absolute commandments and not His commandments which are a response to men's sin and its results, that those who believe in God ought to judge their own lives. So He recalls them from concentration upon the merciful provision contained in Deut 24.1, which takes account of men's hardness of heart and is intended to alleviate its bitter consequences, to the serious consideration of the verses of Genesis which express God's perfect will with regard to marriage (Gen 1.27; 2.21–23), underlining their significance by His prohibition (Mk 10.9), and then in v. 11f directs His disciples' attention to the absolute commandment of Exod 20.14 by His use of 'committeth adultery'.

I shall try now to bring out as clearly as I can what seems to me to be the significance of this passage for us in the light of the biblical witness as a whole.

1. While the special importance for the well-being of society of marriage and the stability of home-life ought most certainly to be recognized, it does not justify the practice of treating marriage, divorce and the re-marriage

of divorced persons as though these matters were somehow on an altogether different level from other matters of morality, a practice which is to be seen in the Church wherever a severity of discipline is applied to those who have openly violated the Seventh Commandment such as is not applied to those who have equally openly and flagrantly violated others of the Ten Commandments. To place the Seventh Commandment on a superior pedestal above the other nine, is not to honour God but by its wilfulness to dishonour Him. We all of us fall very, very far short of adequately obeying any of the Ten Commandments. (Of course, it is possible to interpret them in such a narrow, unimaginative way, that one feels oneself entitled to put a jaunty tick beside each one of them in turn like the rich young ruler (Mk 10.20); but so to deal with them is to fail altogether to take them seriously.) The Ten Commandments have to be understood in the light of such summaries of the divine law as Deut 6.4f; Lev 19.18b; Mic 6.8. We then see the truth of the OT words quoted by Paul in Rom 3.10: 'There is none righteous, no, not one'. The general framework in which we must consider the special matter of broken marriage, divorce, re-marriage, is the clear recognition that all men (including, naturally, all Christians) have to acknowledge that they continually fall far short of true obedience in relation to every one of the Ten Commandments properly understood and that there is no question of their being able to have a righteous status before God except solely by His justification of sinners through Christ.

2. We ought to resist every temptation to tamper with the absoluteness, the perfection, of God's requirement which confronts us in the Genesis verses quoted by Jesus in Mk 10.6–8, in the firm prohibition of Mk 10.9 and in the Seventh Commandment. We must not pretend to

ourselves or to any one else that that requirement is anything less than it is. But this means not only that we must not seek to disguise the seriousness of the sinfulness of infidelity and of the inconsonance of divorce and the re-marriage of divorced persons with the perfect will of God, but also that we must not forget that Jesus included under 'adultery' inward thoughts and desires (Mt 5.27f) and that the standard, by which we ought to judge ourselves and towards which we ought to try to direct our conduct in this whole area of life, is one which goes far beyond conventional respectability and, by its requirement not only of outward fidelity but also of perfect inward loyalty and purity, sets even the happiest of Christian marriages under God's judgment. The sort of ecclesiastical language which gives the impression that those couples whose marriages have not fallen short of ordinary respectability have a right to feel complacent reflects a failure to comprehend the full seriousness of God's commandment.

3. But to refuse to attempt to tamper with the standard which God has set before us, the absoluteness of God's imperative, is not at all the same thing as to be a rigorist. On the contrary, a proper recognition of the distance by which we all fall short of true obedience will incline us to be compassionate towards those whose disobedience is most obvious. To appeal to Mk 10.1–12 as support for the adoption of a rigorist attitude seems to me exceedingly perverse. The statement of Jesus in v. 5, while it certainly forbids all attempts to twist Deut 24.1 into a divine approval of the practice of divorce as of something quite acceptable to God, is surely to be recognized as a testimony to God's merciful concern to limit and alleviate the harsh consequences of men's sinfulness.

4. We have to understand this passage in the light of the biblical witness as a whole; and in that light there can be no doubt that God's message of good news in which He

gives Himself to us and at the same time claims our lives for Himself is addressed to each individual man or woman, not where he or she would like to be, nor where the Church would like him or her to be, but in precisely that situation in which he or she now is, whatever its shame, perplexity and heartbreak. Otherwise it would not be God's good news at all. The pastoral care of the Church, which sincerely believes the gospel, must surely therefore involve trying to help each person (whether among its own members or among those many outside its fellowship whom, if it cares, it can reach) to hear and receive God's healing and saving word, where he or she is.

5. It seems to me that Mk 10.1–12 implies that in a situation in which a particular person's own, and other people's, sinfulness has left him or her (and very often several other people) with only more or less grievously unsatisfactory options open, the Christian pastor has to try, without losing sight of any of the things said above, to help that person to choose the way which, when as far as is possible all that is relevant has been taken into consideration, seems to involve least wrong to others (and the welfare of any children who may be concerned would obviously be of special importance) and to offer the best hope of approximating in the future as nearly as possible to God's perfect will, and then to proceed along that way with humble penitence for all past wrongs and with confidence in God's forgiveness in Christ and His help for the future, and with the understanding support of the Christian fellowship.

6. For the Church rigidly to refuse to solemnize the re-marriage of a divorced person who has accepted God's forgiveness and at the same time God's judgment upon his or her life, who is sincerely penitent for all past wrongs done and sincerely desirous of trying seriously henceforth, with God's help, to order his or her life as

nearly as possible according to God's will, would seem to me to involve a denial of the reality of the forgiveness of sins and therefore of the gospel of Jesus Christ itself. That the Christian solemnization of a re-marriage of a divorced person or of two divorced persons cannot be properly undertaken without careful pastoral inquiry should, of course, be obvious; but, if those who have to make such inquiries have a vivid realization of the fact that they too are sinners before God who stand only by God's forgiveness through Christ, they will approach their difficult task with humility, compassion and sensitiveness, and will fulfil it responsibly, considerately and without trace of self-complacency.

XVIII
UNITY AND LOVE IN THE LIGHT OF JOHN 17:

A NOTE ON THE SITUATION OF THE CHURCHES IN ENGLAND AFTER THE REJECTION OF *TOWARDS VISIBLE UNITY: PROPOSALS FOR A COVENANT*

That John 17, with its repeated use of the word 'one' (vv. 11, 21, 22, 23), should have been so often appealed to in connexion with Church unity is not surprising. It is clear enough from the final clauses of v. 21 ('that the world may believe that thou didst send me') and of v. 23 ('that the world may know that thou didst send me, and lovedst them [i.e. Christ's disciples], even as thou lovedst me') that the unity which is spoken of is not just something invisible and inward but something which the world should be able to observe. There is here a warrant and encouragement for seeking earnestly and unwearyingly, but also soberly, humbly, patiently and prayerfully, the true unity of Christ's Church on earth, and so a scriptural warrant for the existence and continuance of the ecumenical movement. But this passage is surely often grievously abused. It is surely abused whenever it is, so to speak, set on a pedestal, as though it had a peculiar authority superior to that of other parts of the NT. It is abused when it is regarded as conferring an uncritical, undiscriminating, divine approval upon every attempt to bring about a union of churches. It is abused when it is treated as an absolutely conclusive proof that the achievement of full, visible, organic church unity in any particular country is the most urgent task of the churches within it, and that all who dare to urge delay in order that theological issues may be seriously considered must be guilty of an obstinate and disloyal dragging of feet in the doing of the Lord's will.

When we begin to study the chapter more closely, we find that the unity of which it speaks is not just any sort of unity but that unity which is based on, and is at least to some degree comparable with, the unity which is between the Father and the Son. We read: 'that they may be one, even as we *are*' (v. 11); 'that they may all be one; even as thou, Father, *art* in me, and I in thee, that they also may be in us' (v. 21); 'And the glory which thou hast given me I have given unto them; that they may be one, even as we *are* one; I in them, and thou in me, that they may be perfected into one' (vv. 22–23). This might well incline us to be rather humble and sober with regard to assuming that the accomplishment of our union schemes would be the achievement of this unity. And there is something else to be discovered here, the close association of love between the Father and the Son with the oneness of the Father and the Son. The Father's love of the Son is mentioned in vv. 23, 24, 26 (the Son's love of the Father is not explicitly mentioned in this chapter, but there is a reference to it in 14.31). The request that the love with which the Father has loved the Son 'may be in them' (that is, in the disciples) in v. 26 suggests something further, namely, that there is an extremely close connexion between the unity of the disciples which is prayed for and the presence in them of love. And, when 17.11, 20–26, and 13.34f and also 15.12 are carefully compared together (note especially the parallel between 'that they may be perfected into one; that the world may know that thou didst send me, and lovedst them, even as thou lovedst me' in 17.23 and 'A new commandment I give unto you, that ye love one another; even as I have loved you, that ye also love one another. By this shall all men know that ye are my disciples, if ye have love one to another' (13.34f)), the conclusion that the unity of the disciples, to which chapter 17 refers, is inseparable from, or indeed identical with, their – all of them without exception – having true love one to another, would seem to be justified.

If what has just been said is true, it must mean that all of us who have the cause of true Church unity in England at heart need to study afresh with the utmost seriousness, rigorousness and prayerfulness what the NT has to tell us about the nature of Christian love – ἀγάπη. This would obviously involve a careful re-reading of the whole NT with special attention to this question; but a number of passages spring immediately to mind in this connexion, such as Rom 12.3–21; 13.8–10; 14.1–15.13; 1 Cor 13.1–13; Eph 4.1–5.2, to name but a few.

We shall also need to look back over the conversations and schemes of recent years and, in the light of what we learn from this renewed study of the NT teaching about the love which is the mark by which the faithful disciples of Jesus Christ are to be known, to examine ourselves honestly and courageously, as in the presence of God who knows our hearts, as to whether our formal inter-denominational conversations, our debates in church courts, the documents which have been prepared for study, the formulae and procedures which have been proposed, our informal discussions and correspondence, the ways in which we have treated, or were prepared to treat, our brothers and sisters who disagreed with us, have really been characterized by that love of which the Scriptures speak, that love which is concerned for the truth of the gospel and for truthfulness between men (e.g., 1 Cor 13.6; Eph 4.15; Col 3.9), which refuses to grieve one's fellow-Christian's conscience (e.g., Rom 14.15), which is patient, ready to give time, as God gives time, and to refrain from all attempts to hustle the unpersuaded

(1 Cor 13.4), which is kind and gentle (ibid.), which 'doth not behave itself unseemly' and 'is not provoked' (1 Cor 13.5).

I think that, if our study is sufficiently thorough and our self-examination sufficiently honest, we are likely to conclude that there has been much in our recent reunion schemes and in the ways in which they have been constructed and promoted, and also, doubtless, in the ways in which they have been opposed, that has been a denial of Christian love. I think we shall cease to take it for granted that it must necessarily be God's will to give to the churches in England full, visible, organic unity in our time. We shall indeed, I believe, have to reckon with the possibility that it may not be God's wise and merciful will to trust His sinful Christians with the full, visible, organic unity they desire, before the glorious parousia of His Son. To refuse to reckon with that possibility would hardly be evidence of faith. We must surely pray to God both to enable us earnestly to seek that unity which is according to His will and also, in His mercy and faithfulness, to prevent us from pursuing, and, still more, from ever succeeding in obtaining, any full, visible, organic unity, at the cost of sacrificing unfeigned mutual Christian love (and so at the cost of turning our backs on that unity to which the seventeenth chapter of St John's Gospel refers).

And the final clauses of vv. 21 and 23 ('that the world may believe . . .'; 'that the world may know . . .'), to which reference has already been made, should encourage us to look again at the relation between our union schemes and the Church's evangelistic task. The contention that the continued existence of different denominations is the greatest hindrance to the fulfilment of the Church's evangelistic task is surely, at any rate as far as England is concerned, unconvincing. Any evidence of bitter and implacable rivalry or mutual contemptuousness between the denominations would of course be a most serious stumbling-block to those outside; but there has been a vast improvement in relations between the different denominations in recent decades. Such things as regular meetings of the Anglican, Roman and Free Church clergy of a town, with easy and uninhibited discussion and mutual respect, and the holding of united services from time to time, are now quite normal, and are ground indeed for gratitude and joy. But there has been a rapid decline in the number of regular worshippers and a steady growth of an unchurched population almost entirely ignorant of the gospel.

In this situation the more urgent need was surely not to embark on the formulation and discussion of reunion schemes but to try to bring some knowledge of the gospel to the unchurched mass of the population. The great improvement in relations between the denominations had made it perfectly possible for such a mission to be a largely co-operative undertaking, and the denominations' combined resources (with many lay men and women assisting their clergy) would have sufficed to make feasible a systematic visitation of every home and every 'bed-sit' in the country, which would have been not just a matter of pushing a leaflet through the letter-box but of returning again and again until the resident was found at home. The very careful preparation which would have been appropriate to so serious an undertaking would have done much to enlarge and deepen both the clergy's own, and the laity's, understanding of, and therefore confidence in, the gospel; and the involvement in a sustained co-operative effort would have greatly consolidated and enriched the fellowship between the members of the different churches and made them better prepared for intelligent discussion of reunion schemes whenever the time for such schemes might come. Had all the time and all the energy spiritual, mental and physical, which have been spent in recent years on the construction and debating of reunion schemes, been spent on the evangelism of England, the condition of our country might well have been very different today from what it is.

But the other choice was made: priority was given to the quest for full, visible, organic union, and the evangelism of the unchurched was left – not entirely, of course, but to a very large extent – to await the solution of reunion problems. The withdrawal from the churches, far from being halted, has gathered pace, and the bulk of the nation has lived its life without the comfort and support of the gospel and without its challenge. How little those in power are aware of Christian teaching, not to mention giving heed to it, is only too apparent.

The failure of the recent Covenant proposals (coming after the collapse of other union schemes) has left many of the most earnest and active lay church members and many clergy terribly discouraged, bewildered and frustrated. On the one hand, those who had put great hopes in the proposed Covenant have been very cruelly disappointed. On the other hand, those ministers and lay men and women, who were conscientiously opposed to the proposals, not seeing how they could reconcile acceptance of the proposed Covenant with their loyalty to Jesus Christ as they understood it, while relieved by the outcome and thankful to God for it, are not unmarked by their experience of the debate. It will not be surprising if on both sides a painful sense of having been wounded in the house of one's friends is not uncommon. In the circumstances in which we are placed it is surely greatly to be hoped that there will be a sabbath rest from all reunion schemes in England for a quite considerable period. To keep such a sabbath rest is surely required of us, if the obligation of mutual love between Christians is to be honoured and our churches' urgent duty to bring the gospel of Jesus Christ to our fellow-citizens who are living and dying without it is not to be shamefully neglected. That this hoped for sabbath rest will certainly mean no cessation of true ecumenism and no time of taking our ease goes without saying.

LIST OF THE AUTHOR'S
PUBLICATIONS EXCLUDING
REVIEWS

(those republished in this volume are marked by an asterisk)

1941

'Look before you leap', in *Community* 4 (1940–41), pp. 44–45.

' "... but ... therefore ..." or signposts in the Epistle to the Romans',
in *The Student Movement* 44 (1941–42), pp. 22–23.

1942

'Grace: a meditation upon Psalm 90', in *The Student Movement* 45
(1942–43), pp. 13–14.

1943

* 'An interpretation of the Book of Job', in *The Expository Times* 54
(1942–43), pp. 295–298.

1944

'The burden which Habakkuk the prophet did see', in *The Student
Movement* 46 (1943–44), pp. 119–120.

1945

'The vision of the Divine Warrior (Isa 63.1–6)', in *The Student
Movement* 47 (1944–45), pp. 67–68.

1948

'The cup metaphor in Mark 14.36 and parallels', in *The Expository
Times* 59 (1947–48), pp. 137–138.

1949

'The love of God', in *The Student Movement* 51 (1948–49), no. 3,
pp. 6–9.

1950

The First Epistle of Peter, London, 1950; 4th impression, 1958.

'St Mark 9.14–29', in *Scottish Journal of Theology* 3 (1950), pp. 57–67.

'Fellowship', 'Love', etc., in A. Richardson (ed.), *A Theological Word
Book of the Bible*, London, 1950.

AUTHOR'S PUBLICATIONS

1951

'Riches and the kingdom of God: Mark 10.17–31', in *Scottish Journal of Theology* 4 (1951), pp. 302–313.

'St Mark 4.1–34: Part I', in *Scottish Journal of Theology* 4 (1951), pp. 398–414.

1952

'St Mark 4.1–34: Part II', in *Scottish Journal of Theology* 5 (1952), pp. 49–66.

'The first recorded Christian service? (Lk 24.13–35)', in *The Student Movement* 54 (1951–52), no. 4, pp. 11–13.

'A pastor's thanksgiving and intercession for a local church (Phil 1.3–11)', in *The Student Movement* 54 (1951–52), no. 5, pp. 10–13.

'St Mark 16.1–8: Part I' and 'St Mark 16.1–8: Part II', in *Scottish Journal of Theology* 5 (1952), pp. 282–298 and 398–414.

1953

'St Mark 13', in *Scottish Journal of Theology* 6 (1953), pp. 189–196 and 287–303.

1954

'St Mark 13' (continued), in *Scottish Journal of Theology* 7 (1954), pp. 284–303.

'The Good Samaritan (Lk 10.25–37)', in *Theology Today* 11 (1954), pp. 368–372; reprinted, with slight alterations, in *The Service of God* (see under 1965) and in *If God be for us*, 1985.

'Romans 7 reconsidered', in *The Expository Times* 65 (1953–54), p. 221.

1955

'Message of hope: Mark 4.21–32', in *Interpretation* 9 (1955), pp. 150–164.

'The baptism of our Lord – a study of St Mark 1.9–11', in *Scottish Journal of Theology* 8 (1955), pp. 53–63.

'St John' and '1 Peter', in G. H. Davies and A. Richardson (ed.), *The Teachers' Commentary*, revised ed., London, 1955, pp. 439–450 and 504–510.

'St Matthew 25.31–46', in *The Presbyterian Messenger* 110 (1955), no. 1252, pp. 2–3.

1956

'The witness of the New Testament to Christ', in T. H. L. Parker (ed.),
   Essays in Christology for Karl Barth (London, 1956), pp. 71–91.
'Jesus Christ is Lord', in *The Presbyterian Messenger* 111 (1956),
   no. 1265, pp. 2–3.

1957

The Epistle of James: four studies (a brief study outline published by
   the Student Christian Movement), London, 1957.

1958

* 'The interpretation of 1 Peter 3.19 and 4.6', in *The Expository Times*
   69 (1957–58), pp. 369–372.
*'Divine and human action: the biblical concept of worship', in
   Interpretation 12 (1958), pp. 387–398; reprinted, with slight
   alterations and an additional note, in *The Service of God* (see under
   1965).

1959

The Gospel according to Saint Mark (Cambridge Greek Testament
   Commentary), Cambridge, 1959.

1960

'Some observations on Romans 13.1–7', in *New Testament Studies* 6
   (1959–60), pp. 241–249.
I and II Peter and Jude (Torch Bible Commentaries), London, 1960.

1961

'Diakonia (Matthew 25.31–46)', in *The London Quarterly and Holborn
   Review* 186 (1961), pp. 275–281; reprinted in *The Service of God* (see
   under 1965) and in *If God be for us*, 1985.

1962

* 'The Christian's political responsibility according to the New
   Testament', in *Scottish Journal of Theology* 15 (1962), pp. 176–192;
   reprinted in *The Service of God* (see under 1965). A Spanish
   translation was published in C. E. B. Cranfield and A. Skevington
   Wood, *Responsabilidad Social y politica*, Buenos Aires, 1972.
* Μέτρον πίστεως in Romans 12.3', in *New Testament Studies* 8
   (1961–62), pp. 345–351.
Commentary on 1 Peter and general article on the Catholic Epistles, in

M. Black and H. H. Rowley (ed.), *Peake's Commentary on the Bible*, 1962.

'Mark, Gospel of', in G. A. Buttrick (ed.), *The Interpreter's Dictionary of the Bible*, New York and Nashville, 1962, vol. 3, pp. 267–277.

Brief articles in B. Reicke and L. Rost (ed.), *Biblisch-Historisches Handwörterbuch* 1, Göttingen, 1962.

1963

A Ransom for Many, London, 1963; reprinted in *If God be for us*, 1985.

'The Parable of the Unjust Judge and the eschatology of Luke-Acts', in *Scottish Journal of Theology* 16 (1963), pp. 297–301.

The Gospel according to Saint Mark, 2nd impression with supplementary notes, Cambridge, 1963.

1964

'St Paul and the law', in *Scottish Journal of Theology* 17 (1964), pp. 43–68; reprinted in R. Batey (ed.), *New Testament Issues*, New York and Evanston, 1970.

'The Gospel in action: St Luke 14.12–14', in R. J. W. Bevan (ed.), *The Christian Way Explained: sermons on belief and behaviour* by the Archbishop of York and other preachers, London, 1964, pp. 49–56; reprinted in *If God be for us*, 1985.

* 'The significance of διὰ παντός in Romans 11.10', in F. L. Cross (ed.), *Studia Evangelica* II, part 1, Berlin, 1964, pp. 546–550.

Brief articles in B. Reicke and L. Rost (ed.), *Biblisch-Historisches Handwörterbuch* 2, Göttingen, 1964.

1965

A Commentary on Romans 12–13 (*Scottish Journal of Theology* Occasional Papers 12), Edinburgh, 1965.

The Service of God, London, 1965.

'Minister and congregation in the light of 2 Corinthians 4.5–7: an exposition', in *Interpretation* 19 (1965), pp. 163–167.

* 'The message of James', in *Scottish Journal of Theology* 18 (1965), pp. 182–193 and 338–345.

1966

'Romans 8.28', in *Scottish Journal of Theology* 19 (1966), pp. 204–215.

* 'Diakonia in the New Testament', in J. I. McCord and T. H. L. Parker (ed.), *Service in Christ: essays presented to Karl Barth on his 80th birthday*, London, 1966, pp. 37–48.

THE BIBLE AND CHRISTIAN LIFE

The Gospel according to Saint Mark, 3rd impression with additional supplementary notes, Cambridge, 1966.

Brief articles in B. Reicke and L. Rost (ed.), *Biblisch-Historisches Handwörterbuch* 3, Göttingen, 1966.

1967

* 'New church constitutions and diakonia', in *Scottish Journal of Theology* 20 (1967), pp. 338–341.

* 'Hebrews 13.20–21', in *Scottish Journal of Theology* 20 (1967), pp. 437–441.

'What is the Gospel?', in *Outlook* (official magazine of the Presbyterian Church of England) 1 (1967), no. 4, p. 10.

1968

'Romans 1.18', in *Scottish Journal of Theology* 21 (1968), pp. 330–335.

'Are annotated Bibles desirable?', in *The Churchman* 82 (1968), pp. 290–296.

1969

'A reply to Mr. Bradnock', in *The Churchman* 83 (1969), pp. 28–30.

'Postscript on section headings for Bibles', in *The Churchman* 83 (1969), pp. 203–205.

'On some of the problems in the interpretation of Romans 5.12', in *Scottish Journal of Theology* 22 (1969), pp. 324–341.

'True religion: a sermon on Micah 6.8', in *Communio Viatorum* 12 (1969), pp. 191–195; reprinted in *If God be for us*, 1985.

1972

The Gospel according to Saint Mark, 4th impression with revised additional supplementary notes, Cambridge, 1972; reprinted in 1974, and, with further slight revision each time, in 1977, 1979, 1983.

' "You" or "Thou" ' (letter to the editor), in *Outlook* 6 (1972), no. 54, p. 18.

'You and Thou' (letter to the editor), in *Outlook* 6 (1972), no. 56, p. 23.

1974

* 'Some observations on Romans 8.19–21', in R. Banks (ed.), *Reconciliation and Hope: New Testament essays on atonement and eschatology presented to L. L. Morris on his 60th birthday*, Exeter, 1974, pp. 224–230.

'The freedom of the Christian according to Romans 8.2', in M. E.
Glasswell and E. W. Fasholé-Luke (ed.), *New Testament
Christianity for Africa and the world: essays in honour of Harry
Sawyerr*, London, 1974, pp. 91–98.

'Some observations on the interpretation of Romans 14.1–15.13', in
Communio Viatorum 17 (1974), pp. 193–204.

1975

* 'The preacher and his authority', in *Epworth Review* 2 (1975),
pp. 95–106.

'Some notes on Romans 9.30–33', in E. E. Ellis and E. Grässer (ed.),
*Jesus und Paulus: Festschrift für Werner Georg Kümmel zum 70.
Geburtstag*, Göttingen, 1975, pp. 35–43.

A critical and exegetical commentary on the Epistle to the Romans 1
(The International Critical Commentary), Edinburgh, 1975;
reprinted 1977 (with corrections); 1980 (with corrections); 1982;
1985 (with corrections).

1978

'A comment on Mark 10.1–12 on marriage and the remarriage of
divorced people', in a collection of papers, *Marriage, divorce and
remarriage*, United Reformed Church, 1978. (See p. 229.)

1979

A critical and exegetical commentary on the Epistle to the Romans 2,
Edinburgh, 1979; reprinted 1981 (with corrections); 1983 (with
corrections).

* 'A study of 1 Thessalonians 2', in *Irish Biblical Studies* 1 (1979),
pp. 215–226.

1980

'Romans 9.30–10.4', in *Interpretation* 34 (1980), pp. 70–74.

1981

Sermon on Matthew 11.28–30, in *Kingsmen* 35 (Spring term 1981),
pp. 25–29; reprinted in *If God be for us*, 1985.

1982

* 'Light from St Paul on Christian-Jewish relations', in D. W.
Torrance (ed.), *The witness of the Jews to God*, Edinburgh, 1982,
pp. 22–31.

'John 1.14: "became" ', in *The Expository Times* 93 (1981–82), p. 215.
* 'Changes of person and number in Paul's Epistles', in M. D. Hooker and S. G. Wilson (ed.), *Paul and Paulinism: essays in honour of C. K. Barrett*, London, 1982, pp. 280–289.
* 'Thoughts on New Testament eschatology', in *Scottish Journal of Theology* 35 (1982), pp. 497–512.

1983
'Some questions evoked by *Baptism, Eucharist and Ministry*', in *Focus on Unity* (the newsletter of the Ecumenical Response Group in the United Reformed Church), no. 3 (1983), pp. 6–7.

1985
Romans: a shorter commentary, Edinburgh and Grand Rapids, 1985.
If God be for us: a collection of sermons, Edinburgh, 1985.